# Workshop on Graph-Based Algorithms for Natural Language Processing 2006

# (TextGraphs 2006)



**Held at HLT/NAACL 2006**

## New York, New York, USA
## 9 June 2006

**ISBN: 978-1-61738-495-0**

**Printed from e-media with permission by:**

Curran Associates, Inc.
57 Morehouse Lane
Red Hook, NY 12571
www.proceedings.com

**Some format issues inherent in the e-media version may also appear in this print version.**



Printed by Curran Associates, Inc. (2010)



Association for Computational Linguistics
209 N. Eighth Street
Stroudsburg, Pennsylvania 18360

Phone: 1-570-476-8006
Fax: 1-570-476-0860

acl@aclweb.org

# PREFACE

Graph theory is a well studied discipline, and so is the field of natural language processing. Traditionally, these two areas of study have been perceived as distinct, with different algorithms, different applications, and different potential end-users. However, as recent research work has shown, the two disciplines are in fact intimately connected, with a large variety of natural language processing applications finding efficient solutions within graph-theoretical frameworks.

This volume contains papers accepted for presentation at the Textgraphs 2006 Workshop on Graph-based Algorithms for Natural Language Processing. This event took place on June 9, 2006, in New York City, immediately following the HLT-NAACL Human Language Technologies Conference. The workshop was centered around the topic of using graph-based algorithms for natural language processing, and it brought together people working on areas as diverse as lexical semantics, text summarization, text mining, ontology construction, clustering and learning, connected by the common underlying theme consisting of the use of graph-theoretical methods for text processing tasks.

We issued calls for both regular and short, late–breaking papers. After careful review by our program committee, eleven regular papers and four short papers were accepted for presentation. We were truly impressed by the high quality of the reviews provided by all the members of the program committee, particularly since deadlines were very tight. All of the committee members provided timely and thoughtful reviews, and the papers that appear have certainly benefited from that expert feedback.

Finally, when we first started planning this workshop, we agreed that having a high quality invited speaker was crucial. We thank Lillian Lee not only for her talk, but also for the boost of confidence provided by her quick and enthusiastic acceptance.

Rada Mihalcea and Dragomir Radev
June 2006

**CHAIRS:**

Dragomir Radev, University of Michigan
Rada Mihalcea, University of North Texas

**INVITED SPEAKER:**

Lillian Lee, Cornell University

**PROGRAM COMMITTEE:**

Lada Adamic, University of Michigan
Răzvan Bunescu, University of Texas at Austin
Timothy Chklovski, USC / Information Sciences Institute
Diane Cook, University of Texas at Arlington
Inderjit Dhillon, University of Texas at Austin
Beate Dorow, University of Stuttgart
Gael Dias, Universidade da Beira Interior Portugal
Kevin Gee, University of Texas at Arlington
Lise Getoor, University of Maryland
Güneş Erkan, University of Michigan
John Lafferty, Carnegie Mellon University
Lillian Lee, Cornell University
Andrew McCallum, University of Massachusetts
Bo Pang, Cornell University
Patrick Pantel, USC / Information Sciences Institute
Paul Tarau, University of North Texas
Simone Teufel, University of Cambridge
Lucy Vanderwende, Microsoft Research
Florian Wolf, F-W Consulting
Dominic Widdows, Maya Design
Hongyuan Zha, Penn State
Xiaojin Zhu, University of Wisconsin

**WEBSITE:**

http://www.textgraphs.org/ws06

# Table of Contents

# Conference Program

**Friday, June 9, 2006**

08:45–09:00 Introduction

**Session 1: Session One**



10:30–11:00 Coffee break

**Session 2: Session Two**



11:30–12:30 Invited talk "Sense and Sensibility" by Lillian Lee

12:30–14:00 Lunch break

**Friday, June 9, 2006 (continued)**

**Session 3: Session Three**



**Session 4: Session Four**

# A Graphical Framework for Contextual Search and Name Disambiguation in Email

**Einat Minkov**
Language Technologies Inst.
Carnegie Mellon University
Pittsburgh, PA 15213
einatm@cs.cmu.edu

**William W. Cohen**
Machine Learning Dept.
Carnegie Mellon University
Pittsburgh, PA 15213
wcohen@cs.cmu.edu

**Andrew Y. Ng**
Computer Science Dept.
Stanford University
Stanford, CA 94305
ang@cs.stanford.edu

## Abstract

Similarity measures for text have historically been an important tool for solving information retrieval problems. In this paper we consider extended similarity metrics for documents and other objects embedded in graphs, facilitated via a lazy graph walk. We provide a detailed instantiation of this framework for email data, where content, social networks and a timeline are integrated in a structural graph. The suggested framework is evaluated for the task of disambiguating names in email documents. We show that reranking schemes based on the graph-walk similarity measures often outperform baseline methods, and that further improvements can be obtained by use of appropriate learning methods.

## 1 Introduction

Many tasks in information retrieval can be performed by clever application of textual similarity metrics. In particular, The canonical IR problem of *ad hoc* retrieval is often formulated as the task of finding documents "similar to" a query. In modern IR settings, however, documents are usually not isolated objects: instead, they are frequently connected to other objects, via hyperlinks or meta-data. (An email message, for instance, is connected via header information to other emails in the same thread and also to the recipient's social network.) Thus it is important to understand how text-based document similarity measures can be extended to documents embedded in complex structural settings.

Our similarity metric is based on a lazy graph walk, and is closely related to the well-known PageRank algorithm (Page et al., 1998). PageRank and its variants are based on a graph walk of infinite length with random resets. In a *lazy* graph walk, there is a fixed probability of halting the walk at each step. In previous work (Toutanova et al., 2004), lazy walks over graphs were used for estimating word dependency distributions: in this case, the graph was one constructed especially for this task, and the edges in the graph represented different flavors of word-to-word similarity. Other recent papers have also used walks over graphs for query expansion (Xi et al., 2005; Collins-Thompson and Callan, 2005). In these tasks, the walk propagates similarity to a start node through edges in the graph—incidentally accumulating evidence of similarity over multiple connecting paths.

In contrast to this previous work, we consider schemes for propogating similarity across a graph that naturally models a structured dataset like an email corpus: entities correspond to objects including email addresses and dates, (as well as the usual types of documents and terms), and edges correspond to relations like *sent-by*. We view the similarity metric as a *tool for performing search* across this structured dataset, in which related entities that are not directly similar to a query can be reached via multi-step graph walk.

In this paper, we formulate and evaluate this extended similarity metric. The principal problem we



*Workshop on TextGraphs, at HLT-NAACL 2006*, pages 1–8,
New York City, June 2006. 

consider is *disambiguating personal names in email*, which we formulate as the task of retrieving the person most related to a particular name mention. We show that for this task, the graph-based approach improves substantially over plausible baselines. After retrieval, learning can be used to adjust the ranking of retrieved names based on the edges in the paths traversed to find these names, which leads to an additional performance improvement. Name disambiguation is a particular application of the suggested general framework, which is also applicable to any real-world setting in which structural data is available as well as text.

This paper proceeds as follows. Sections 2 and 3 formalize the general framework and its instantiation for email. Section 4 gives a short summary of the learning approach. Section 5 includes experimental evaluation, describing the corpora and results for the person name disambiguation task. The paper concludes with a review of related work, summary and future directions.

## 2 Email as a Graph

A graph $G$ consists of a set of nodes, and a set of labeled directed edges. Nodes will be denoted by letters like $x$, $y$, or $z$, and we will denote an edge from $x$ to $y$ with label $\ell$ as $x \xrightarrow{\ell} y$. Every node $x$ has a type, denoted $T(x)$, and we will assume that there are a fixed set of possible types. We will assume for convenience that there are no edges from a node to itself (this assumption can be easily relaxed.)

We will use these graphs to represent real-world data. Each node represents some real-world entity, and each edge $x \xrightarrow{\ell} y$ asserts that some binary relation $\ell(x, y)$ holds. The entity types used here to represent an email corpus are shown in the leftmost column of Table 1. They include the traditional types in information retrieval systems, namely *file* and *term*. In addition, however, they include the types *person*, *email-address* and *date*. These entities are constructed from a collection of email messages in the obvious way–for example, a recipient of "Einat Minkov <einat@cs.cmu.edu>" indicates the existence of a person node "Einat Minkov" and an email-address node "einat@cs.cmu.edu". (We assume here that person names are unique identifiers.)

The graph edges are directed. We will assume that edge labels determine the source and target node types: i.e., if $x \xrightarrow{\ell} z$ and $w \xrightarrow{\ell} y$ then $T(w) = T(x)$ and $T(y) = T(z)$. However, multiple relations can hold between any particular pair of nodes types: for instance, it could be that $x \xrightarrow{\ell} y$ or $x \xrightarrow{\ell'} y$, where $\ell \neq \ell'$. (For instance, an email message $x$ could be *sent-from* $y$, or *sent-to* $y$.) Note also that edges need not denote functional relations: for a given $x$ and $\ell$, there may be many distinct nodes $y$ such that $x \xrightarrow{\ell} y$. For instance, for a file $x$, there are many distinct terms $y$ such that $x \xrightarrow{\textit{has-term}} y$ holds.

In representing email, we also create an *inverse label* $\ell^{-1}$ for each edge label (relation) $\ell$. Note that this means that the graph will definitely be cyclic. Table 1 gives the full set of relations used in our email represention scheme.

## 3 Graph Similarity

### 3.1 Edge weights

Similarity between two nodes is defined by a lazy walk process, and a walk on the graph is controlled by a small set of parameters $\Theta$. To walk away from a node $x$, one first picks an edge label $\ell$; then, given $\ell$, one picks a node $y$ such that $x \xrightarrow{\ell} y$. We assume that the probability of picking the label $\ell$ depends only on the type $T(x)$ of the node $x$, i.e., that the outgoing probability from node $x$ of following an edge type $\ell$ is:

$$Pr(\ell \mid x) = Pr(\ell \mid T_i) \equiv \theta_{\ell,T_i}$$

Let $S_{T_i}$ be the set of possible labels for an edge leaving a node of type $T_i$. We require that the weights over all outgoing edge types given the source node type form a probability distribution, i.e., that

$$\sum_{\ell \in S_{T_i}} \theta_{\ell,T_i} = 1$$

In this paper, we will assume that once $\ell$ is picked, $y$ is chosen uniformly from the set of all $y$ such that $x \xrightarrow{\ell} y$. That is, the weight of an edge of type $l$ connecting source node $x$ to node $y$ is:

$$Pr(x \xrightarrow{\ell} y \mid \ell) = \frac{\theta_{\ell,T_i}}{\mid y : x \xrightarrow{\ell} y \mid}$$

This assumption could easily be generalized, however: for instance, for the type $T(x) =$ *file* and

| source type | edge type | target type |
|---|---|---|
| *file* | sent-from | *person* |
| | sent-from-email | *email-address* |
| | sent-to | *person* |
| | sent-to-email | *email-address* |
| | date-of | *date* |
| | has-subject-term | *term* |
| | has-term | *term* |
| *person* | sent-from inv. | *file* |
| | sent-to$^{-1}$ | *file* |
| | alias | *email-address* |
| | has-term | *term* |
| *email-address* | sent-to-email$^{-1}$ | *file* |
| | sent-from-email$^{-1}$ | *file* |
| | alias-inverse | *person* |
| | is-email$^{-1}$ | *term* |
| *term* | has-term$^{-1}$ | *file* |
| | has subject-term$^{-1}$ | *file* |
| | is-email | *email-address* |
| | has-term$^{-1}$ | *person* |
| *date* | date-of$^{-1}$ | *file* |

Table 1: Graph structure: Node and relation types

$\ell = \textit{has-term}$, weights for terms $y$ such that $x \xrightarrow{\ell} y$ might be distributed according to an appropriate language model (Croft and Lafferty, 2003).

### 3.2 Graph walks

Conceptually, the edge weights above define the probability of moving from a node $x$ to some other node $y$. At each step in a lazy graph walk, there is also some probability $\gamma$ of staying at $x$. Putting these together, and denoting by $\mathbf{M}_{xy}$ the probability of being at node $y$ at time $t+1$ given that one is at $x$ at time $t$ in the walk, we define

$$\mathbf{M}_{xy} = \begin{cases} (1-\gamma)\sum_{\ell} Pr(x \xrightarrow{\ell} y|\ell) \cdot Pr(\ell|T(x)) & x \neq y \\ \gamma & x = y \end{cases}$$

If we associate nodes with integers, and make $\mathbf{M}$ a matrix indexed by nodes, then a walk of $k$ steps can then be defined by matrix multiplication: specifically, if $V_0$ is some initial probability distribution over nodes, then the distribution after a $k$-step walk is proportional to $V_k = V_0\mathbf{M}^k$. Larger values of $\gamma$ increase the weight given to shorter paths between $x$ and $y$. In the experiments reported here, we consider small values of $k$, and this computation is carried out directly using sparse-matrix multiplication methods.[1] If $V_0$ gives probability 1 to some node $x_0$ and probability 0 to all other nodes, then the value given to $y$ in $V_k$ can be interpreted as a similarity measure between $x$ and $y$.

In our framework, a *query* is an initial distribution $V_q$ over nodes, plus a desired output type $T_{out}$, and the answer is a list of nodes $y$ of type $T_{out}$, ranked by their score in the distribution $V_k$. For instance, for an ordinary *ad hoc* document retrieval query (like "economic impact of recycling tires") would be an appropriate distribution $V_q$ over query terms, with $T_{out} = \textit{file}$. Replacing $T_{out}$ with *person* would find the person most related to the query—e.g., an email contact heavily associated with the retread economics. Replacing $V_q$ with a point distribution over a particular document would find the people most closely associated with the given document.

### 3.3 Relation to TF-IDF

It is interesting to view this framework in comparison to more traditional IR methods. Suppose we restrict ourselves to two types, terms and files, and allow only *in-file* edges. Now consider an initial query distribution $V_q$ which is uniform over the two terms "the aardvark". A one-step matrix multiplication will result in a distribution $V_1$, which includes file nodes. The common term "the" will spread its probability mass into small fractions over many file nodes, while the unusual term "aardvark" will spread its weight over only a few files: hence the effect will be similar to use of an IDF weighting scheme.

## 4 Learning

As suggested by the comments above, this graph framework could be used for many types of tasks, and it is unlikely that a single set of parameter values will be best for all tasks. It is thus important to consider the problem of *learning* how to better rank graph nodes.

Previous researchers have described schemes for adjusting the parameters $\theta$ using gradient descent-like methods (Diligenti et al., 2005; Nie et al., 2005). In this paper, we suggest an alternative approach of learning to re-order an initial ranking. This reranking approach has been used in the past for meta-search (Cohen et al., 1999) and also several natural-

[1] We have also explored an alternative approach based on sampling; this method scales better but introduces some additional variance into the procedure, which is undesirable for experimentation.

language related tasks (Collins and Koo, 2005). The advantage of reranking over parameter tuning is that the learned classifier can take advantage of "global" features that are not easily used in walk.

Note that node reranking, while can be used as an alternative to weight manipulation, it is better viewed as a complementary approach, as the techniques can be naturally combined by first tuning the parameters $\theta$, and then reranking the result using a classifier which exploits non-local features. This hybrid approach has been used successfully in the past on tasks like parsing (Collins and Koo, 2005).

We here give a short overview of the reranking approach, that is described in detail elsewhere (Collins and Koo, 2005). The reranking algorithm is provided with a training set containing $n$ examples. Example $i$ (for $1 \leq i \leq n$) includes a ranked list of $l_i$ nodes. Let $w_{ij}$ be the $j$th node for example $i$, and let $p(w_{ij})$ be the probability assigned to $w_{ij}$ by the graph walk. A candidate node $w_{ij}$ is represented through $m$ features, which are computed by $m$ feature functions $f_1, \ldots, f_m$. We will require that the features be binary; this restriction allows a closed form parameter update. The *ranking function* for node $x$ is defined as:

$$F(x, \bar{\alpha}) = \alpha_0 L(x) + \sum_{k=1}^{m} \alpha_k f_k(x)$$

where $L(x) = log(p(x))$ and $\bar{\alpha}$ is a vector of real-value parameters. Given a new test example, the output of the model is the given node list re-ranked by $F(x, \bar{\alpha})$.

To learn the parameter weights $\bar{\alpha}$, we use a boosting method (Collins and Koo, 2005), which minimizes the following loss function on the training data:

$$ExpLoss(\bar{\alpha}) = \sum_i \sum_{j=2}^{l_i} e^{-(F(x_{i,1},\bar{\alpha}) - F(x_{i,j},\bar{\alpha}))}$$

where $x_{i,1}$ is, without loss of generality, a correct target node. The weights for the function are learned with a boosting-like method, where in each iteration the feature $f_k$ that has the most impact on the loss function is chosen, and $\alpha_k$ is modified. Closed form formulas exist for calculating the optimal additive updates and the impact per feature (Schapire and Singer, 1999).

# 5 Evaluation

We experiment with three separate corpora.

The **Cspace** corpus contains email messages collected from a management course conducted at Carnegie Mellon University in 1997 (Minkov et al., 2005). In this course, MBA students, organized in teams of four to six members, ran simulated companies in different market scenarios. The corpus we used here includes the emails of all teams over a period of four days. The **Enron** corpus is a collection of mail from the Enron corpus that has been made available for the research community (Klimt and Yang, 2004). Here, we used the saved email of two different users.[2] To eliminate spam and news postings we removed email files sent from email addresses with suffix ".com" that are not Enron's; widely distributed email files (sent from "enron.announcement", to "all.employees@enron.com" etc.). Text from forwarded messages, or replied-to messages were also removed from the corpus.

Table 2 gives the size of each processed corpus, and the number of nodes in the graph representation of it. In deriving terms for the graph, terms were Porter-stemmed and stop words were removed. The processed Enron corpora are available from the first author's home page.

| | **corpus** | | Person set | |
|---|---|---|---|---|
| | **files** | **nodes** | train | test |
| **Cspace** | 821 | 6248 | 26 | 80 |
| **Sager-E** | 1632 | 9753 | 11 | 51 |
| **Shapiro-R** | 978 | 13174 | 11 | 49 |

Table 2: Corpora Details

## 5.1 Person Name Disambiguation

### 5.1.1 Task definition

Consider an email message containing a common name like "Andrew". Ideally an intelligent mailer would, like the user, understand which person "Andrew" refers to, and would rapidly perform tasks like retrieving Andrew's prefered email address or home page. Resolving the referent of a person name is also an important complement to the ability to perform named entity extraction for tasks like social network analysis or studies of social interaction in email.

[2]Specifially, we used the "all_documents" folder, including both incoming and outgoing files.

However, although the referent of the name is unambiguous to the recipient of the email, it can be non-trivial for an automated system to find out which "Andrew" is indicated. Automatically determining that "Andrew" refers to "Andrew Y. Ng" and not "Andrew McCallum" (for instance) is especially difficult when an informal nickname is used, or when the mentioned person does not appear in the email header. As noted above, we model this problem as a search task: based on a name-mention in an email message $m$, we formulate query distribution $V_q$, and then retrieve a ranked list of *person* nodes.

### 5.1.2 Data preparation

Unfortunately, building a corpus for evaluating this task is non-trivial, because (if trivial cases are eliminated) determining a name's referent is often non-trivial for a human other than the intended recipient. We evaluated this task using three labeled datasets, as detailed in Table 2.

The Cspace corpus has been manually annotated with personal names (Minkov et al., 2005). Additionally, with the corpus, there is a great deal of information available about the composition of the individual teams, the way the teams interact, and the full names of the team members. Using this extra information it is possible to manually resolve name mentions. We collected 106 cases in which single-token names were mentioned in the the body of a message but did not match any name from the header. Instances for which there was not sufficient information to determine a unique person entity were excluded from the example set. In addition to names that refer to people that are simply not in the header, the names in this corpus include people that are in the email header, but cannot be matched because they are referred to using: *initials*–this is commonly done in the sign-off to an email; *nicknames*, including common nicknames (e.g., "Dave" for "David"), unusual nicknames (e.g., "Kai" for "Keiko"); or American names adopted in place of a foreign name (e.g., "Jenny" for "Qing").

For Enron, two datasets were generated automatically. We collected name mentions which correspond uniquely a names that is in the email "Cc" header line; then, to simulate a non-trivial matching task, we eliminate the collected person name from the email header. We also used a small dictionary of 16 common American nicknames to identify nicknames that mapped uniquely to full person names on the "Cc" header line.

For each dataset, some examples were picked randomly and set aside for learning and evaluation purposes.

| | **initials** | **nicknames** | **other** |
|---|---|---|---|
| **Cspace** | 11.3% | 54.7% | 34.0% |
| **Sager-E** | - | 10.2% | 89.8% |
| **Shapiro-R** | - | 15.0% | 85.0% |

Table 3: Person Name Disambiguation Datasets

## 5.2 Results for person name disambiguation

### 5.2.1 Evaluation details

All of the methods applied generate a ranked list of person nodes, and there is exactly one correct answer per example.[3] Figure 1 gives results[4] for two of the datasets as a function of recall at rank $k$, up to rank 10. Table 4 shows the mean average precision (MAP) of the ranked lists as well as accuracy, which we define as the percentage of correct answers at rank 1 (i.e., precision at rank 1.)

### 5.2.2 Baseline method

To our knowledge, there are no previously reported experiments for this task on email data. As a baseline, we apply a reasonably sophisticated string matching method (Cohen et al., 2003). Each name mention in question is matched against all of the person names in the corpus. The similarity score between the name term and a person name is calculated as the maximal Jaro similarity score (Cohen et al., 2003) between the term and any single token of the personal name (ranging between 0 to 1). In addition, we incorporate a nickname dictionary[5], such that if the name term is a known nickname of a name, the similarity score of that pair is set to 1.

The results are shown in Figure 1 and Table 4. As can be seen, the baseline approach is substantially less effective for the more informal Cspace dataset. Recall that the Cspace corpus includes many cases such as initials, and also nicknames that have no literal resemblance to the person's name (section

[3]If a ranking contains a block of items with the same score, a node's rank is counted as the average rank of the "block".

[4]Results refer to test examples only.

[5]The same dictionary that was used for dataset generation.

5.1.2), which are not handled well by the string similarity approach. For the Enron datasets, the baseline approach perfoms generally better (Table 4). In all the corpora there are many ambiguous instances, e.g., common names like "Dave" or "Andy" that match many people with equal strength.

### 5.2.3 Graph walk methods

We perform two variants of graph walk, corresponding to different methods of forming the query distribution $V_q$. Unless otherwise stated, we will use a uniform weighting of labels—i.e., $\theta_{\ell,T} = 1/S_T$; $\gamma = 1/2$; and a walk of length 2.

In the first variant, we concentrate all the probability in the query distribution on the name term. The column labeled **term** gives the results of the graph walk from this probability vector. Intuitively, using this variant, the name term propagates its weight to the files in which it appears. Then, weight is propagated to person nodes which co-occur frequently with these files. Note that in our graph scheme there is a direct path between terms to person names, so that they recieve weight as well.

As can be seen in the results, this leads to very effective performance: e.g., it leads to 61.3% vs. 41.3% accuracy for the baseline approach on the CSpace dataset. However, it does not handle ambiguous terms as well as one would like, as the query does not include any information of the *context* in which the name occurred: the top-ranked answer for ambiguous name terms (e.g., "Dave") will always be the same person. To solve this problem, we also used a **file+term** walk, in which the query $V_q$ gives equal weight to the name term node and the file in which it appears.

We found that adding the file node to $V_q$ provides useful context for ambiguous instances—e.g., the correct "David" would in general be ranked higher than other persons with this same name. On the other hand, though, adding the file node reduces the the contribution of the term node. Although the MAP and accuracy are decreased, file+term has better performance than term at higher recall levels, as can be seen in Figure 1.

### 5.2.4 Reranking the output of a walk

We now examine reranking as a technique for improving the results. After some preliminary experimentation, we adopted the following types of features $f$ for a node $x$. The set of features are fairly generic. *Edge unigram features* indicate, for each edge label $\ell$, whether $\ell$ was used in reaching $x$ from $V_q$. *Edge bigram features* indicate, for each pair of edge labels $\ell_1$, $\ell_2$, whether $\ell_1$ and $\ell_2$ were used (in that order) in reaching $x$ from $V_q$. *Top edge bigram features* are similar but indicate if $\ell_1, \ell_2$ were used in one of the two highest-scoring paths between $V_q$ and $x$ (where the "score" of a path is the product of $\Pr(y \xrightarrow{\ell} z)$ for all edges in the path.)

We believe that these features could all be computed using dynamic programming methods. Currently, however, we compute features by using a method we call *path unfolding*, which is similar to the *back-propagation through time* algorithm (Haykin, 1994; Diligenti et al., 2005) used in training recurrent neural networks. Graph unfolding is based on a backward breadth-first visit of the graph, starting at the target node at time step $k$, and expanding the unfolded paths by one layer per each time step. This procedure is more expensive, but offers more flexibility in choosing alternative features, and was useful in determining an optimal feature set.

In addition, we used for this task some additional problem-specific features. One feature indicates whether the set of paths leading to a node originate from one or two nodes in $V_q$. (We conjecture that in the file+term walk, nodes are connected to both the source term and file nodes are more relevant comparing to nodes that are reached from the file node or term node only.) We also form features that indicate whether the given term is a nickname of the person name, per the nicknames dictionary; and whether the Jaro similarity score between the term and the person name is above 0.8. This information is similar to that used by the baseline method.

The results (for the test set, after training on the train set) are shown in Table 4 and (for two representative cases) Figure 1. In each case the top 10 nodes were reranked. Reranking substantially improves performance, especially for the file+term walk. The accuracy rate is higher than 75% across all datasets. The features that were assigned the highest weights by the re-ranker were the literal similarity features and the *source count* feature.

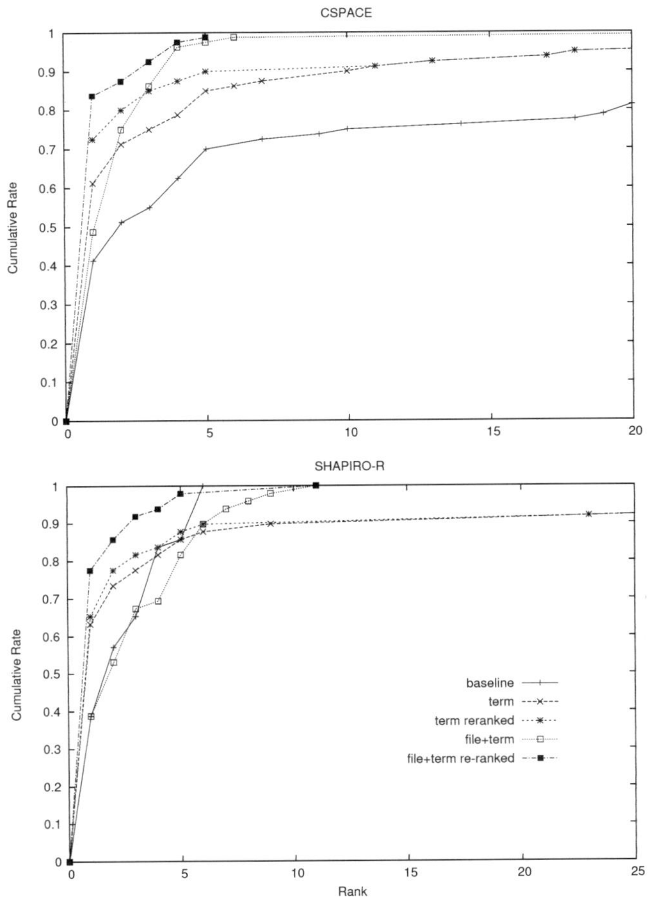


Figure 1: Person name disambiguation results: Recall at rank k

| | MAP | Accuracy |
|---|---|---|
| **Cspace** | | |
| Baseline | 49.0 | 41.3 |
| Graph - term | 72.6 | 61.3 |
| Graph - file+term | 66.3 | 48.8 |
| Reranking - term | 85.6 | 72.5 |
| Reranking - file+term | **89.0** | **83.8** |
| **Sager-E** | | |
| Baseline | 67.5 | 39.2 |
| Graph - term | 82.8 | 66.7 |
| Graph - file+term | 61.7 | 41.2 |
| Reranking - term | 83.2 | 68.6 |
| Reranking - file+term | **88.9** | **80.4** |
| **Shapiro-R** | | |
| Baseline | 60.8 | 38.8 |
| Graph - term | 84.1 | 63.3 |
| Graph - file+term | 56.5 | 38.8 |
| Reranking - term | **87.9** | 65.3 |
| Reranking - file+term | 85.5 | **77.6** |

Table 4: Person Name Disambiguation Results

## 6 Related Work

As noted above, the similarity measure we use is based on graph-walk techniques which have been adopted by many other researchers for several different tasks. In the information retrieval community, infinite graph walks are prevalent for determining document centrality (e.g., (Page et al., 1998; Diligenti et al., 2005; Kurland and Lee, 2005)). A related venue of research is of *spreading activation* over semantic or association networks, where the underlying idea is to propagate activation from source nodes via weighted links through the network (Berger et al., 2004; Salton and Buckley, 1988).

The idea of representing structured data as a graph is widespread in the data mining community, which is mostly concerned with relational or semi-structured data. Recently, the idea of PageRank has been applied to keyword search in structured databases (Balmin et al., 2004). Analysis of inter-object relationships has been suggested for entity disambiguation for entities in a graph (Kalashnikov et al., 2005), where edges are unlabelled. It has been suggested to model similarity between objects in relational data in terms of structural-context similarity (Jeh and Widom, 2002).

We propose the use of learned re-ranking schemes to improve performance of a lazy graph walk. Earlier authors have considered instead using hill-climbing approaches to adjust the parameters of a graph-walk (Diligenti et al., 2005). We have not compared directly with such approaches; preliminary experiments suggest that the performance gain of such methods is limited, due to their inability to exploit the global features we used here[6]. Related research explores random walks for semi supervised learning (Zhu et al., 2003; Zhou et al., 2005).

The task of person disambiguation has been studied in the field of social networks (e.g., (Malin et al., 2005)). In particular, it has been suggested to perform name disambiguation in email using traffic information, as derived from the email headers (Diehl et al., 2006). Our approach differs in that it allows integration of email content and a timeline in addition to social network information in a unified

[6] For instance, re-ranking using a set of simple locally-computable features only modestly improved performance of the "random" weight set for the CSpace threading task.

framework. In addition, we incorporate learning to tune the system parameters automatically.

## 7 Conclusion

We have presented a scheme for representing a corpus of email messages with a graph of typed entities, and an extension of the traditional notions of document similarity to documents embedded in a graph. Using a boosting-based learning scheme to rerank outputs based on graph-walk related, as well as other domain-specific, features provides an additional performance improvement. The final results are quite strong: for the explored name disambiguation task, the method yields MAP scores in the mid-to-upper 80's. The person name identification task illustrates a key advantage of our approach—that context can be easily incorporated in entity disambiguation.

In future work, we plan to further explore the scalability of the approach, and also ways of integrating this approach with language-modeling approaches for document representation and retrieval. An open question with regard to contextual (multi-source) graph walk in this framework is whether it is possible to further focus probability mass on nodes that are reached from multiple source nodes. This may prove beneficial for complex queries.

## References


Andrey Balmin, Vagelis Hristidis, and Yannis Papakonstantinou. 2004. ObjectRank: Authority-based keyword search in databases. In *VLDB*.

Helmut Berger, Michael Dittenbach, and Dieter Merkl. 2004. An adaptive information retrieval system. based on associative networks. In *APCCM*.

William W. Cohen, Robert E. Schapire, and Yoram Singer. 1999. Learning to order things. *Journal of Artificial Intelligence Research (JAIR)*, 10:243–270.

William W. Cohen, Pradeep Ravikumar, and Stephen Fienberg. 2003. A comparison of string distance metrics for name-matching tasks. In *IIWEB*.

Michael Collins and Terry Koo. 2005. Discriminative reranking for natural language parsing. *Computational Linguistics*, 31(1):25–69.

Kevyn Collins-Thompson and Jamie Callan. 2005. Query expansion using random walk models. In *CIKM*.

W. Bruce Croft and John Lafferty. 2003. *Language Modeling for Information Retrieval*. Springer.

Christopher P. Diehl, Lise Getoor, and Galileo Namata. 2006. Name reference resolution in organizational email archives. In *SIAM*.

Michelangelo Diligenti, Marco Gori, and Marco Maggini. 2005. Learning web page scores by error back-propagation. In *IJCAI*.

Simon Haykin. 1994. *Neural Networks*. Macmillan College Publishing Company.

Glen Jeh and Jennifer Widom. 2002. Simrank: A measure of structural-context similarity. In *SIGKDD*.

Dmitri Kalashnikov, Sharad Mehrotra, and Zhaoqi Chen. 2005. Exploiting relationship for domain independent data cleaning. In *SIAM*.

Brown Klimt and Yiming Yang. 2004. The enron corpus: A new dataset for email classification research. In *ECML*.

Oren Kurland and Lillian Lee. 2005. Pagerank without hyperlinks: Structural re-ranking using links induced by language models. In *SIGIR*.

Bradely Malin, Edoardo M. Airoldi, and Kathleen M. Carley. 2005. A social network analysis model for name disambiguation in lists. *Journal of Computational and Mathematical Organization Theory*, 11(2).

Einat Minkov, Richard Wang, and William Cohen. 2005. Extracting personal names from emails: Applying named entity recognition to informal text. In *HLT-EMNLP*.

Zaiqing Nie, Yuanzhi Zhang, Ji-Rong Wen, and Wei-Ying Ma. 2005. Object-level ranking: Bringing order to web objects. In *WWW*.

Larry Page, Sergey Brin, R. Motwani, and T. Winograd. 1998. The pagerank citation ranking: Bringing order to the web. In *Technical Report, Computer Science department, Stanford University*.

Gerard Salton and Chris Buckley. 1988. On the use of spreading activation methods in automatic information retrieval. In *SIGIR*.

Robert E. Schapire and Yoram Singer. 1999. Improved boosting algorithms using confidence-rated predictions. *Machine Learning*, 37(3):297–336.

Kristina Toutanova, Christopher D. Manning, and Andrew Y. Ng. 2004. Learning random walk models for inducing word dependency distributions. In *ICML*.

Wensi Xi, Edward Allan Fox, Weiguo Patrick Fan, Benyu Zhang, Zheng Chen, Jun Yan, and Dong Zhuang. 2005. Simfusion: Measuring similarity using unified relationship matrix. In *SIGIR*.

Dengyong Zhou, Bernhard Scholkopf, and Thomas Hofmann. 2005. Semi-supervised learning on directed graphs. In *NIPS*.

Xiaojin Zhu, Zoubin Ghahramani, and John Lafferty. 2003. Semi-supervised learning using gaussian fields and harmonic functions. In *ICML*.

# Graph Based Semi-Supervised Approach for Information Extraction

**Hany Hassan** **Ahmed Hassan** **Sara Noeman**

IBM Cairo Technology Development Center
Giza, Egypt
P.O. Box 166 Al-Ahram

hanyh@eg.ibm.com hasanah@eg.ibm.com noemans@eg.ibm.com

## Abstract

Classification techniques deploy supervised labeled instances to train classifiers for various classification problems. However labeled instances are limited, expensive, and time consuming to obtain, due to the need of experienced human annotators. Meanwhile large amount of unlabeled data is usually easy to obtain. Semi-supervised learning addresses the problem of utilizing unlabeled data along with supervised labeled data, to build better classifiers. In this paper we introduce a semi-supervised approach based on mutual reinforcement in graphs to obtain more labeled data to enhance the classifier accuracy. The approach has been used to supplement a maximum entropy model for semi-supervised training of the ACE Relation Detection and Characterization (RDC) task. ACE RDC is considered a hard task in information extraction due to lack of large amounts of training data and inconsistencies in the available data. The proposed approach provides 10% relative improvement over the state of the art supervised baseline system.

## 1 Introduction

Classification techniques use labeled data to train classifiers for various classification problems. Yet they often face a shortage of labeled training data. Labeled instances are often difficult, expensive, and /or time consuming to obtain. Meanwhile large numbers of unlabeled instances are often available. Semi-supervised learning addresses the problem of how unlabeled data can be usefully employed, along with labeled data, to build better classifiers.

In this paper we propose a semi-supervised approach for acquiring more training instances similar to some labeled instances. The approach depends on constructing generalized extraction patterns, which could match many instances, and deploying graph based mutual reinforcement to weight the importance of these patterns. The mutual reinforcement is used to automatically identify the most informative patterns; where patterns that match many instances tend to be correct. Similarly, instances matched by many patterns also tend to be correct. The labeled instances should have more effect in the mutual reinforcement weighting process. The problem can therefore be seen as hubs (instances) and authorities (patterns) problem which can be solved using the Hypertext Induced Topic Selection (HITS) algorithm (Kleinberg, 1998 ).

HITS is an algorithmic formulation of the notion of authority in web pages link analysis, based on a relationship between a set of relevant "authoritative pages" and a set of "hub pages". The HITS algorithm benefits from the following observation: when a page (hub) links to another page (authority), the former confers authority over the latter.

By analogy to the authoritative web pages problem, we could represent the patterns as authorities and instances as hubs, and use mutual reinforcement between patterns and instances to weight the most authoritative patterns. Instances from unsu-



*Workshop on TextGraphs, at HLT-NAACL 2006*, pages 9–16,
New York City, June 2006. ©2006 Association for Computational Linguistics

pervised data matched with the highly weighted patterns are then used in retraining the system.

The paper proceeds as follows: in Section 2 we discuss previous work followed by a brief definition of our general notation in Section 3. A detailed description of the proposed approach then follows in Section 4. Section 5 discusses the application of the proposed approach to the problem of detecting semantic relations from text. Section 6 discusses experimental results while the conclusion is presented in Section 7.

## 2 Previous Work

(Blum and Mitchell, 1998) proposed an approach based on co-training that uses unlabeled data in a particular setting. They exploit the fact that, for some problems, each example can be described by multiple representations. They develop a boosting scheme which exploits conditional independence between these representations.

(Blum and Chawla, 2001) proposed a general approach utilizing unlabeled data by constructing a graph on all the data points based on distance relationships among examples, and then to use the known labels to perform a graph partitioning using the minimum cut that agrees with the labeled data. (Zhu et al., 2003) extended this approach by proposing a cut based on the assumption that labels are generated according to a Markov Random Field on the graph , (Joachims, 2003) presented an algorithm based on spectral graph partitioning. (Blum et al., 2004) extended the min-cut approach by adding randomness to the graph structure, their algorithm addresses several shortcomings of the basic mincut approach, yet it may not help in cases where the graph does not have small cuts for a given classification problem.

## 3 Background

In graph theory, a graph is a set of objects called vertices joined by links called edges. A bipartite graph, also called a bigraph, is a special graph where the set of vertices can be divided into two disjoint sets with no two vertices of the same set sharing an edge.

The Hypertext Induced Topic Selection (HITS) algorithm is an algorithm for rating, and therefore ranking, web pages. The HITS algorithm makes use of the following observation: when a page (hub) links to another page (authority), the former confers authority over the latter. HITS uses two values for each page, the *"authority value"* and the *"hub value"*. "*Authority value*" and "*hub value*" are defined in terms of one another in a mutual recursion. An authority value is computed as the sum of the scaled hub values that point to that authority. A hub value is the sum of the scaled authority values of the authorities it points to.

A *template*, as we define for this work, is a sequence of generic forms that could generalize over the given training instance. An example template is:

*COUNTRY NOUN_PHRASE PERSON VERB_PHRASE*

This template could represent the sentence:

*"American vice President Al Gore visited ... ".*

This template is derived from the representation of the Named Entity tags, Part-of-Speech (POS) tags and semantic tags. The choice of the template representation here is for illustration purpose only; any combination of tags, representations and tagging styles might be used.

A *pattern* is more specific than a template. A pattern specifies the role played by the tags (first entity, second entity, or relation). An example of a pattern is:

*COUNTRY(E2) NOUN_PHRASE(R) PERSON(E1) VERB_PHRASE*

This pattern indicates that the word(s) with the tag *COUNTRY* in the sentence represents the second entity (Entity 2) in the relation, while the word(s) tagged *PERSON* represents the first entity (Entity 1) in this relation. Finally, the word(s) with the tag *NOUN_PHRASE* represents the relation between the two previous entities.

A *tuple*, in our notation during this paper, is the result of the application of a pattern to unstructured text. In the above example, one result of applying the pattern to some raw text is the following tuple:

*Entity 1: Al Gore*
*Entity 2: United States*
*Relation: vice President*

## 4 The Approach

The semi-supervised graph-based approach we propose depends on the construction of generalized extraction patterns that could match many training instances. The patterns are then weighted according to their importance by deploying graph based mutual reinforcement techniques. Patterns derived from the supervised training instances should have a superior effect in the reinforcement weighting process. This duality in patterns and tuples relation could be stated that patterns could match different tuples, and tuples in turn could be matched by different patterns. The proposed approach is composed of two main steps namely, pattern extraction and pattern weighting or induction. Both steps are detailed in the next subsections.

### 4.1 Patterns Extraction

As shown in Figure 1, several syntactic, lexical, and semantic analyzers could be applied to the training instances. The resulting analyses could be employed in the construction of extraction patterns. Any extraction pattern could match different relations and hence could produce several tuples. As an example let's consider the pattern depicted in figure 1:

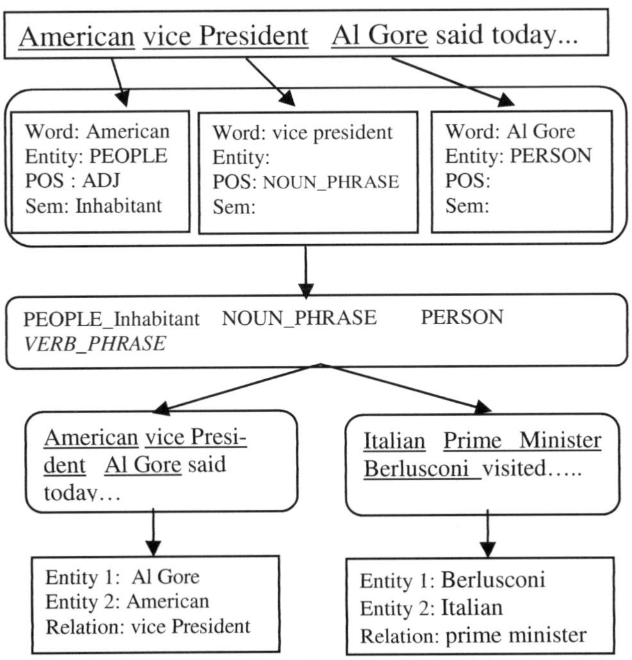


Figure 1: An example of a pattern and its possible tuples.

*PEOPLE_Inhabitant(E2) NOUN_PHRASE(R) PERSON(E1) VERB_PHRASE*

This pattern could extract the tuple:

*Entity 1: Al Gore*
*Entity 2: American*
*Relation: vice President*

Another tuple that could be extracted by the same pattern is:

*Entity 1: Berlusconi*
*Entity 2: Italian*
*Relation: Prime Minister*

On the other hand, many other patterns could extract the same information in the tuple from different contexts. It is worth mentioning that the proposed approach is general enough to accommodate any pattern design; the introduced pattern design is for illustration purposes only.

To further increase the number of patterns that could match a single tuple, the tuple space might be reduced i.e. by grouping tuples conveying the same information content together into a single tuple. This will be detailed further in the experimental setup section.

### 4.2 Pattern Induction

The inherent duality in the patterns and tuples relation suggests that the problem could be interpreted as a hub authority problem. This problem could be solved by applying the HITS algorithm to iteratively assign authority and hub scores to patterns and tuples respectively.

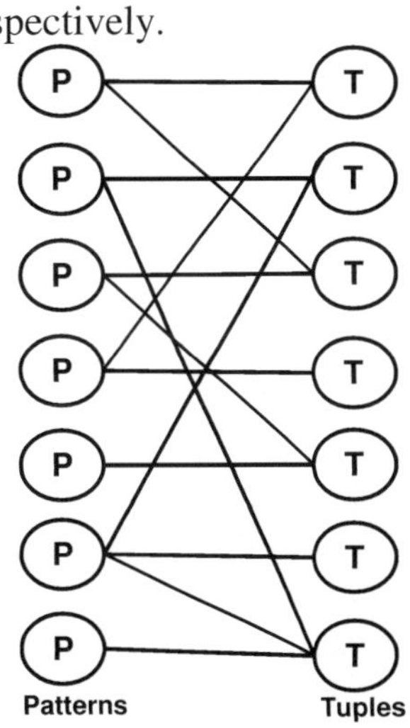


Figure 2: A bipartite graph representing patterns and tuples

Patterns and tuples are represented by a bipartite graph as illustrated in figure 2. Each pattern or tuple is represented by a node in the graph. Edges represent matching between patterns and tuples.

The pattern induction problem can be formulated as follows: Given a very large set of data *D* containing a large set of patterns *P* which match a large set of tuples T, the problem is to identify $\widetilde{P}$, the set of patterns that match the set of the most correct tuples $\widetilde{T}$. The intuition is that the tuples matched by many different patterns tend to be correct and the patterns matching many different tuples tend to be good patterns. In other words; we want to choose, among the large space of patterns in the data, the most informative, highest confidence patterns that could identify correct tuples; i.e. choosing the most *"authoritative"* patterns in analogy with the hub authority problem. However, both $\widetilde{P}$ and $\widetilde{T}$ are unknown. The induction process proceeds as follows: each pattern *p* in *P* is associated with a numerical authority weight $a_v$ which expresses how many tuples match that pattern. Similarly, each tuple *t* in *T* has a numerical hub weight $h_t$ which expresses how many patterns were matched by this tuple. The weights are calculated iteratively as follows:

$$a^{(i+1)}(p) = \sum_{u=1}^{T(p)} \frac{h^{(i)}(u)}{H^{(i)}} \quad (1)$$

$$h^{(i+1)}(t) = \sum_{u=1}^{P(t)} \frac{a^{(i)}(u)}{A^{(i)}} \quad (2)$$

where *T(p)* is the set of tuples matched by *p*, *P(t)* is the set of patterns matching *t*, $a^{(i+1)}(p)$ is the authoritative weight of pattern $p$ at iteration $(i+1)$, and $h^{(i+1)}(t)$ is the hub weight of tuple $t$ at iteration $(i+1)$. *H(i)* and *A(i)* are normalization factors defined as:

$$H^{(i)} = \sum_{p=1}^{|P|} \sum_{u=1}^{T(p)} h^{(i)}(u) \quad (3)$$

$$A^{(i)} = \sum_{v=1}^{|T|} \sum_{u=1}^{P(t)} a^{(i)}(u) \quad (4)$$

Patterns with weights lower than a predefined threshold are rejected, and examples associated with highly ranked patterns are then used in unsupervised training.

It is worth mentioning that both *T* and *P* contain supervised and unsupervised examples, however the proposed method could assign weights to the correct examples (tuples and patterns) in a completely unsupervised setup. For semi-supervised data some supervised examples are provided, which are associated in turn with tuples and patterns.

We adopt the HITS extension introduced in (White and Smyth, 2003) to extend HITS with *Priors*. By analogy, we handle the supervised examples as priors to the HITS induction algorithm.

A prior probabilities vector $pr = \{pr_1, \ldots, pr_n\}$ is defined such that the probabilities sum to 1, where $pr_v$ denotes the relative importance (or "prior bias") we attach to node *v*. A pattern $P_i$ is assigned a prior $pr_i = 1/n$ if pattern $P_i$ matches a supervised tuple, otherwise $pr_i$ *is set to zero*, *n* is the total number of patterns that have a supervised match. We also define a *"back probability"* $\beta$, $0 \leq \beta \leq 1$ which determines how often we bias the supervised nodes:

$$a^{(i+1)}(p) = (1-\beta)\left(\sum_{u=1}^{T(p)} \frac{h^{(i)}(u)}{H^{(i)}}\right) + \beta * pr_p \quad (5)$$

$$h^{(i+1)}(t) = (1-\beta)\left(\sum_{u=1}^{P(t)} \frac{a^{(i)}(u)}{A^{(i)}}\right) + \beta * pr_t \quad (6)$$

where *T(p)* is the set of tuples matched by *p* , *P(t)* is the set of patterns matching *t*, and *H(i)* and *A(i)* are normalization factors defined as in equations (3) and (4)

Thus each node in the graph (pattern or tuple) has an associated prior weight depending on its supervised data. The induction process proceeds to iteratively assign weights to the patterns and tuples. In the current work we used $\beta = 0.5$.

## 5 Experimental Setup

### 5.1 ACE Relation Detection and Characterization

In this section, we describe Automatic Content Extraction (ACE). ACE is an evaluation conducted by NIST to measure Entity Detection and Tracking (EDT) and Relation Detection and Characterization (RDC). The EDT task is concerned with the detection of mentions of entities, and grouping them together by identifying their coreference. The RDC task detects relations between entities identified by the EDT task. We choose the RDC task to show the performance of the graph based semi-supervised information extraction approach we propose. To this end we need to introduce the notion of mentions and entities. Mentions are any instances of textual references to objects like people, organizations, geo-political entities (countries, cities ...etc), locations, or facilities. On the other hand, entities are objects containing all mentions to the same object.

| Type | Subtype | Number of Instances |
|---|---|---|
| ART | User-Owner | 331 |
| | Inventor | |
| | Other | |
| DISC | DISC | 143 |
| EMP-ORG | Employ-Exec | 1673 |
| | Employ-Staff | |
| | Employ-Undetermined | |
| | Member-of-Group | |
| | Subsidiary | |
| | Other | |
| Other-AFF | Ethnic | 153 |
| | Ideology | |
| | Other | |
| GPE-AFF | Citizen-Resident | 695 |
| | Based-in | |
| | Other | |
| PER-SOC | Business | 358 |
| | Family | |
| | Other | |
| PHYS | Located | 1411 |
| | Near | |
| | Part-Whole | |

Table 1. Types and subtypes of ACE relations

Table 1 lists the types and subtypes of relations for the ACE RDC task. Here, we present an example for those relations:

```
Spain's Interior Minister an-
nounced this evening the ar-
rest of separatist
organization Eta's presumed
leader Ignacio Garcia Ar-
regui. Arregui, who is con-
sidered to be the Eta
organization's top man, was
arrested at 17h45 Greenwich.
The Spanish judiciary sus-
pects Arregui of ordering a
failed attack on King Juan
Carlos in 1995.
```

In this fragment, all the underlined phrases are mentions to *Eta* organization, or to *"Garcia Arregui"*. There is a management relation between *leader* which references to *"Garcia Arregui"* and *Eta*.

### 5.2 Baseline System

The base line system uses a Maximum Entropy model that combines diverse lexical, syntactic and semantic features derived from text, like the system described in (Nanda, 2004). The system was trained on the ACE training data provided by LDC. The training set contained 145K words, and 4764 instances of relations, the number of instances corresponding to each relation is shown in Table 1.

The test set contained around 41K words, and 1097 instances of relations. The system was evaluated using standard ACE evaluation procedure. ACE evaluation procedure assigns the system an ACE value for each relation type and a total ACE value. The ACE value is a standard NIST metric for evaluating relation extraction. The reader is referred to the ACE web site (ACE, 2004) for more details.

### 5.3 Pattern Construction

We used the baseline system described in the previous section to label a large amount of unsupervised data. The data comes from LDC English Gigaword corpus, Agence France Press English Service (AFE). The data contains around 3M words, from which 80K instances of relations have been extracted.

We start by extracting a set of patterns that represent the supervised and unsupervised data. We consider each relation type separately and extract a pattern for each instance in the selected relation. The pattern we used consists of a mix between the part of speech (POS) tags and the mention tags for the words in the training instance. We use the mention tag, if it exists; otherwise we use the part of speech tag. An example of a pattern is:

```
Text: Eta's presumed leader
Arregui …
Pos: NNP POS JJ NN NNP
Mention: ORG 0 0 0 PERSON
Pattern: ORG(E2) POS JJ NN(R)
PERSON(E1)
```

### 5.4 Tuples Clustering

As discussed in the previous section, the tuple space should be reduced to allow more matching between pattern-tuple pairs. This space reduction could be accomplished by seeking a tuple similarity measure, and constructing a weighted undirected graph of tuples. Two tuples are linked with an edge if their similarity measure exceeds a certain threshold. Graph clustering algorithms could be deployed to partition the graph into a set of homogeneous communities or clusters. To reduce the space of tuples, we seek a matching criterion that group similar tuples together. Using WordNet, we can measure the semantic similarity or relatedness between a pair of concepts (or word senses), and by extension, between a pair of sentences. We use the similarity measure described in (Wu and Palmer, 1994) which finds the path length to the root node from the least common subsumer (LCS) of the two word senses which is the most specific word sense they share as an ancestor. The similarity score of two tuples, $S_T$, is calculated as follows:.

$$S_T = \sqrt{S_{E1}^2 + S_{E2}^2} \qquad (9)$$

where $S_{E1}$, and $S_{E2}$ are the similarity scores of the first entities in the two tuples, and their second entitles respectively.

The tuple matching procedure assigns a similarity measure to each pair of tuples in the dataset. Using this measure we can construct an undirected graph G. The vertices of G are the tuples. Two vertices are connected with an edge if the similarity measure between their underlying tuples exceeds a certain threshold. It was noticed that the constructed graph consists of a set of semi isolated groups as shown in figure 3. Those groups have a very large number of inter-group edges and meanwhile a rather small number of intra-group edges. This implies that using a graph clustering algorithm would eliminate those weak intra-group edges and produce separate groups or clusters representing similar tuples. We used Markov Cluster Algorithm (MCL) for graph clustering (Dongen, 2000). MCL is a fast and scalable unsupervised cluster algorithm for graphs based on simulation of stochastic flow.

A bipartite graph of patterns and tuple clusters is constructed. Weights are assigned to patterns and tuple clusters by iteratively applying the HITS with Priors' algorithm. Instances associated with highly ranked patterns are then added to the training data and the model is retrained. Samples of some highly ranked patterns and corresponding matching text are introduced in Table 2.

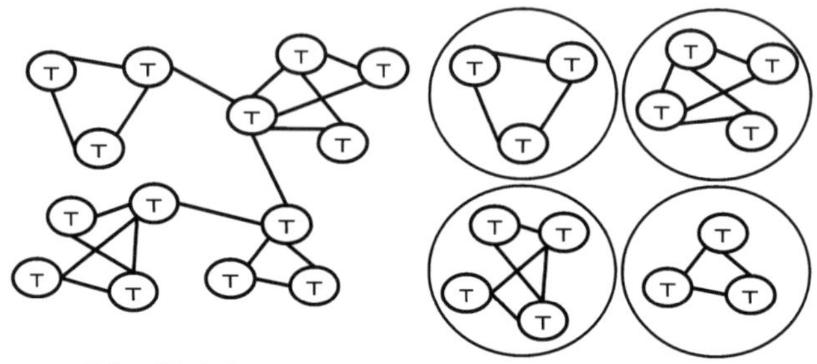


Figure 3: Applying Clustering Algorithms to Tuple graph

| Pattern | Matches |
|---|---|
| GPE PERSON PERSON PERSON | Zimbabwean President Robert Mugabe |
| GPE POS PERSON PERSON | Zimbabwe 's President Robert Mugabe |
| GPE JJ PERSON | American diplomatic personnel |
| PERSON IN JJ GPE | candidates for local government |
| ORGANIZATION PERSON | Airways spokesman |
| ORGANIZATION PERSON | Ajax players |
| PERSON IN DT JJ ORGANIZATION | chairman of the opposition parties |
| ORGANIZATION PERSON | parties chairmans |

Table 2: Examples of patterns with high weights

## 6 Results and Discussion

We train several models like the one described in section 5.2 on different training data sets. In all experiments, we use both the LDC ACE training data and the labeled unsupervised data induced with the graph based approach we propose. We use the ACE evaluation procedure and ACE test corpus, provided by LDC, to evaluate all models.

We incrementally added labeled unsupervised data to the training data to determine the amount of data after which degradation in the system performance occurs. We sought this degradation point separately for each relation type. Figure 4 shows the effect of adding labeled unsupervised data on the ACE value for each relation separately. We notice from figure 4 and table 1 that relations with a small number of training instances had a higher gain in performance compared to relations with a large number of training instances. This implies that the proposed approach achieves significant improvement when the number of labeled training instances is small but representative.

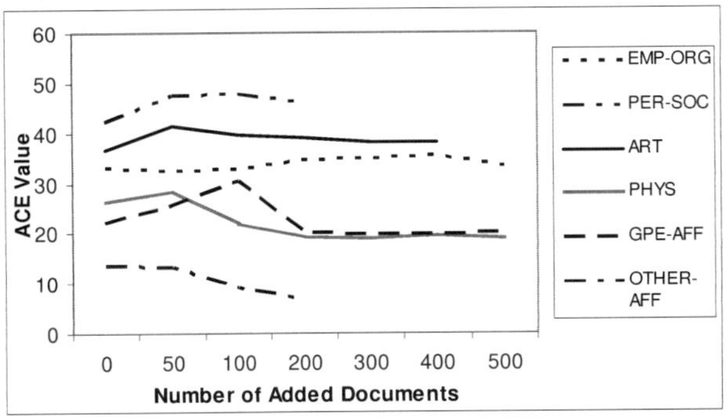


Figure 4: The effect of adding labeled unsupervised data on the ACE value for each relation. The average number of relations per document is 4.

From figure 4, we determined the number of training instances resulting in the maximum boost in performance for each relation. We added the training instances corresponding to the maximum boost in performance for all relations to the supervised training data and trained a new model on them. Figure 5 compares the ACE values for each relation in the base line model and the final model

The total system ACE value has been improved by 10% over the supervised baseline system. All relation types, except the DSC relation, had significant improvement ranging from 7% to 30% over the baseline supervised system. The DISC relation type had a small degradation; noting that it already has a low ACE value with the baseline system. We think this is due to the fact that the DISC relation has few and inconsistent examples in the supervised data set.

To assess the usefulness of the smoothing method employing WordNet distance, we repeated the experiment on EMP-ORG relation without it. We found out that it contributed to almost 30% of the total achieved improvement. We also repeated the experiment but with considering hub scores instead of authority scores. We added the examples associated with highly ranked tuples to the training set. We noticed that using hub scores yielded very little variation in the ACE value (i.e. 0.1 point for EMP-ORG relation).

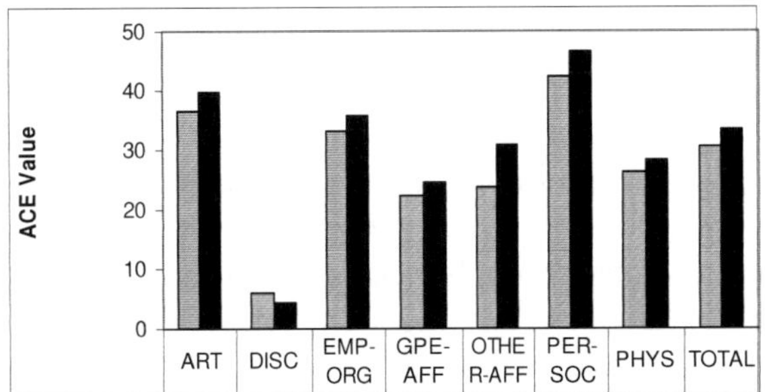


| | ART | DISC | EMP-ORG | GPE-AFF | OTHER-AFF | PER-SOC | PHYS | TOTAL |
|---|---|---|---|---|---|---|---|---|
| BaseLine | 36.7 | 6 | 33.1 | 22.3 | 23.6 | 42.2 | 26.4 | 30.5 |
| Final Model | 39.6 | 4.2 | 35.8 | 24.7 | 30.8 | 46.6 | 28.2 | 33.5 |

Figure 5: A comparison of base line ACE values, and final ACE values for each relation.

To evaluate the quality and representativeness of the labeled unsupervised data, acquired using the proposed approach, we study the effect of replacing supervised data with unsupervised data while holding the amount of training data fixed. Several systems have been built using mixture of the supervised and the unsupervised data. In Figure 6, the dotted line shows the degradation in the system performance when using a reduced amount of supervised training data only, while the solid line shows the effect of replacing supervised training data with unsupervised labeled data on the system performance. We notice from Figure 6 that the unsupervised data could replace more than 50% of the supervised data without any degradation in the system performance. This is an indication that the induced unsupervised data is good for training the classifier.

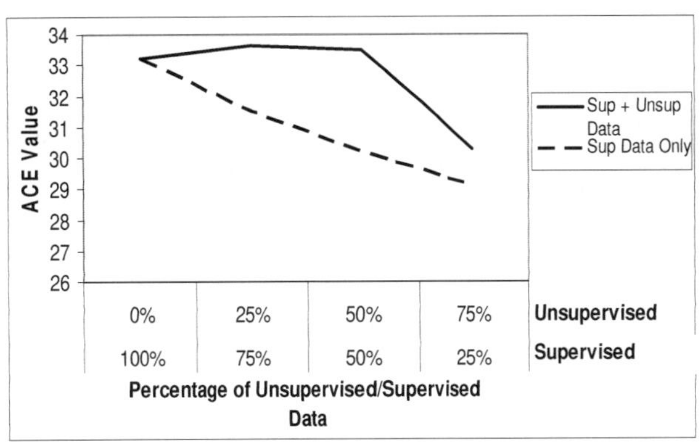


Figure 6: The effect of removing portions of the supervised data on the ACE value. And the effect

of replacing portions of the supervised data with labeled training data.

## 7 Conclusion

We introduce a general framework for semi-supervised learning based on mutual reinforcement in graphs. We construct generalized extraction patterns and deploy graph based mutual reinforcement to automatically identify the most informative patterns. We provide motivation for our approach from a graph theory and graph link analysis perspective.

We present experimental results supporting the applicability of the proposed approach to ACE Relation Detection and Characterization (RDC) task, demonstrating its applicability to hard information extraction problems. Our approach achieves a significant improvement over the base line supervised system especially when the number of labeled instances is small.

## 8 Acknowledgements

We would like to thank Nanda Kambhatla for providing the ACE baseline system. We would also like to thank Salim Roukos for several invaluable suggestions and guidance. Finally we would like to thank the anonymous reviewers for their constructive criticism and helpful comments.

## References

ACE. 2004. The NIST ACE evaluation website. http://www.nist.gov/speech/tests/ace/

Avrim Blum, and Tom Mitchell. 1998. *Combining Labeled and Unlabeled data with Co-training*. Proceedings of the 11th Annual Conference on Computational Learning Theory.

Avrim Blum and Shuchi Chawla. 2001. *Learning From Labeled and Unlabeled Data Using Graph Mincuts.* Proceedings of International Conference on Machine Learning (ICML).

Avrim Blum, John Lafferty, Mugizi Rwebangira, and Rajashekar Reddy. 2004. *Semi-supervised Learning Using Randomized Mincuts*. Proceedings of the International Conference on Machine Learning (ICML).

Stijn van Dongen. 2000. *A Cluster Algorithm for Graphs.* Technical Report INS-R0010, National Research Institute for Mathematics and Computer Science in the Netherlands.

Stijn van Dongen. 2000. *Graph Clustering by Flow Simulation*. PhD thesis, University of Utrecht

Radu Florian, Hany Hassan, Hongyan Jing, Nanda Kambhatla, Xiaqiang Luo, Nicolas Nicolov, and Salim Roukos. 2004. *A Statistical Model for multilingual entity detection and tracking.* Proceedings of the Human Language Technologies Conference (HLT-NAACL'04).

Dayne Freitag, and Nicholas Kushmerick. 2000. *Boosted wrapper induction*. The 14th European Conference on Artificial Intelligence Workshop on Machine Learning for Information Extraction

Taher Haveliwala. 2002. *Topic-sensitive PageRank.* Proceedings of the 11th International World Wide Web Conference

Thorsten Joachims. 2003. *Transductive Learning via Spectral Graph Partitioning*. Proceedings of the International Conference on Machine Learning (ICML).

John Kleinberg. 1998. *Authoritative Sources in a Hyperlinked Environment.* Proceedings of the. 9th ACM-SIAM Symposium on Discrete Algorithms.

Nanda Kambhatla. 2004. *Combining Lexical, Syntactic, and Semantic Features with Maximum Entropy Models for Information Extraction*. Proceedings of the $42^{nd}$ Annual Meeting of the Association for Computational Linguistics

Ted Pedersen, Siddharth Patwardhan, and Jason Michelizzi, 2004, *WordNet::Similarity - Measuring the Relatedness of Concepts*. Proceedings of Fifth Annual Meeting of the North American Chapter of the Association for Computational Linguistics (NAACL-2004)

Scott White, and Padhraic Smyth. 2003. *Algorithms for Discoveing Relative Importance in Graphs*. Proceedings of Ninth ACM SIGKDD International Conference on Knowledge Discovery and Data Mining.

Zhibiao Wu, and Martha Palmer. 1994. *Verb semantics and lexical selection*. Proceedings of the 32nd Annual Meeting of the Association for Computational Linguistics.

Xiaojin Zhu, Zoubin Ghahramani, and John Lafferty. 2003. *Semi-supervised Learning using Gaussian Fields and Harmonic Functions*. Proceedings of the 20th International Conference on Machine Learning.

# Graph-Based Text Representation for Novelty Detection

**Michael Gamon**
Microsoft Research
Redmond, WA 98052
mgamon@microsoft.com

## Abstract

We discuss several feature sets for novelty detection at the sentence level, using the data and procedure established in task 2 of the TREC 2004 novelty track. In particular, we investigate feature sets derived from graph representations of sentences and sets of sentences. We show that a highly connected graph produced by using sentence-level term distances and pointwise mutual information can serve as a source to extract features for novelty detection. We compare several feature sets based on such a graph representation. These feature sets allow us to increase the accuracy of an initial novelty classifier which is based on a bag-of-word representation and KL divergence. The final result ties with the best system at TREC 2004.

## 1 Introduction

Novelty detection is the task of identifying novel information given a set of already accumulated background information. Potential applications of novelty detection systems are abundant, given the "information overload" in email, web content etc. Gabrilovich et al (2004), for example, describe a scenario in which a newsfeed is personalized based on a measure of information novelty: the user can be presented with pieces of information that are novel, given the documents that have already been reviewed. This will spare the user the task of sifting through vast amounts of duplicate and redundant information on a topic to find bits and pieces of information that are of interest.

In 2002 TREC introduced a novelty track (Harman 2002), which continued — with major changes — in 2003 (Soboroff and Harman 2003) and 2004 (Voorhees 2004). In 2002 the task was to identify the set of relevant and novel sentences from an ordered set of documents within a TREC topic. Novelty was defined as "providing new information that has not been found in any previously picked sentences". Relevance was defined as "relevant to the question or request made in the description section of the topic". Inter-annotator agreement was low (Harman 2002). There were 50 topics for the novelty task in 2002. For the 2003 novelty track a number of major changes were made. Relevance and novelty detection were separated into different tasks, allowing a separate evaluation of relevance detection and novelty detection. In the 2002 track, the data proved to be problematic since the percentage of relevant sentences in the documents was small. This, in turn, led to a very high percentage of relevant sentences being novel, given that amongst the small set of relevant sentences there was little redundancy. 50 new topics were created for the 2003 task, with a better balance of relevant and novel sentences. Slightly more than half of the topics dealt with "events," the rest with "opinions."

The 2004 track used the same tasks, the same number of topics and the same split between event and opinion topics as the 2003 track.

For the purpose of this paper, we are only concerned with novelty detection, specifically with task 2 of the 2004 novelty track, as described in more detail in the following section.



*Workshop on TextGraphs, at HLT-NAACL 2006*, pages 17–24,
New York City, June 2006. ©2006 Association for Computational Linguistics

The question that we investigate here is: what is a meaningful feature set for text representation for novelty detection? This is obviously a far-reaching and loaded question. Possibilities range from simple bag-of-word features to features derived from sophisticated linguistic representations. Ultimately, the question is open-ended since there will always be another feature or feature combination that could/should be exploited. For our experiments, we have decided to focus more narrowly on the usefulness of features derived from graph representations and we have restricted ourselves to representations that do not require linguistic analysis. Simple bag-of-word metrics like KL divergence establish a baseline for classifier performance. More sophisticated metrics can be defined on the basis of graph representations. Graph representations of text can be constructed without performing linguistic analysis, by using term distances in sentences and pointwise mutual information between terms to form edges between term-vertices. A term-distance based representation has been used successfully for a variety of tasks in Mihalcea (2004) and Mihalcea and Tarau (2004).

## 2 Previous work

There were 13 participants and 54 submitted runs for the 2004 TREC novelty track task 2. Each participant submitted up to five runs with different system configurations. Metrics and approaches varied widely, from purely string based approaches to systems that used sophisticated linguistic components for synonymy resolution, coreference resolution and named entity recognition. Many systems employed a thresholding approach to the task, defining a novelty metric and then determining a sentence to be novel if the threshold is exceeded (e.g. Blott et al. 2004, Zhang et al. 2004, Abdul-Jaleel et al. 2004, Eichmann et al. 2004, Erkan 2004). Thresholds are either determined on the 2003 data, are based on a notion of mean score, or are determined in an ad hoc manner[1]. Tomiyama et al (2004), similar to our approach, use an SVM classifier to make the binary classification of a sentence as novel or not.

The baseline result for the 2004 task 2 was an average F-measure of 0.577. This baseline is achieved if all relevant sentences are categorized as novel. The difficulty of the novelty detection task is evident from the relatively low score achieved by even the best systems. The five best-performing runs were:

1. Blott et al. (2004) (Dublin City University): using a tf.idf based metric of "importance value" at an ad hoc threshold: **0.622.**
2. Tomiyama et al. (2004) (Meiji University): using an SVM classifier trained on 2003 data, features based on conceptual fuzzy sets derived from a background corpus: **0.619**.
3. Abdul-Jaleel et al. (2004) (UMass): using named entity recognition, using cosine similarity as a metric and thresholds derived from the 2003 data set: **0.618**.
4. Schiffman and McKeown (2004) (Columbia): using a combination of tests based on weights (derived from a background corpus) for previously unseen words with parameters trained on the 2003 data set, and taking into account the novelty status of the previous sentence: **0.617**.
5. Tomiyama et al (2004) (Meiji University): slight variation of the system described above, with one of the features (scarcity measure) eliminated: **0.617**.

As this list shows, there was no clear tendency of any particular kind of approach outperforming others. Among the above four systems and five runs, there are thresholding and classification approaches, systems that use background corpora and conceptual analysis and systems that do not.

## 3 Experimental setup

### 3.1 The task

Task 2 of the 2004 novelty track is formulated as follows:

> Task 2: Given the relevant sentences in the complete document set (for a given topic), identify all novel sentences.

The procedure is sequential on an ordered list of sentences per topic. For each Sentence $S_i$ the determination needs to be made whether it is novel given the previously seen sentences $S_1$ through $S_{i-1}$.

[1] Unfortunately, some of the system descriptions are unclear about the exact rationale for choosing a particular threshold.

The evaluation metric for the novelty track is $F_1$-measure, averaged over all 50 topics.

## 3.2 Novelty detection as classification

For the purpose of this paper we view novelty detection as a supervised classification task. While the supervised approach has its limitations in real-life scenarios where annotated data are hard to come by, it can serve as a testing ground for the question we are interested in: the evaluation of feature sets and text representations.

At training time, a feature vector is created for each tagged sentence S and the set of sentences that comprise the already seen information that S is compared to. Features in the vector can be features of the tagged sentence, features of the set of sentences comprising the given background information and features that capture a relation between the tagged sentence and the set of background sentences. A classifier is trained on the set of resulting feature vectors. At evaluation time, a feature vector is extracted from the sentence to be evaluated and from the set of sentences that form the background knowledge. The classifier then determines whether, given the feature values of that vector, the sentence is more likely to be novel or not.

We use the TREC 2003 data set for training, since it is close to the 2004 data set in its makeup. We train Support Vector Machines (SVMs) on the 2003 data, using the LibSVM tool (Chang and Lin 2001). Following the methodology outlined in Chang and Lin 2003, we use radial basis function (RBF) kernels and perform a grid search on two-fold cross validated results on the training set to identify optimal parameter settings for the penalty parameter C and the RBF parameter $\gamma$. Continuously valued features are scaled to values between -1 and 1. The scaling range is determined on the training set and the same range is applied to the test set.

The text was minimally preprocessed before extracting features: stop words were removed, tokens were lowercased and punctuation was stripped from the strings.

# 4 Text representations and features

## 4.1 KL divergence as a feature

Treating sentences as an unordered collection of terms, the information-theoretic metric of KL divergence (or relative entropy) has been successfully used to measure "distance" between documents by simply comparing the term distributions in a document compared to another document or set of documents. The notions of distance and novelty are closely related: if a new document is very distant from the collection of documents that has been seen previously, it is likely to contain new, previously unseen information. Gabrilovich et al. (2004), for example, report on a successful use of KL divergence for novelty detection. KL divergence is defined in Equation 1:

$$\sum_{w} p_d(w) \log \frac{p_d(w)}{p_R(w)}$$

Equation 1: KL divergence.

$w$ belongs to the set of words that are shared between document $d$ and document (set) $R$. $p_d$ and $p_R$ are the probability distributions of words in $d$ and $R$, respectively. Both $p_d(w)$ and $p_R(w)$ need to be non-zero in the equation above. We used simple add-one smoothing to ensure non-zero values. While it is conceivable that KL divergence could take into account other features than just bag-of-words information, we restrict ourselves to this particular use of the measure since it corresponds to the typical use in novelty detection.

## 4.2 Term distance graphs: from text to graph without linguistic analysis

KL divergence as described above treats a document or sentence as an unordered collection of words. Language obviously provides more structure than that. Linguistic resources can impose structure on a string of words through consultation of linguistic knowledge (either hand-coded or learned from a tagged corpus). Even without any outside knowledge, however, the order of words in a sentence provides a means to construct a highly connected undirected graph with the words as vertices. The intuition here is:

1. All words in a sentence have some relationship to all other words in the sentence, modulo a "window size" outside of which the relationship is not taken into consideration
2. The closer two words are to each other, the stronger their connection tends to be[2]

It follows from (2) that weights on the edges will be inversely proportional to the distance between two words (vertices). In the remainder of the paper we will refer to these graphs as TD (term distance) graphs. Of course (1) and (2) are rough generalizations with many counterexamples, but without the luxury of linguistic analysis this seems to be a reasonable step to advance beyond simple bag-of-word assumptions. Multiple sentence graphs can then be combined into a highly connected graph to represent text. Mihalcea (2004) and Mihalcea and Tarau (2004) have successfully explored very similar graph representations for extractive summarization and key word extraction.

In addition to distance, we also employ pointwise mutual information as defined in Equation 2 between two words/vertices to enter into the calculation of edge weight[3]. This combination of distance and a cooccurrence measure such as PMI is reminiscent of decaying language models, as described for IR, for example, in Gao et al. (2002)[4]. Cooccurrence is counted at the sentence level, i.e. $P(i, j)$ is estimated by the number of sentences that contain both terms $w_i$ and $w_j$, and $P(i)$ and $P(j)$ are estimated by counting the total sentences containing $w_i$ and $w_j$, respectively. As the set of seen sentences grows and cooccurrence between words becomes more prevalent, PMI becomes more influential on edge weights, strengthening edges between words that have high PMI.

$$PMI_{(i,j)} = \log_2 \frac{P(i,j)}{P(i)P(j)}$$

Equation 2: Pointwise Mutual Information (PMI) between two terms *i* and *j*.

Formally, the weight *wt* for each edge in the graph is defined as in Equation 3, where $d_{i,j}$ is the distance between words $w_i$ and $w_j$.and PMI(i,j) is the pointwise mutual information between words $w_i$ and $w_j$, given the sentences seen so far. For the purpose of Equation 3 we ignored negative PMI values, i.e. we treated negative PMI values as 0.

$$wt_{i,j} = \frac{1 + PMI(i,j)}{d_{i,j}^2}$$

Equation 3: Assigning weight to an edge between two vertices.

We imposed a "window size" as a limit on the maximum distance between two words to enter an edge relationship. Window size was varied between 3 and 8; on the training set a window size of 6 proved to be optimal.

On a TD graph representation, we can calculate various features based on the strengths and number of connections between words. In novelty detection, we can model the growing store of background information by adding each "incoming" sentence graph to the existing background graph. If an "incoming" edge already exists in the background graph, the weight of the "incoming" edge is added to the existing edge weight.

Figure 1 shows a subset of a TD graph for the first two sentences of topic N57. The visualization is generated by the Pajek tool (Bagatelj and Mrvar).

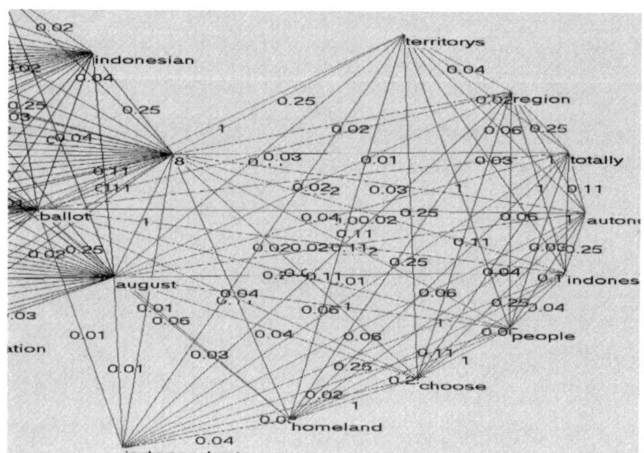


Figure 1: A subset of a TD graph of the first two sentences of topic N57.

---

[2] This view is supported by examining dependency structures derived from the Penn Tree Bank and mapping the probability of a dependency to the distance between words. See also Eisner and Smith (2005) who explore this generalization for dependency parsing.

[3] We also computed results from a graph where the edge weight is determined only by term distance, without PMI. These results were consistently worse than the ones reported here.

[4] We are grateful to an anonymous reviewer for pointing this out.

### 4.3 Graph features

#### 4.3.1 Simple Graph features

In novelty detection, graph based features allow to assess the change a graph undergoes through the addition of a new sentence. The intuition behind these features is that the more a graph changes when a sentence is added, the more likely the added sentence is to contain novel information. After all, novel information may be conveyed even if the terms involved are not novel. Establishing a new relation (i.e. edge in the graph) between two previously seen terms would have exactly that effect: old terms conveying new information. KL divergence or any other measure of distributional similarity is not suited to capture this scenario. As an example consider a news story thread about a crime. The various sentences in the background information may mention the victim, multiple suspects, previous convictions, similar crimes etc. When a new sentence is encountered where one suspect's name is mentioned in the same sentence with the victim, at a close distance, none of these two terms are new. The fact that suspect and victim are mentioned in one sentence, however, may indicate a piece of novel information: a close relationship between the two that did not exist in the background story.

We designed 21 graph based features, based on the following definitions:

- *Background graph:* the graph representing the previously seen sentences.
- *G(S):* the graph of the sentence that is currently being evaluated.
- *Reinforced background edge:* an edge that exists both in the background graph and in G(*S*).
- *Added background edge:* a new edge in G(S) that connects two vertices that already exist in the background graph.
- *New edge:* an edge in G(S) that connects two previously unseen vertices.
- *Connecting edge:* an edge in G(S) between a previously unseen vertex and a previously seen vertex.

The 21 features are:

- number of new edges
- number of added background edges
- number of background edges
- number of background vertices
- number of connecting edges
- sum of weights on new edges
- sum of weights on added background edges
- sum of weights on connecting edges
- background connectivity (ratio between edges and vertices)
- connectivity added by *S*
- ratio between added background edges and new edges
- ratio between new edges and connecting edges
- ratio between added background edges and connecting edges
- ratio between the sum of weights on new edges and the sum of weights on added background edges
- ratio between the sum of weights on new edges and the sum of weights on connecting edges
- ratio between the sum of weights on added background edges and the sum of weights on connecting edges
- ratio between sum of weights on added background edges and the sum of pre-existing weights on those edges
- ratio between sum of weights on new edges and sum of weight on background edges
- ratio between sum of weights added to reinforced background edges and sum of background weights
- ratio between number of added background edges and reinforced background edges
- number of background edges leading from those background vertices that have been connected to new vertices by G(*S*)

We refer to this set of 21 features as *simple graph features*, to distinguish them from a second set of graph-based features that are based on TextRank.

#### 4.3.2 TextRank features

The TextRank metric, as described in Mihalcea and Tarau (2004) is inspired by the PageRank metric which is used for web page ranking[5]. TextRank is designed to work well in text graph representations: it can take edge weights into account and it works on undirected graphs. TextRank calculates a weight for each vertex, based on Equation 4.

$$TR(V_i) = (1-d) + d * \left( \sum_{V_j \in NB(V_i)} \frac{wt_{ji}}{\sum_{V_k \in NB(V_j)} wt_{jk}} TR(V_j) \right)$$

Equation 4: The TextRank metric.

where $TR(V_i)$ is the TextRank score for vertex i, $NB(V_i)$ is the set of neighbors of $V_i$, i.e. the set of nodes connected to $V_i$ by a single edge, $wt_{xy}$ is the weight of the edge between vertex x and vertex y, and d is a constant "dampening factor", set at 0.85[6]. To calculate TR, an initial score of 1 is assigned to all vertices, and the formula is applied iteratively until the difference in scores between iterations falls below a threshold of 0.0001 for all vertices (as in Mihalcea and Tarau 2004).

The TextRank score itself is not particularly enlightening for novelty detection. It measures the "importance" rather than the novelty of a vertex - hence its usefulness in keyword extraction. We can, however, derive a number of features from the TextRank scores that measure the change in scores as a result of adding a sentence to the graph of the background information. The rationale is that the more the TextRank scores are "disturbed" by the addition of a new sentence, the more likely it is that the new sentence carries novel information. We normalize the TextRank scores by the number of vertices to obtain a probability distribution. The features we define on the basis of the (normalized) TextRank metric are:

1. sum of TR scores on the nodes of S, after adding S
2. maximum TR score on any nodes of S
3. maximum TR score on any background node before adding S
4. delta between 2 and 3
5. sum of TR scores on the background nodes (after adding S)
6. delta between 5 and 1
7. variance of the TR scores before adding S
8. variance of TR scores after adding S
9. delta between 7 and 8
10. ratio of 1 to 5
11. KL divergence between the TR scores before and after adding S

## 5 Results

To establish a baseline, we used a simple bag-of-words approach and KL divergence as a feature for classification. Employing the protocol described above, i.e. training the classifier on the 2003 data set, and optimizing the parameters on 2 folds of the training data, we achieve a surprisingly high result of 0.618 average F-measure on the 2004 data. This result would place the run at a tie for third place with the UMass system in the 2004 competition.

In the tables below, *KL* refers to the KL divergence feature, *TR* to the TextRank based features and *SG* to the simple graph based features.

Given that the feature sets we investigate possibly capture orthogonal properties, we were also interested in using combinations of the three feature sets. For the graph based features we determined on the training set that results were optimal at a "window size" of 6, i.e. if graph edges are produced only if the distance between terms is six tokens or less. All results are tabulated in Table 1, with the best results boldfaced.

| Feature set | Average F measure |
|---|---|
| KL | 0.618 |
| TR | 0.600 |
| SG | 0.619 |
| **KL + SG** | **0.622** |
| **KL + SG + TR** | **0.621** |
| SG + TR | 0.615 |
| TR + KL | 0.618 |

Table 1: Performance of the different feature sets.

We used the McNemar test to determine pairwise statistical significance levels between the novelty classifiers based on different feature sets[7]. The two (boldfaced) best results from Table 1 are significantly different from the baseline at 0.999 confidence. Individual sentence level

[5] Erkan and Radev (2005) introduced *LexRank* where a graph representation of a set of sentences is derived from the cosine similarity between sentences. Kurland and Lee (2004) derive a graph representation for a set of documents by linking documents X and Y with edges weighted by the score that a language model trained on X assigns to Y.

[6] Following Mihalcea and Tarau (2004), who in turn base their default setting on Brin and Page (1998).

[7] We could not use the Wilcoxon rank test for our results since we only had binary classification results for each sentence, as opposed to individual (class probability) scores.

classifications from the official 2004 runs were not available to us, so we were not able to test for statistical significance on our results versus TREC results.

## 6 Summary and Conclusion

We showed that using KL divergence as a feature for novelty classification establishes a surprisingly good result at an average F-measure of 0.618, which would top all but 3 of the 54 runs submitted for task 2 in the TREC novelty track in 2004. To improve on this baseline we computed graph features from a highly connected graph built from sentence-level term cooccurrences with edges weighted by distance and pointwise mutual information. A set of 21 "simple graph features" extracted directly from the graph perform slightly better than KL divergence, at 0.619 average F-measure. We also computed TextRank features from the same graph representation. TextRank features by themselves achieve 0.600 average F-measure. The best result is achieved by combining feature sets: Using a combination of KL features and simple graph features produces an average F-measure of 0.622.

Being able to establish a very high baseline with just the use of KL divergence as a feature was surprising to us: it involves a minimal approach to novelty detection. We believe that the high baseline indicates that a classification approach to novelty detection is promising. This is corroborated by the very good performance of the runs from Meiji University which also used a classifier.

The second result, i.e. the benefit obtained by using graph based features was in line with our expectations. It is a reasonable assumption that the graph features would be able to add to the information that a feature like KL divergence can capture. The gains were statistically significant but very modest, which poses a number of questions. First, our feature engineering may be less than optimal, missing important information from a graph-based representation. Second, the classification approach may be suffering from inherent differences between the training data (TREC 2003) and the test data (TREC 2004). To explore this hypothesis, we trained SVMs on the KL + SG feature set with default settings on three random folds of the 2003 and 2004 data. For these experiments we simply measured accuracy. The baseline accuracy (predicting the majority class label) was 65.77% for the 2003 data and 58.59% for the 2004 data. Average accuracy for the threefold crossvalidation on 2003 data was 75.72%, on the 2004 data it was 64.88%. Using the SVMs trained on the 2003 data on the three folds of the 2004 data performed below baseline at 55.07%. These findings indicate that the 2003 data are indeed not an ideal fit as training material for the 2004 task.

With these results indicating that graph features can be useful for novelty detection, the question becomes which graph representation is best suited to extract these features from. A highly connected term-distance based graph representation, with the addition of pointwise mutual information, is a computationally relatively cheap approach. There are at least two alternative graph representations that are worth exploring.

First, a "true" dependency graph that is based on linguistic analysis would provide a less connected alternative. Such a graph would, however, contain more information in the form of directed edges and edge labels (labels of semantic relations) that could prove useful for novelty detection. On the downside, it would necessarily be prone to errors and domain specificity in the linguistic analysis process.

Second, one could use the parse matrix of a statistical dependency parser to create the graph representation. This would yield a dependency graph that has more edges than those coming from a "1-best" dependency parse. In addition, the weights on the edges could be based on dependency probability estimates, and analysis errors would not be as detrimental since several alternative analyses enter into the graph representations.

It is beyond the scope of this paper to present a thorough comparison between these different graph representations. However, we were able to demonstrate that a computationally simple graph representation, which is based solely on pointwise mutual information and term distance, allows us to successfully extract useful features for novelty detection. The results that can be achieved in this manner only present a modest gain over a simple approach using KL divergence as a classification feature. The best achieved result, however, would tie for first place in the 2004 TREC novelty track, in comparison to many systems which relied on relatively heavy analysis machinery and additional data resources.

## References


Nasreen Abdul-Jaleel, James Allan, W. Bruce Croft, Fernando Diaz, Leah Larkey, Xiaoyan Li, Mark D. Smucker and Courtney Wade. 2004. UMass at TREC 2004: Novelty and HARD. *NIST Special Publication 500-261: The Thirteenth Text REtrieval Conference (TREC 2004).*

Vladimir Batagelj, Andrej Mrvar: Pajek - Program for Large Network Analysis. Home page http://vlado.fmf.uni-lj.si/pub/networks/pajek/.

Stephen Blott, Oisin Boydell, Fabrice Camous, Paul Ferguson, Georgina Gaughan, Cathal Gurrin, Gareth J. F. Jones, Noel Murphy, Noel O'Connor, Alan F. Smeaton, Barry Smyth, Peter Wilkins. 2004. Experiments in Terabyte Searching, Genomic Retrieval and Novelty Detection for TREC-2004. *NIST Special Publication 500-261: The Thirteenth Text REtrieval Conference (TREC 2004).*

Sergey Brin and Lawrence Page. 1998. The anatomy of a large-scale hypertextual web search engine. *Computer Networks and ISDN Systems 30: 107-117.*

Chih-Chung Chang and Chih-Jen Lin. LIBSVM: a library for support vector machines, 2001. Software available at http://www.csie.ntu.edu.tw/~cjlin/libsvm.

Chih-Chung Chang and Chih-Jen Lin. 2003. A Practical Guide to Support Vector Classification.

David Eichmann, Yi Zhang, Shannon Bradshaw, Xin Ying Qiu, Li Zhou, Padmini Srinivasan, Aditya Kumar Sehgal and Hudon Wong. 2004. Novelty, Question Answering and Genomics: The University of Iowa Response. *NIST Special Publication 500-261: The Thirteenth Text REtrieval Conference (TREC 2004).*

Jason Eisner and Noah A. Smith. 2005. Parsing with Soft and Hard Constraints on Dependency Length. *Proceedings of the International Workshop on Parsing Technologies (IWPT).*

Güneş Erkan. 2004. The University of Michigan in Novelty 2004. *NIST Special Publication 500-261: The Thirteenth Text REtrieval Conference (TREC 2004).*

Güneş Erkan and Dragomir Radev. 2004. LexRank: Graph-based Centrality as Salience in Text Summarization. *Journal of Artificial Intelligence Research 22, pp. 457-479.*

Evgeniy Gabrilovich, Susan Dumais and Eric Horvitz. 2004. Newsjunkie: Providing Personalized Newsfeeds via Analysis of Information Novelty. WWW13, 2004.

Jianfeng Gao, Jian-Yun Nie, Hongzhao He, Weijun Chena and Ming Zhou. 2002. Resolving Query Translation Ambiguity using a Decaying Co-occurrence Model and Syntactic Dependency Relations. Proceedings of SIGIR 2002, 183-190.

Donna Harman. 2002. Overview of the TREC 2002 Novelty Track. *NIST Special Publication 500-251: The Eleventh Text REtrieval Conference (TREC 2002).*

Oren Kurland and Lillian Lee. 2004. PageRank without hyperlinks: structural re-ranking using links induced by language models. *Proceedings of SIGIR 2005, pp. 306-313.*

Rada Mihalcea. 2004. Graph-based Ranking Algorithms for Sentence Extraction, Applied to Text Summarization. *Proceedings of the 42nd Annual Meeting of the Association for Computational Linguistics, companion volume (ACL 2004).*

Rada Mihalcea and Paul Tarau. 2004. TextRank: Bringing Order into Texts. *Proceedings of the Conference on Empirical Methods in Natural Language Processing (EMNLP 2004).*

Barry Schiffman and Kathleen R. McKeown. 2004. Columbia University in the Novelty Track at TREC 2004. *NIST Special Publication 500-261: The Thirteenth Text REtrieval Conference (TREC 2004).*

Ian Soboroff and Donna Harman. 2003. Overview of the TREC 2003 Novelty Task. *NIST Special Publication 500-255: The Twelfth Text REtrieval Conference (TREC 2003).*

Tomoe Tomiyama, Kosuke Karoji, Takeshi Kondo, Yuichi Kakuta and Tomohiro Takagi. 2004. Meiji University Web, Novelty and Genomics Track Experiments. *NIST Special Publication 500-261: The Thirteenth Text REtrieval Conference (TREC 2004).*

Ellen M. Voorhees. 2004. Overview of TREC 2004. *NIST Special Publication 500-261: The Thirteenth Text REtrieval Conference (TREC 2004).*

Hua-Ping Zhang, Hong-Bo Xu, Shuo Bai, Bin Wang and Xue-Qi Cheng. 2004. Experiments in TREC 2004 Novelty Track at CAS-ICT. *NIST Special Publication 500-261: The Thirteenth Text REtrieval Conference (TREC 2004).*

# Measuring Aboutness of an Entity in a Text

**Marie-Francine Moens**
Legal Informatics and Information Retrieval
Katholieke Universiteit Leuven, Belgium
marie-france.moens@law.kuleuven.be

**Patrick Jeuniaux**
Department. of Psychology
University of Memphis, USA
pjeuniaux@mail.psyc.memphis.edu

**Roxana Angheluta**
Legal Informatics and Information Retrieval
Katholieke Universiteit Leuven, Belgium
anghelutar@yahoo.com

**Rudradeb Mitra**
Mission Critical, IT
Brussels, Belgium
rdm@missioncriticalit.com

## Abstract

In many information retrieval and selection tasks it is valuable to score how much a text is about a certain entity and to compute how much the text discusses the entity with respect to a certain viewpoint. In this paper we are interested in giving an aboutness score to a text, when the input query is a person name and we want to measure the aboutness with respect to the biographical data of that person. We present a graph-based algorithm and compare its results with other approaches.

## 1 Introduction

In many information processing tasks one is interested in measuring how much a text or passage is about a certain entity. This is called *aboutness* or topical relevance (Beghtol 1986; Soergel 1994). Simple word counts of the entity term often give only a rough estimation of aboutness. The true frequency of the entity might be hidden by coreferents. Two entities are considered as coreferents when they both refer to the same entity in the situation described in the text (e.g., in the sentences: "Dan Quayle met his wife in college. The Indiana senator married her shortly after he finished his studies": "his", "Indiana senator" and "he" all corefer to "Dan Quayle"). If we want to score the aboutness of an entity with respect to a certain viewpoint, the aboutness is also obfuscated by the referents that refer to the chosen viewpoint and in which context the entity is mentioned. In the example "Dan Quayle ran for presidency", "presidency" can be considered as a referent for "Dan Quayle". Because, coreferents and referents can be depicted in a graphical representation of the discourse content, it seems interesting to exploit this graph structure in order to compute aboutness. This approach is inspired by studies in cognitive science on text comprehension (van Dijk and Kintsch, 1983). When humans read a text, they make many inferences about and link information that is found in the text, a behavior that influences aboutness assessment. Automated aboutness computation has many applications such as text indexing, summarization, and text linking.

We focus on estimating the aboutness score of a text given an input query in the form of a person proper name. The score should reflect how much the text deals with biographical information about the person. We present an algorithm based on eigenvector analysis of the link matrix of the discourse graph built by the noun phrase coreferents and referents. We test the approach with a small set of documents, which we rank by decreasing aboutness of the input entity. We compare the results with results obtained by traditional approaches such as a normalized term frequency (possibly corrected by coreference resolution and augmented with other referent information). Although the results on a small test set do not pretend to give firm evidence on the validity of our approach, our contribution lies in the reflection of using graph based document representations of discourse content and exploiting this structure in content recognition.

## 2 Methods

Our approach involves the detection of entities and their noun phrase coreferents, the generation of terms that are correlated with biographical infor-



*Workshop on TextGraphs, at HLT-NAACL 2006*, pages 25–28,
New York City, June 2006. 

mation, the detection of references between entities, and the computation of the aboutness score. As linguistic resources we used the LT-POS tagger developed at the University of Edinburgh and the Charniak parser developed at Brown University.

### 2.1 Noun Phrase Coreference Resolution

Coreference resolution focuses on detecting "identity" relationships between noun phrases (i.e. not on is-a or whole/part links). It is natural to view coreferencing as a partitioning or clustering of the set of entities. The idea is to group coreferents into the same cluster, which is accomplished in two steps: 1) detection of the entities and extraction of their features set; 2) clustering of the entities. For the first subtask we use the same set of features as in Cardie and Wagstaff (1999). For the second step we used the progressive fuzzy clustering algorithm described in Angheluta et al. (2004).

### 2.2 Learning Biographical Terms

We learn a term's biographical value as the correlation of the term with texts of biographical nature. There are different ways of learning associations present in corpora (e.g., use of the mutual information statistic, use of the chi-square statistic). We use the likelihood ratio for a binomial distribution (Dunning 1993), which tests the hypothesis whether the term occurs independently in texts of biographical nature given a large corpus of biographical and non-biographical texts. For considering a term as biography-related, we set a likelihood ratio threshold such that the hypothesis can be rejected with a certain significance level.

### 2.3 Reference Detection between Entities

We assume that the syntactic relationships between entities (proper or common nouns) in a text give us information on their semantic reference status. In our simple experiment, we consider reference relationships found within a single sentence, and more specifically we take into account relationships between two noun phrase entities. The analysis requires that the sentences are syntactically analyzed or parsed. The following syntactic relationships are detected in the parse tree of each sentence:

1) **Subject-object**: An object refers to the subject (e.g., in the sentence *He eats an apple*, *an apple* refers to *He*). This relationship type also covers prepositional phrases that are the argument of a verb (e.g., in the sentence *He goes to Hollywood*, *Hollywood* refers to *He*). The relationship holds between the heads of the respective noun phrases in case other nouns modify them.

2) **NP-PP{NP}**: A noun phrase is modified by a prepositional noun phrase: the head of the prepositional noun phrase refers to the head of the dominant noun phrase (e.g., in the chunk *The nominee for presidency*, *presidency* refers to *The nominee*).

3) **NP-NP**: A noun phrase modifies another noun phrase: the head of the modifying noun phrase refers to the head of the dominant noun phrase (e.g., in the chunk *Dan Quayle's sister*, *Dan Quayle* refers to *sister*, in the chunk *sugar factory*, *sugar* refers to *factory*).

When a sentence is composed of different subclauses and when one of the components of the first two relationships has the form of a subclause, the first noun phrase of the subclause is considered. When computing a reference relation with an entity term, we only consider biographical terms found as described in (2.2).

### 2.4 Computing the Aboutness Score

The aboutness of a document text $D$ for the input entity $E$ is computed as follows:

$$aboutness(D,E) = \frac{entity\_score(E)}{\sum_{F \in \text{distinctentities of } D} entity\_score(F)}$$

*entity_score* is zero when $E$ does not occur in $D$. Otherwise we compute the entity score as follows. We represent $D$ as a graph, where nodes represent the entities as mentioned in the text and the weights of the connections represent the reference score (in our experiments set to 1 when the entities are coreferents, 0.5 when the entities are other referents). The values 1 and 0.5 were selected ad hoc. Future fine-tuning of the weights of the edges of the discourse graph based on discourse features could be explored (cf. Givón 2001). The edge values are stored in a link matrix $A$. The authority of an entity is computed by considering the values of the principal eigenvector of $A^TA$. (cf. Kleinberg 1998) (in the results below this approach is referred to as LM). In this way we compute the authority of each entity in a text.

We implemented four other entity scores: the term frequency (TF), the term frequency augmented with noun phrase coreference information (TFCOREF), the term frequency augmented with reference information (weighted by 0.5) (TFREF) and the term frequency augmented with coreference and reference information (TFCOREFREF). The purpose is not that the 4 scoring functions are mutually comparable, but that the ranking of the documents that is produced by each of them can be compared against an ideal ranking built by humans.

## 3 Experiments and Results

For learning person related words we used a training corpus consisting of biographical texts of persons obtained from the Web (from http://www.biography.com) and biographical and non-biographical texts from DUC-2002 and DUC-2003. For considering a term as biography-related, we set a likelihood ratio threshold such that the hypothesis of independence can be rejected with a significance level of less than 0.0025, assuring that the selected terms are really biography-related.

In order to evaluate the aboutness computation, we considered five input queries consisting of a proper person name phrase ("Dan Quayle" (D), "Hillary Clinton" (H), "Napoleon" (N), "Sadam Hussein" (S) and "Sharon Stone" (ST)) and downloaded for each of the queries 5 texts from the Web (each text contains minimally once an exact match with the input query). Two persons were asked to rank the texts according to relevancy, if they were searching biographical information on the input person (100% agreement was obtained). Two aspects are important in determining relevancy: a text should really and almost exclusively contain biographical information of the input person in order not to lose time with other information. For each query, at least one of the texts is a biographical text and one of the texts only marginally mentions the person in question. All texts except for the biography texts speak about other persons, and pronouns are abundantly used. The "Hillary Clinton" texts do not contain many other persons except for Hillary, in contrast with the "Dan Quayle", "Napoleon" and "Sadam Hussein" texts. The "Hillary Clinton" texts are in general quite relevant for this first lady. For "Napoleon" there is one biographical text on Napoleon's surgeon that mentions Napoleon only marginally. The “Dan Quayle” texts contain a lot of direct speech. For "Sharon Stone" 4 out of the 5 texts described a movie in which this actress played a role, thus being only marginally relevant for a demand of biographical data of the actress.

Then we ranked the texts based on the TF, TFCOREF, TFREF, TFCOREFREF and LM scores and computed the congruence of each ranking ($R_x$) with the manual ranking ($R_m$). We used the following measure of similarity of the rankings:

$$sim(R_x, R_m) = 1 - \frac{\sum_i |r_{x,i} - r_{m,i}|}{floor\frac{n^2}{2}} * 100$$

where $n$ is the number of items in the 2 rankings and $r_{x,i}$ and $r_{m,i}$ denote the position of the $i$th item in $R_x$ and $R_m$ respectively. Table 1 shows the results.

## 4 Discussion of the Results and Related Research

From our limited experiments we can draw the following findings. It is logical that erroneous coreference resolution worsens the results compared to the TF baseline. In one of the "Napoleon" texts, one mention of Napoleon and one mention of the name of his surgeon entail that a large number of pronouns in the text are wrongly resolved. They all refer to the surgeon, but the system considers them as referring to Napoleon, making that the ranking of this text is completely inversed compared to the ideal one. Adding other reference information gives some mixed results. The ranking based on the principal eigenvector computation of the link matrix of the text that represents reference relationships between entities provides a natural way of computing a ranking of the texts with regard to the person entity. This can be explained as follows. Decomposition into eigenvectors breaks down the original relationships into linear independent components. Sorting them according to their corresponding eigenvalues sorts the components from the most important information to the less important one. When keeping the principal eigenvector, we keep the most important information which best distinguishes it from other information while ignoring marginal information. In this way we hope to smooth some noise that is generated when building the links. On the other hand, when relationships that are wrongly detected are dominant, they will be reinforced (as is the case in the "Napoleon" text). Although an aboutness score is normalized by the sum of a text's entity scores, the effect of this normalization and the behavior of eigenvectors in case of texts of different length should be studied.

The work is inspired by link analysis algorithms such as HITS, which uses theories of spectral partitioning of a graph for detecting authoritative pages in a graph of hyperlinked pages (Kleinberg 1998). Analogically, Zha (2002) detects terms and sentences with a high salience in a text and uses these for summarization. The graph here is made of linked term and sentence nodes. Other work on text summarization computes centrality on graphs (Erkan and Radev 2004; Mihalcea and Tarau 2004). We use a linguistic motivation for linking terms in texts founded in reference relationships such as coreference and reference by biographical terms in certain syntactical constructs. Intuitively, an important entity is linked to many referents; the more important the referents are, the more important the entity is. Latent semantic indexing (LSI) is also used to detect main topics in a set of documents/sentences, it will not explicitly model the weights of the edges between entities.

Our implementation aims at measuring the aboutness of an entity from a biographical viewpoint. One can easily focus upon other viewpoints when determining the terms that enter into a reference relationship with the input entity (e.g., computing the aboutness of an input animal name with regard to its reproductive activities).

## 5 Conclusion

In this paper we considered the problem of ranking texts when the input query is in the form of a person proper name and when we are interested in biographical information. The ranking based on the computation of the principal eigenvector of the link matrix that represents coreferent and other referent relationships between noun phrase entities offers novel directions for future research.

## 6 Acknowledgements

The research was sponsored by the IWT-grant Nr. ADV/000135/KUL).

**Table 1.** Similarity of the system made rankings compared to the ideal ranking for the methods used with regard to the input queries.

| | TF | TFCOREF | TFREF | TFCOREFREF | LM |
|---|---|---|---|---|---|
| D | 0.33 | 0.00 | 0.33 | 0.00 | 0.50 |
| H | 0.33 | 0.50 | 0.33 | 0.33 | 0.66 |
| N | 0.66 | 0.33 | 0.66 | 0.66 | 0.33 |
| S | 0.83 | 0.66 | 0.66 | 0.66 | 1.00 |
| ST | 0.00 | 0.33 | 0.16 | 0.50 | 0.83 |

## 7 References

Angheluta, R., Jeuniaux, P., Mitra, R. and Moens, M.-F. (2004). Clustering algorithms for noun phrase coreference resolution. In *Proceedings JADT - 2004. 7èmes Journées internationales d'Analyse statistique des Données Textuelles.* Louvain-La-Neuve, Belgium.

Beghtol, C. (1986). Bibliographic classification theory and text linguistics: Aboutness analysis, intertextuality and the cognitive act of classifying documents. *Journal of Documentation*, 42(2): 84-113.

Cardie C. and Wagstaff K. (1999). Noun phrase coreference as clustering. In *Proceedings of the Joint Conference on Empirical Methods in NLP and Very Large Corpora.*

Dunning, T. (1993). Accurate methods for the statistics of surprise and coincidence. *Computational Linguistics*, 19: 61-74.

Erkan, G. and Radev, D.R. (2004). LexRank: Graph-based lexical centrality as salience in text summarization. *Journal of Artificial Intelligence Research*, 22: 457-479.

Givón, T. (2001). *Syntax. An Introduction.* Amsterdam: John Benjamins.

Kleinberg, J.M. (1998). Authoritative sources in a hyperlinked environment. In *Proceedings 9th ACM-SIAM Symposium on Discrete Algorithms* (pp. 668-677).

Mihalcea, R. and Tarau, P. (2004). TextRank : Bringing order into texts. In *Proceedings of EMNLP* (pp. 404-411).

Soergel, D. (1994). Indexing and retrieval performance: The logical evidence. *Journal of the American Society for Information Science*, 45 (8): 589-599.

Van Dijk, T. A. and Kintsch, W. (1983). *Strategies of Discourse Comprehension.* New York: Academic Press.

Zha, H. (2002). Generic summarization and keyphrase extraction using mutual reinforcement principle and sentence clustering. In *Proceedings of the 25th Annual International ACM SIGIR Conference on Research and Development in Information Retrieval* (pp. 113-120). New York : ACM.

# A Study of Two Graph Algorithms in Topic-driven Summarization

**Vivi Nastase**[1] and **Stan Szpakowicz**[1,2]
[1] School of Information Technology and Engineering,
University of Ottawa, Ottawa, Canada
[2] Institute of Computer Science,
Polish Academy of Sciences, Warsaw, Poland
{vnastase, szpak}@site.uottawa.ca

## Abstract

We study how two graph algorithms apply to topic-driven summarization in the scope of Document Understanding Conferences. The DUC 2005 and 2006 tasks were to summarize into 250 words a collection of documents on a topic consisting of a few statements or questions. Our algorithms select sentences for extraction. We measure their performance on the DUC 2005 test data, using the Summary Content Units made available after the challenge. One algorithm matches a graph representing the entire topic against each sentence in the collection. The other algorithm checks, for pairs of open-class words in the topic, whether they can be connected in the syntactic graph of each sentence. Matching performs better than connecting words, but a combination of both methods works best. They also both favour longer sentences, which makes summaries more fluent.

## 1 Introduction

The DUC 2005 and 2006 summarization challenges were motivated by the desire to make summarization relevant to real users. The task was focussed by specifying an information need as a *topic*: one or a few statements or questions (Dang, 2005). Systems usually employ such data as a source of key words or phrases which then help rank document sentences by relevance to the topic.

We explore other information that can be extracted from a topic description. In particular, we look at connections between open-class words. A dependency parser, MiniPar (Lin, 1998), builds a dependency relation graph for each sentence. We apply such graphs in two ways. We match a graph that covers the entire topic description against the graph for each sentence in the collection. We also extract all pairs of open-class words from the topic description, and check whether they are connected in the sentence graphs. Both methods let us rank sentences; the top-ranking ones go into a summary of at most 250 words. We evaluate the summaries with the summary content units (SCU) data made available after DUC 2005 (Nenkova and Passonneau, 2004; Copeck and Szpakowicz, 2005). The experiments show that using more information than just keywords leads to summaries with more SCUs (total and unique) and higher SCU weight.

We present related work in section 2, and the data and the representation we work with in section 3. Section 4 shows the algorithms in more detail. We describe the experiments and their results in section 5, and draw a few conclusions in section 6.

## 2 Related work

Erkan and Radev (2004), Mihalcea (2004), Mihalcea and Tarau (2004) introduced graph methods for summarization, word sense disambiguation and other NLP applications.

The summarization graph-based systems implement a form of sentence ranking, based on the idea of prestige or centrality in social networks. In this case the network consists of sentences, and significantly similar sentences are interconnected. Various measures (such as node degree) help find the most *central* sentences, or to score each sentence.

In topic-driven summarization, one or more sentences or questions describe an information need which the summaries must address. Previous systems extracted key words or phrases from topics and used them to focus the summary (Fisher et al., 2005).

Our experiments show that there is more to topics than key words or phrases. We will experiment with using grammatical dependency relations for the task of extractive summarization.

In previous research, graph-matching using grammatical relations was used to detect textual entailment (Haghighi et al., 2005).

## 3 Data

### 3.1 Topics

We work with a list of topics from the test data in the DUC 2005 challenge. A topic has an identifier, category (general/specific), title and a sequence of statements or questions, for example:



*Workshop on TextGraphs, at HLT-NAACL 2006*, pages 29–32,
New York City, June 2006. 

```
d307b
specific
New Hydroelectric Projects
What hydroelectric projects are planned
or in progress and what problems are
associated with them?
```

We apply MiniPar to the titles and contents of the topics, and to all documents. The output is post-processed to produce dependency pairs only for open-class words. The dependency pairs bypass prepositions and subordinators/coordinators between clauses, linking the corresponding open-class words. After post-processing, the topic will be represented like this:

```
QUESTION NUMBER: d307b
LIST OF WORDS:
associate, hydroelectric, in, plan,
problem, progress, project, new, them
LIST OF PAIRS:
relation(project, hydroelectric)
relation(project, new)
relation(associate, problem)
relation(plan, project)
relation(in, progress)
relation(associate, them)
```

The parser does not always produce perfect parses. In this example it did not associate the phrase *in progress* with the noun *projects*, so we missed the connection between *projects* and *progress*.

In the next step, we expand each open-class word in the topic with all its *WordNet* synsets and one-step hypernyms and hyponyms. We have two variants of the topic file: with all open-class words from the topic description $Topics_{all}$, and only with nouns and verbs $Topics_{NV}$.

### 3.2 Documents

For each topic, we summarize a collection of up to 50 news items. In our experiments, we build a file with all documents for a given topic, one sentence per line, cleaned of XML tags. We process each file with MiniPar, and post-process the output similarly to the topics. For documents we keep the list of dependency relations but not a separate list of words. This processing also gives one file per topic, each sentence followed by its list of dependency relations.

### 3.3 Summary Content Units

The DUC 2005 summary evaluation included an analysis based on *Summary Content Units*. SCUs are manually-selected topic-specific summary-worthy phrases which the summarization systems are expected to include in their output (Nenkova and Passonneau, 2004; Copeck and Szpakowicz, 2005). The SCUs for 20 of the test topics became available after the challenge. We use the SCU data to measure the performance of our graph-matching and path-search algorithms: the total number, weight and number of unique SCUs per summary, and the number of negative SCU sentences, explicitly marked as not relevant to the summary.

## 4 Algorithms

### 4.1 Topic↔sentence graph matching (GM)

We treat a sentence and a topic as graphs. The nodes are the open-class words in the sentence or topic (we also refer to them as keywords), and the edges are the dependency relations extracted from MiniPar's output. In order to maximize the matching score, we replace a word $w_S$ in the sentence with $w_Q$ from the query, if $w_S$ appears in the *WordNet* expansion of words in $w_Q$.

To score a match between a sentence and a graph, we compute and then combine two partial scores:

$S_N$ (node match score) the node (keyword) overlap between the two text units. A keyword count is equal to the number of dependency pairs it appears with in the document sentence;

$S_E$ (edge match score) the edge (dependency relation) overlap.

The overall score is $S = S_N + WeightFactor * S_E$, where $WeightFactor \in \{0, 1, 2, ..., 15, 20, 50, 100\}$. Varying the weight factor allows us to find various combinations of node and edge score matches which work best for sentence extraction in summarization. When $WeightFactor = 0$, the sentence scores correspond to keyword counts.

### 4.2 Path search for topic keyword pairs (PS)

Here too we look at sentences as graphs. We only take the list of words from the topic representation. For each pair of those words, we check whether they both appear in the sentence and are connected in the sentence graph. We use the list of *WordNet*-expanded terms again, to maximize matching. The final score for the sentence has two components: the node-match score $S_N$, and $S_P$, the number of word pairs from the topic description connected by a path in the sentence graph. The final score is $S = S_N + WeightFactor * S_P$. $WeightFactor$, in the same range as previously, is meant to boost the contribution of the path score towards the final score of the sentence.

## 5 Experiments and results

We produce a summary for each topic and each experimental configuration. We take the most highly ranked (complete) sentences for which the total number of words does not exceed the 250-word limit. Next, we gather SCU data for each sentence in each summary from the SCU information files. For a specific experimental configuration – topic representation, graph algorithm – we produce summaries for the 20 documents with the weight factor values $0, 1, 2, ..., 15, 20, 50, 100$. Each experimental configuration generates 19 sets of average results, one

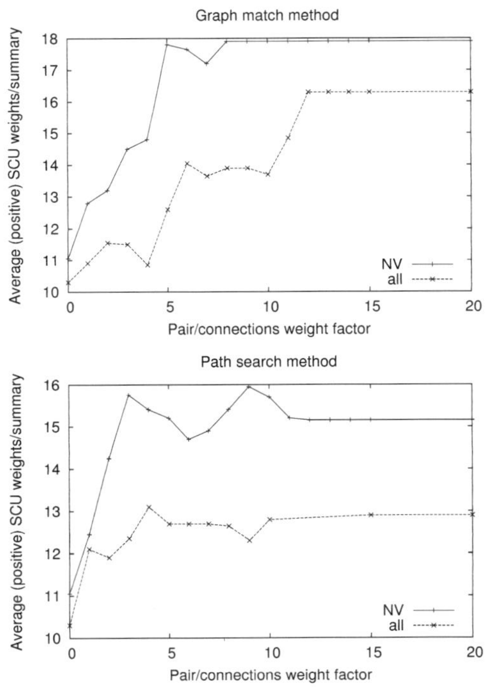


Figure 1: Average SCU weights for graph matching (GM) and path search (PS) with different topic representations

per weight factor. For one weight factor, we generate summaries for the 20 topics, and then average their SCU statistics, including SCU weight, number of unique SCUs and total number of SCUs. In the results which follow we present average SCU weight per summary. The number of unique SCUs and the number of SCUs closely follow the presented graphs. The overlap of SCUs (number of SCUs / number of unique SCUs) reaches a maximum of 1.09. There was no explicit redundancy elimination, mostly because the SCU overlap was so low.

We compare the performance of the two algorithms, GM and PS, on the two topic representations – with all open-class words and only with nouns and verbs. Figure 1 shows the performance of the methods in terms of average SCU weights per summary for each weight factor considered [1].

The results allow us to make several observations.

- Keyword-only match performs worse that either GM or PS. The points corresponding to keyword (node) match only are the points for which the weight factor is 0. In this case the dependency pairs match and paths found in the graph do not contribute to the overall score.
- Both graph algorithms achieve better performance for only the nouns and verbs from the topic than for all open-class words. If, however, the topic requests entities or events with specific properties, described by adjectives or adverbs, using only nouns and verbs may produce worse results.
- GM performs better than PS for both types of topic descriptions. In other words, looking at the same words that appear in the topic, connected in the same way, leads to better results than finding pairs of words that are "somehow" connected.
- Higher performance for higher weight factors further supports the point that looking for word connections, instead of isolated words, helps find sentences with information content more related to the topic.

For the following set of experiments, we use the topics with the word list containing only nouns and verbs. We want to compare graph matching and path search further. One issue that comes to mind is whether a combination of the two methods will perform better than each of them individually. Figure 2 plots the average of SCU weights per summary.

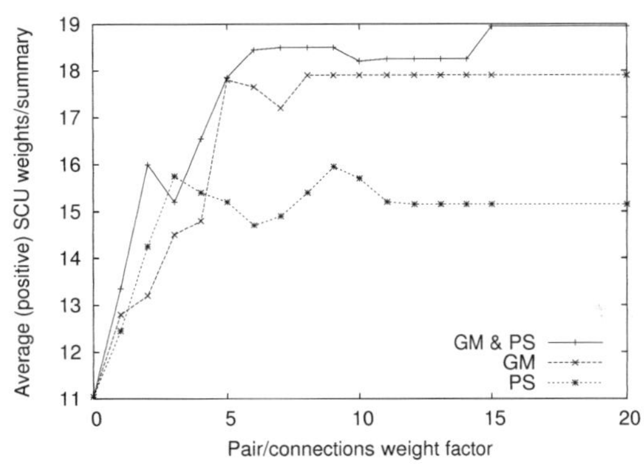


Figure 2: Graph matching, path search and their combination

We observe that the combination of graph matching and path search gives better results than either method alone. The sentence score combines the number of edges matched and the number of connections found with equal weight factors for the edge match and path score. This raises the question whether different weights for the edge match and path would lead to better scores. Figure 3 plots the results produced using the score computation formula $S = S_N + WeightFactor_E * S_E + WeightFactor_P * S_P$, where both $WeightFactor_E$ and $WeightFactor_P$ are integers from 0 to 30.

The lowest scores are for the weight factors 0, when sentence score depends only on the keyword score. There is an increase in average SCU weights

[1] The summary statistics level off above a certain weight factor, so we include only the non-flat part of the graph.

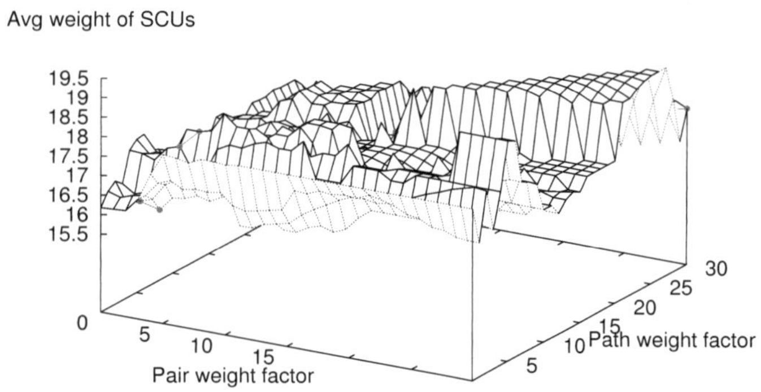


Figure 3: Graph match and path search combined with different weight factors

towards higher values of weight factors. A transparent view of the 3D graph shows that graph match has higher peaks toward higher weight factors than path search, and higher also than the situation when path search and graph match have equal weights.

The only sentences in the given documents tagged with SCU information are those which appeared in the summaries generated by the competing teams in 2005. Our results are therefore actually a lower bound – more of the sentences selected may include relevant information. A manual analysis of the summaries generated using only keyword counts showed that, for these summaries, the sentences not containing SCUs were not informative. We cannot check this for all the summaries generated in these experiments, because the number is very large, above 1000. An average summary had 8.24 sentences, with 3.19 sentences containing SCUs. We cannot say much about the sentences that do not contain SCUs. This may raise doubts about our results. Support for the fact that the results reflect a real increase in performance comes from the weights of the SCUs added: the average SCU weight increases from 2.5 when keywords are used to 2.75 for path search algorithm, and 2.91 for graph match and the combination of path search and graph match. This shows that by increasing the weight of graph edges and paths in the scoring of a sentence, the algorithm can pick more and better SCUs, SCUs which more people see as relevant to the topic. It would be certainly interesting to have a way of assessing the "SCU-less" sentences in the summary. We leave that for future work, and possibly future developments in SCU annotation.

## 6 Conclusions

We have studied how two algorithms influence summarization by sentence extraction. They match the topic description and sentences in a document. The results show that using connections between the words in the topic description improves the accuracy of sentence scoring compared to simple keyword match. Finding connections between query words in a sentence depends on finding the corresponding words in the sentence. In our experiments, we have used one-step extension in *WordNet* (along IS-A links) to find such correspondences. It is, however, a limited solution, and better word matches should be attempted, such as for example word similarity scores in *WordNet*.

In summarization by sentence extraction, other scores affect sentence ranking, for example position in the document and paragraph or proximity to other high-ranked sentences. We have analyzed the effect of connections in isolation, to reduce the influence of other factors. A summarization system would combine all these scores, and possibly produce better results. Word connections or pairs could also be used just as keywords were, as part of a feature description of documents, to be automatically ranked using machine learning.

## References

Terry Copeck and Stan Szpakowicz. 2005. Leveraging pyramids. http://duc.nist.gov/pubs/2005papers/uottawa.copeck2.pdf.

Hoa Trang Dang. 2005. Overview of DUC 2005. http://duc.nist.gov/pubs/2005papers/OVERVIEW05.pdf.

Güneş Erkan and Dragomir Radev. 2004. LexRank: Graph-based centrality as salience in text summarization. *Journal of Artificial Intelligence Research*, (22).

Seeger Fisher, Brian Roark, Jianji Yang, and Bill Hersh. 2005. Ogi/ohsu baseline query-directed multi-document summarization system for duc-2005. http://duc.nist.gov/pubs/2005papers/ohsu.seeger.pdf.

Aria Haghighi, Andrew Ng, and Christopher Manning. 2005. Robust textual inference via graph matching. In *Proc. of HLT-EMNLP 2005*, Vancouver, BC, Canada.

Dekang Lin. 1998. Dependency-based evaluation of MiniPar. In *Workshop on the Evaluation of Parsing Systems*, Granada, Spain.

Rada Mihalcea and Paul Tarau. 2004. Textrank: Bringing order into texts. In *Proc. of EMNLP 2004*, Barcelona, Spain.

Rada Mihalcea. 2004. Graph-based ranking algorithms for sentence extraction, applied to text summarization. In *Proc. of ACL 2004*, Barcelona, Spain.

Ani Nenkova and Rebecca Passonneau. 2004. Evaluating content selection in summarization: the pyramid method. In *Proc. of NAACL-HLT 2004*.

# Similarity between Pairs of Co-indexed Trees for Textual Entailment Recognition

**Fabio Massimo Zanzotto**
DISCo
University Of Milan-Bicocca
Milano, Italy
zanzotto@disco.unimib.it

**Alessandro Moschitti**
DISP
University Of Rome "Tor Vergata"
Roma, Italy
moschitti@info.uniroma2.it

## Abstract

In this paper we present a novel similarity between pairs of co-indexed trees to automatically learn textual entailment classifiers. We defined a kernel function based on this similarity along with a more classical intra-pair similarity. Experiments show an improvement of 4.4 absolute percent points over state-of-the-art methods.

## 1 Introduction

Recently, a remarkable interest has been devoted to textual entailment recognition (Dagan et al., 2005). The task requires to determine whether or not a text $T$ entails a hypothesis $H$. As it is a binary classification task, it could seem simple to use machine learning algorithms to learn an entailment classifier from training examples. Unfortunately, this is not. The learner should capture the similarities between different pairs, $(T', H')$ and $(T'', H'')$, taking into account the relations between sentences within a pair. For example, having these two learning pairs:

$T_1 \Rightarrow H_1$

| | |
|---|---|
| $T_1$ | *"At the end of the year, all solid companies pay dividends"* |
| $H_1$ | *"At the end of the year, all solid insurance companies pay dividends."* |

$T_1 \nRightarrow H_2$

| | |
|---|---|
| $T_1$ | *"At the end of the year, all solid companies pay dividends"* |
| $H_2$ | *"At the end of the year, all solid companies pay cash dividends."* |

determining whether or not the following implication holds:

$T_3 \Rightarrow H_3$?

| | |
|---|---|
| $T_3$ | *"All wild animals eat plants that have scientifically proven medicinal properties."* |
| $H_3$ | *"All wild mountain animals eat plants that have scientifically proven medicinal properties."* |

requires to detect that:

1. $T_3$ is structurally (and somehow lexically) similar to $T_1$ and $H_3$ is more similar to $H_1$ than to $H_2$;
2. relations between the sentences in the pairs $(T_3, H_3)$ (e.g., $T_3$ and $H_3$ have the same noun governing the subject of the main sentence) are similar to the relations between sentences in the pairs $(T_1, H_1)$ and $(T_1, H_2)$.

Given this analysis we may derive that $T_3 \Rightarrow H_3$.

The example suggests that graph matching tecniques are not sufficient as these may only detect the structural similarity between sentences of textual entailment pairs. An extension is needed to consider also if two pairs show compatible relations between their sentences.

In this paper, we propose to observe textual entailment pairs as pairs of syntactic trees with co-indexed nodes. This shuold help to cosider both the structural similarity between syntactic tree pairs and the similarity between relations among sentences within a pair. Then, we use this *cross-pair* similarity with more traditional *intra-pair* similarities (e.g., (Corley and Mihalcea, 2005)) to define a novel kernel function. We experimented with such kernel using Support Vector Machines on the Recognizing Textual Entailment (RTE) challenge test-beds. The comparative results show that (a) we have designed an effective way to automatically learn entailment rules



*Workshop on TextGraphs, at HLT-NAACL 2006*, pages 33–36,
New York City, June 2006. 

from examples and (b) our approach is highly accurate and exceeds the accuracy of the current state-of-the-art models.

In the remainder of this paper, Sec. 2 introduces the cross-pair similarity and Sec. 3 shows the experimental results.

## 2 Learning Textual Entailment from examples

To carry out automatic learning from examples, we need to define a cross-pair similarity $K((T', H'), (T'', H''))$. This function should consider pairs similar when: (1) texts and hypotheses are structurally and lexically similar (*structural similarity*); (2) the relations between the sentences in the pair $(T', H')$ are compatible with the relations in $(T'', H'')$ (*intra-pair word movement compatibility*). We argue that such requirements could be met by augmenting syntactic trees with *placeholders* that co-index related words within pairs. We will then define a cross-pair similarity over these pairs of co-indexed trees.

### 2.1 Training examples as pairs of co-indexed trees

Sentence pairs selected as possible sentences in entailment are naturally co-indexed. Many words (or expressions) $w_h$ in $H$ have a referent $w_t$ in $T$. These pairs $(w_t, w_h)$ are called *anchors*. Possibly, it is more important that the two words in an anchor are related than the actual two words. The entailment could hold even if the two words are substitued with two other related words. To indicate this we co-index words associating *placeholders* with anchors. For example, in Fig. 1, $\boxed{2''}$ indicates the *(companies,companies)* anchor between $T_1$ and $H_1$. These placeholders are then used to augment tree nodes. To better take into account argument movements, placeholders are propagated in the syntactic trees following constituent heads (see Fig. 1).

In line with many other researches (e.g., (Corley and Mihalcea, 2005)), we determine these anchors using different similarity or relatedness dectors: the exact matching between tokens or lemmas, a similarity between tokens based on their edit distance, the derivationally related form relation and the verb entailment relation in WordNet, and, finally, a WordNet-based similarity (Jiang and Conrath, 1997). Each of these detectors gives a different weight to the anchor: the actual computed similarity for the last and 1 for all the others. These weights will be used in the final kernel.

### 2.2 Similarity between pairs of co-indexed trees

Pairs of syntactic trees where nodes are co-indexed with placeholders allow the design a cross-pair similarity that considers both the structural similarity and the intra-pair word movement compatibility.

Syntactic trees of texts and hypotheses permit to verify the structural similarity between pairs of sentences. Texts should have similar structures as well as hypotheses. In Fig. 1, the overlapping subtrees are in bold. For example, $T_1$ and $T_3$ share the subtree starting with **S** $\rightarrow$ **NP VP**. Although the lexicals in $T_3$ and $H_3$ are quite different from those $T_1$ and $H_1$, their bold subtrees are more similar to those of $T_1$ and $H_1$ than to $T_1$ and $H_2$, respectively. $H_1$ and $H_3$ share the production **NP** $\rightarrow$ **DT JJ NN NNS** while $H_2$ and $H_3$ do not. To decide on the entailment for $(T_3, H_3)$, we can use the value of $(T_1, H_1)$.

Anchors and placeholders are useful to verify if two pairs can be aligned as showing compatible intra-pair word movement. For example, $(T_1, H_1)$ and $(T_3, H_3)$ show compatible constituent movements given that the dashed lines connecting placeholders of the two pairs indicates structurally equivalent nodes both in the texts and the hypotheses. The dashed line between $\boxed{3}$ and $\boxed{b}$ links the main verbs both in the texts $T_1$ and $T_3$ and in the hypotheses $H_1$ and $H_3$. After substituting $\boxed{3}$ to $\boxed{b}$ and $\boxed{2}$ to $\boxed{a}$, $T_1$ and $T_3$ share the subtree **S** $\rightarrow$ **NP**$\boxed{2}$ **VP**$\boxed{3}$. The same subtree is shared between $H_1$ and $H_3$. This implies that words in the pair $(T_1, H_1)$ are correlated like words in $(T_3, H_3)$. Any different mapping between the two anchor sets would not have this property.

Using the structural similarity, the placeholders, and the connection between placeholders, the overall similarity is then defined as follows. Let $A'$ and $A''$ be the placeholders of $(T', H')$ and $(T'', H'')$, respectively. The similarity between two co-indexed syntactic tree pairs $K_s((T', H'), (T'', H''))$ is defined using a classical similarity between two trees $K_T(t_1, t_2)$ when the best alignment between the $A'$ and $A''$ is given. Let $C$ be the set of all bijective

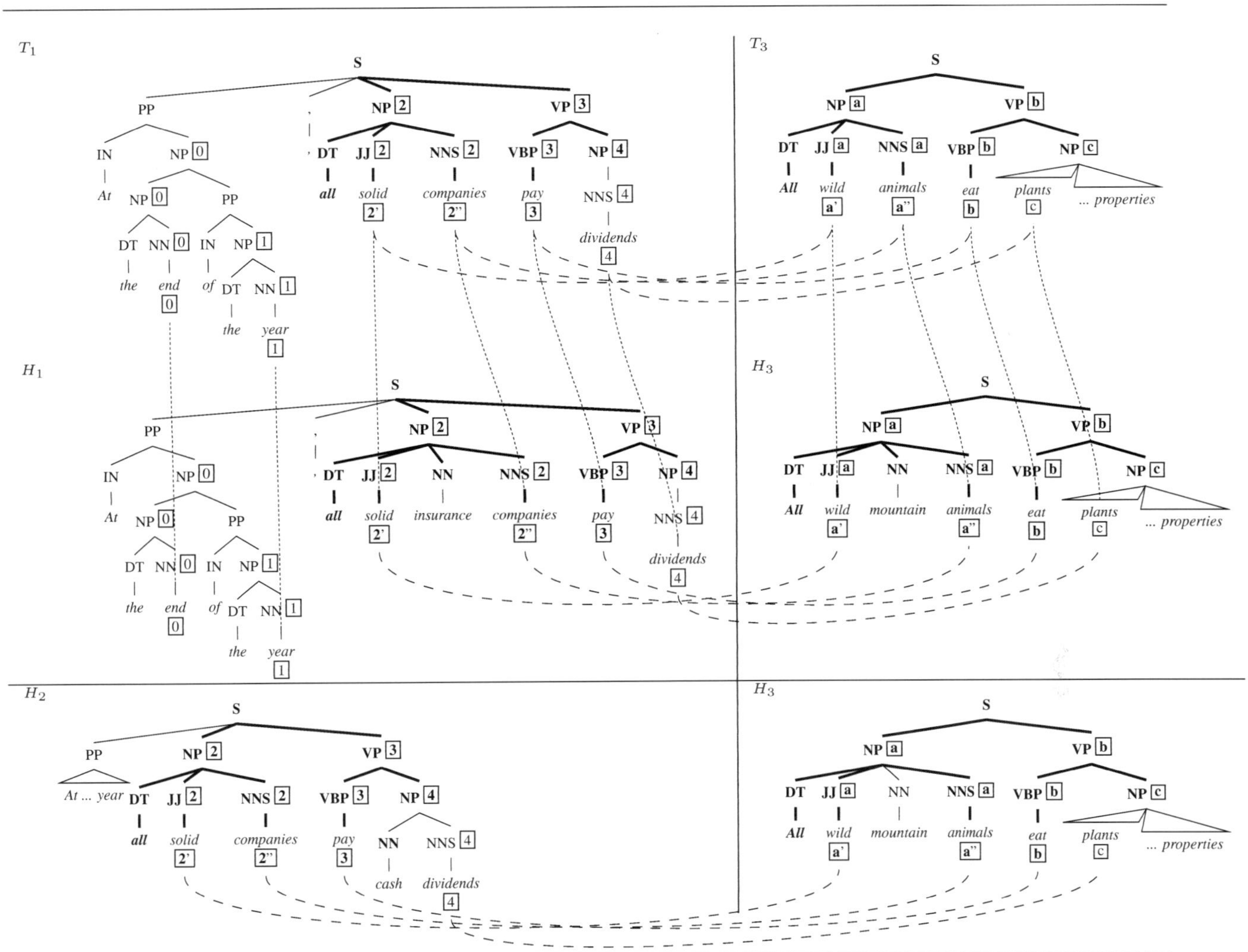


Figure 1: Relations between $(T_1, H_1)$, $(T_1, H_2)$, and $(T_3, H_3)$.

mappings from $a' \subseteq A' : |a'| = |A''|$ to $A''$, an element $c \in C$ is a substitution function. The co-indexed tree pair similarity is then defined as:

$$K_s((T', H'), (T'', H'')) = max_{c \in C}(K_T(t(H', c), t(H'', i)) + K_T(t(T', c), t(T'', i))$$

where (1) $t(S, c)$ returns the syntactic tree of the hypothesis (text) $S$ with placeholders replaced by means of the substitution $c$, (2) $i$ is the identity substitution and (3) $K_T(t_1, t_2)$ is a function that measures the similarity between the two trees $t_1$ and $t_2$.

### 2.3 Enhancing cross-pair syntactic similarity

As the computation cost of the similarity measure depends on the number of the possible sets of correspondences $C$ and this depends on the size of the anchor sets, we reduce the number of *placeholders* used to represent the anchors. Placeholders will have the same name if these are in the same *chunk* both in the text and the hypothesis, e.g., the placeholders 2' and 2" are collapsed to 2.

## 3 Experimental investigation

The aim of the experiments is twofold: we show that (a) entailments can be learned from examples and (b) our kernel function over syntactic structures is effective to derive syntactic properties. The above goals can be achieved by comparing our cross-pair similarity kernel against (and in combination with) other methods.

### 3.1 Experimented kernels

We compared three different kernels: (1) the kernel $K_l((T', H'), (T'', H''))$ based on the intra-pair

| Datasets | $K_l$ | $K_l + K_t$ | $K_l + K_s$ |
|---|---|---|---|
| Train:$D1$ Test:$T1$ | 0.5888 | 0.6213 | **0.6300** |
| Train:$T1$ Test:$D1$ | 0.5644 | 0.5732 | **0.5838** |
| Train:$D2(50\%)'$ Test:$D2(50\%)''$ | 0.6083 | 0.6156 | **0.6350** |
| Train:$D2(50\%)''$ Test:$D2(50\%)'$ | 0.6272 | 0.5861 | **0.6607** |
| Train:$D2$ Test:$T2$ | 0.6038 | 0.6238 | **0.6388** |
| Mean | 0.5985 ($\pm$ 0.0235 ) | 0.6040 ($\pm$ 0.0229 ) | **0.6297** ($\pm$ 0.0282 ) |

Table 1: Experimental results

lexical similarity $sim_l(T, H)$ as defined in (Corley and Mihalcea, 2005). This kernel is defined as $K_l((T', H'), (T'', H'')) = sim_l(T', H') \times sim_l(T'', H'')$. (2) the kernel $K_l + K_s$ that combines our kernel with the lexical-similarity-based kernel; (3) the kernel $K_l + K_t$ that combines the lexical-similarity-based kernel with a basic tree kernel. This latter is defined as $K_t((T', H'), (T'', H'')) = K_T(T', T'') + K_T(H', H'')$. We implemented these kernels within SVM-light (Joachims, 1999).

### 3.2 Experimental settings

For the experiments, we used the Recognizing Textual Entailment (RTE) Challenge data sets, which we name as $D1$, $T1$ and $D2$, $T2$, are the development and the test sets of the first and second RTE challenges, respectively. $D1$ contains 567 examples whereas $T1$, $D2$ and $T2$ have all the same size, i.e. 800 instances. The positive examples are the $50\%$ of the data. We produced also a random split of $D2$. The two folds are $D2(50\%)'$ and $D2(50\%)''$.

We also used the following resources: the Charniak parser (Charniak, 2000) to carry out the syntactic analysis; the `wn::similarity` package (Pedersen et al., 2004) to compute the Jiang&Conrath (J&C) distance (Jiang and Conrath, 1997) needed to implement the lexical similarity $sim_l(T, H)$ as defined in (Corley and Mihalcea, 2005); SVM-light-TK (Moschitti, 2004) to encode the basic tree kernel function, $K_T$, in SVM-light (Joachims, 1999).

### 3.3 Results and analysis

Table 1 reports the accuracy of different similarity kernels on the different training and test split described in the previous section. The table shows some important result.

First, as observed in (Corley and Mihalcea, 2005) the lexical-based distance kernel $K_l$ shows an accuracy significantly higher than the random baseline, i.e. $50\%$. This accuracy (second line) is comparable with the best systems in the first RTE challenge (Dagan et al., 2005). The accuracy reported for the best systems, i.e. $58.6\%$ (Glickman et al., 2005; Bayer et al., 2005), is not significantly far from the result obtained with $K_l$, i.e. $58.88\%$.

Second, our approach (last column) is significantly better than all the other methods as it provides the best result for each combination of training and test sets. On the "Train:$D1$-Test:$T1$" testbed, it exceeds the accuracy of the current state-of-the-art models (Glickman et al., 2005; Bayer et al., 2005) by about 4.4 absolute percent points (63% vs. 58.6%) and 4% over our best lexical similarity measure. By comparing the average on all datasets, our system improves on all the methods by at least 3 absolute percent points.

Finally, the accuracy produced by our kernel based on co-indexed trees $K_l + K_s$ is higher than the one obtained with the plain syntactic tree kernel $K_l + K_t$. Thus, the use of placeholders and co-indexing is fundamental to automatically learn entailments from examples.

## References


Samuel Bayer, John Burger, Lisa Ferro, John Henderson, and Alexander Yeh. 2005. MITRE's submissions to the eu pascal rte challenge. In *Proceedings of the 1st Pascal Challenge Workshop*, Southampton, UK.

Eugene Charniak. 2000. A maximum-entropy-inspired parser. In *Proc. of the 1st NAACL*, pages 132–139, Seattle, Washington.

Courtney Corley and Rada Mihalcea. 2005. Measuring the semantic similarity of texts. In *Proc. of the ACL Workshop on Empirical Modeling of Semantic Equivalence and Entailment*, pages 13–18, Ann Arbor, Michigan, June. Association for Computational Linguistics.

Ido Dagan, Oren Glickman, and Bernardo Magnini. 2005. The PASCAL RTE challenge. In *PASCAL Challenges Workshop*, Southampton, U.K.

Oren Glickman, Ido Dagan, and Moshe Koppel. 2005. Web based probabilistic textual entailment. In *Proceedings of the 1st Pascal Challenge Workshop*, Southampton, UK.

Jay J. Jiang and David W. Conrath. 1997. Semantic similarity based on corpus statistics and lexical taxonomy. In *Proc. of the 10th ROCLING*, pages 132–139, Tapei, Taiwan.

Thorsten Joachims. 1999. Making large-scale svm learning practical. In B. Schlkopf, C. Burges, and A. Smola, editors, *Advances in Kernel Methods-Support Vector Learning*. MIT Press.

Alessandro Moschitti. 2004. A study on convolution kernels for shallow semantic parsing. In *proceedings of the ACL*, Barcelona, Spain.

Ted Pedersen, Siddharth Patwardhan, and Jason Michelizzi. 2004. Wordnet::similarity - measuring the relatedness of concepts. In *Proc. of 5th NAACL*, Boston, MA.

# Learning of Graph-based Question Answering Rules

**Diego Mollá**
Department of Computing
Macquarie University
Sydney 2109, Australia
diego@ics.mq.edu.au

## Abstract

In this paper we present a graph-based approach to question answering. The method assumes a graph representation of question sentences and text sentences. Question answering rules are automatically learnt from a training corpus of questions and answer sentences with the answer annotated. The method is independent from the graph representation formalism chosen. A particular example is presented that uses a specific graph representation of the logical contents of sentences.

## 1 Introduction

Text-based question answering (QA) is the process of automatically finding the answers to arbitrary questions in plain English by searching collections of text files. Recently there has been intensive research in this area, fostered by evaluation-based conferences such as the Text REtrieval Conference (TREC) (Voorhees, 2001b), the Cross-Lingual Evaluation Forum (CLEF) (Vallin et al., 2005), and the NII-NACSIS Test Collection for Information Retrieval Systems workshops (NTCIR) (Kando, 2005). Current research focuses on factoid question answering, whereby the answer is a short string that indicates a fact, usually a named entity. An example of a factoid question is *Who won the 400m race in the 2000 Summer Olympic games?*, which has a short answer: *Cathy Freeman*.

There are various approaches to question answering. The focus of this paper is on **rule-based systems**. A rule could be, say, "if the question is of the form *Who is the <position> of <country>*" and a text sentence says *<position> of <country> Y* and Y consists of two capitalised words, then Y is the answer"). Such a rule was used by Soubbotin (2001), who developed a system who obtained the best accuracy in the 2001 Text REtrieval Conference (Voorhees, 2001a). The system developed by Soubbotin (2001) relied on the development of a large set of patterns of potential answer expressions, and the allocation of those patterns to types of questions. The patterns were developed by hand by examining the data.

Soubbotin (2001)'s work shows that a rule-based QA system can produce good results if the rule set is comprehensive enough. Unfortunately, if the system is ported to a new domain the set of rules needs to be ported as well. It has not been proven that rules like the ones developed by Soubbotin (2001), which were designed for the TREC QA task, can be ported to other domains. Furthermore, the process of producing the rules was presumably very labour intensive. Consequently, the cost of manually producing new rules for a specialised domain could become too expensive for some domains.

In this paper we present a method for the automatic learning of question answering rules by applying graph manipulation methods. The method relies on the representation of questions and answer sentences as graphs. Section 2 describes the general format of the graph-based QA rules and section 3 describes the method to learn the rules. The methods described on the above two sections are independent of the actual sentence representation formalism,



*Workshop on TextGraphs, at HLT-NAACL 2006*, pages 37–44,
New York City, June 2006. 

as long as the representation is a graph. Section 4 presents a specific application using logical graphs. Finally, sections 5 and 6 focus on related research and final conclusions, respectively.

## 2 Question Answering Rules

In one form or another, a question answering rule must contain the following information:

1. a pattern that matches the question;
2. a pattern that matches the corresponding answer sentence; and
3. a pointer to the answer in the answer sentence

The patterns in our rules are expressed as graphs with vertices containing variables. A vertex with a variable can unify with a subgraph. For example, Figure 1 shows two graphs and a pattern that matches both graphs.

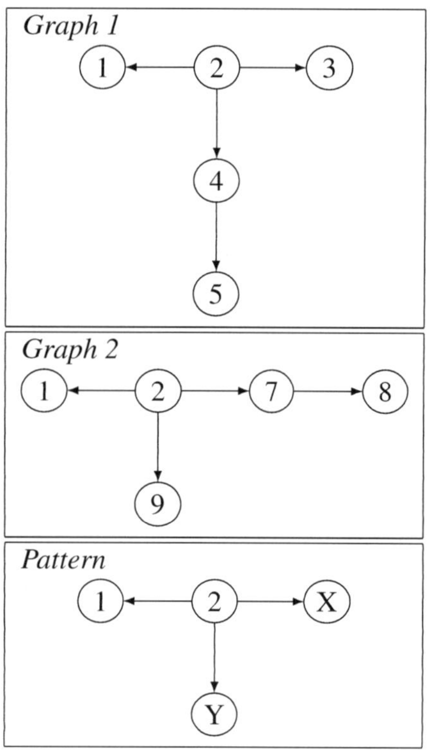


Figure 1: Two graphs and a pattern (variables in uppercase)

Such patterns are used to match the graph representation of the question. If a pattern defined in a rule matches a question sentence, then the rule applies to the sentence.

Our rules specify the pattern of the answer sentence in an unusual way. Instead of keeping a pattern to match the answer sentence, our rules define an *extension* graph that will be added to the graph of the question. The rationale for this is that we want to reward answer sentences that have a high similarity with the question. Therefore, the larger the number of vertices and edges that are shared between the question and the answer, the better. The extension graph contains information that simulates the difference between a question sentence and a sentence containing an answer.

For example, lets us use graph representations of syntactic dependency structures. We will base our representation on the output of Connexor (Tapanainen and Järvinen, 1997), but the choice of parser is arbitrary. The same method applies to the output of any parser, as long as it can be represented as a graph. In our choice, the dependency structure is represented as a bipartite graph where the lexical entries are the vertices represented in boxes and the dependency labels are the vertices represented in ovals. Figure 2 shows the graphs of a question and an answer sentence, and an extension of the question graph. The answer is shown in thick lines, and the extension is shown in dashed lines. This is what we aim to reproduce with our graph rules. In particular, the extension of the question graph is such that the graph of the answer sentence becomes a subgraph of the extended question graph.

The question and answer sentence of Figure 2 have an almost identical dependency graph and consequently the extension required to the question graph is very small. Sentence pairs with more differences would induce a more substantial extension graph.

Note that the extended graph still contains the representation of information that does not appear in the answer sentence, namely the question term *what book*. There is no need to remove any element from the question graph because, as we will see later, the criteria to score the answer extracted are based on the overlap between graphs.

In sum, a graph rule has the following components:

$R_p$ a question pattern;

$R_e$ an extension graph, which is a graph to be added

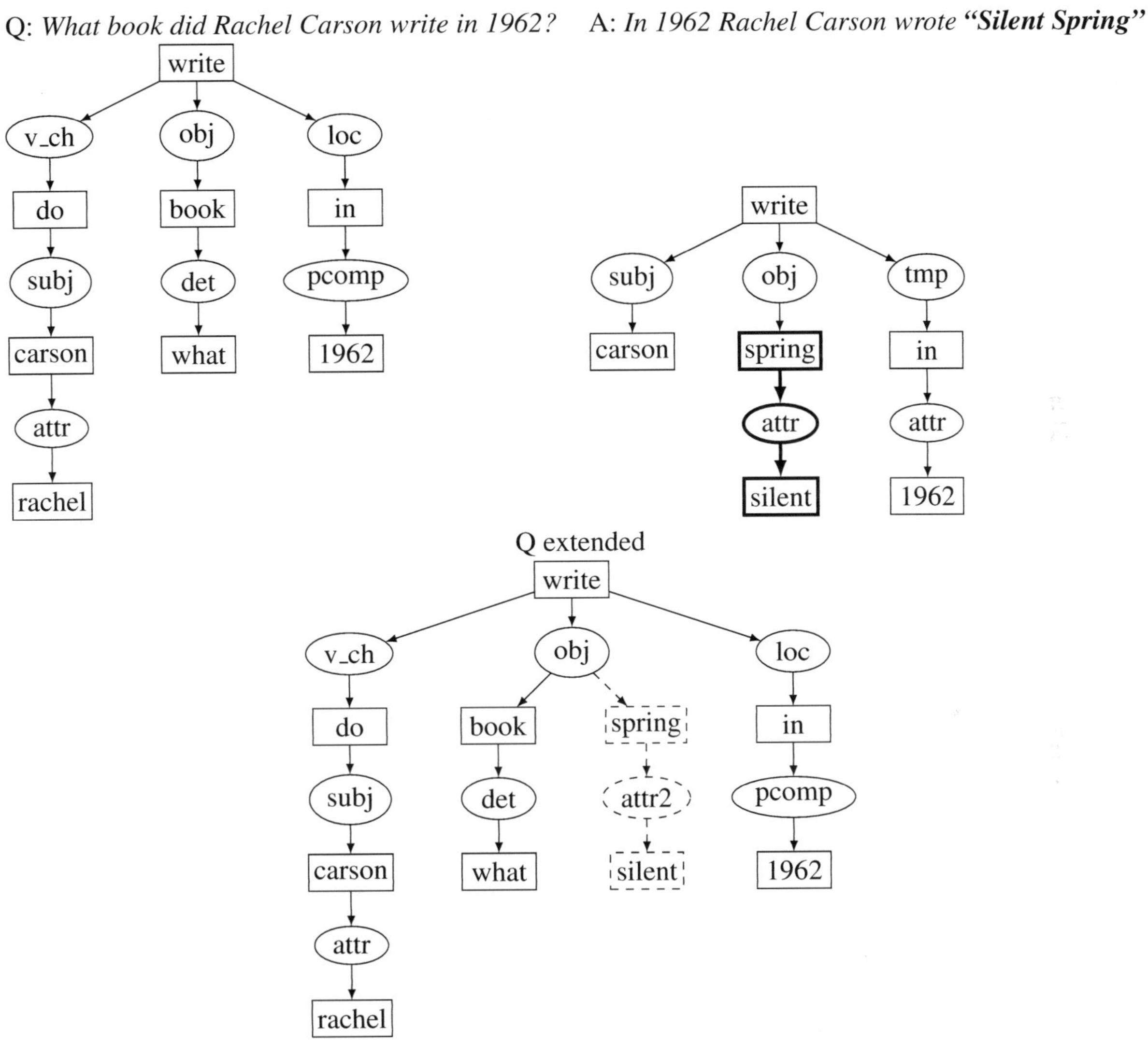


Figure 2: Graph of a question, an answer sentence, and an extension of the question graph

to the question graph; and

$R_a$ a pointer to the answer in the extension graph

An example of a rule is shown in Figure 3. This rule is derived from the pair of question and answer sentence shown in Figure 2.

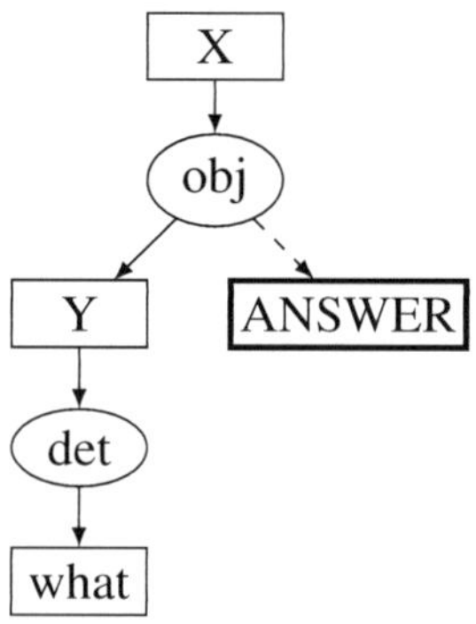


Figure 3: Example of a QA rule. $R_p$ is in solid lines, $R_e$ is in dashed lines, and $R_a$ is in thick lines.

The rule can be used with a fresh pair of question $q_i$ and answer sentence $as_i$. Let us use the notation $Gr(s)$ to denote the graph that represents the string $s$. Also, unless said explicitly, names starting with uppercase denote graphs, and names starting with lowercase denote strings. Informally, the process to find the answer is:

1. If $Gr(q_i)$ matches $R_p$ then the rule applies. Otherwise try a new rule.
2. Extend $Gr(q_i)$ with $r_e$ to produce a new graph $E_{q_i}^{R_e}$.
3. Compute the overlap between $E_{q_i}^{R_e}$ and $Gr(as_i)$.
4. If a part of $R_a$ is in the resulting overlap, then expand its projection on $Gr(as_i)$.

The crucial point in the process is to determine the projection of an overlap on the answer sentence, and then to extend it. Once the overlap is found in step 3, if this overlap includes part of the annotated answer, that is if it includes $R_a$, then part of the answer will be the string in the answer sentence that corresponds to the overlap. The full answer can be retrieved by expanding the answer found in the overlap by following the outgoing edges in the graph of

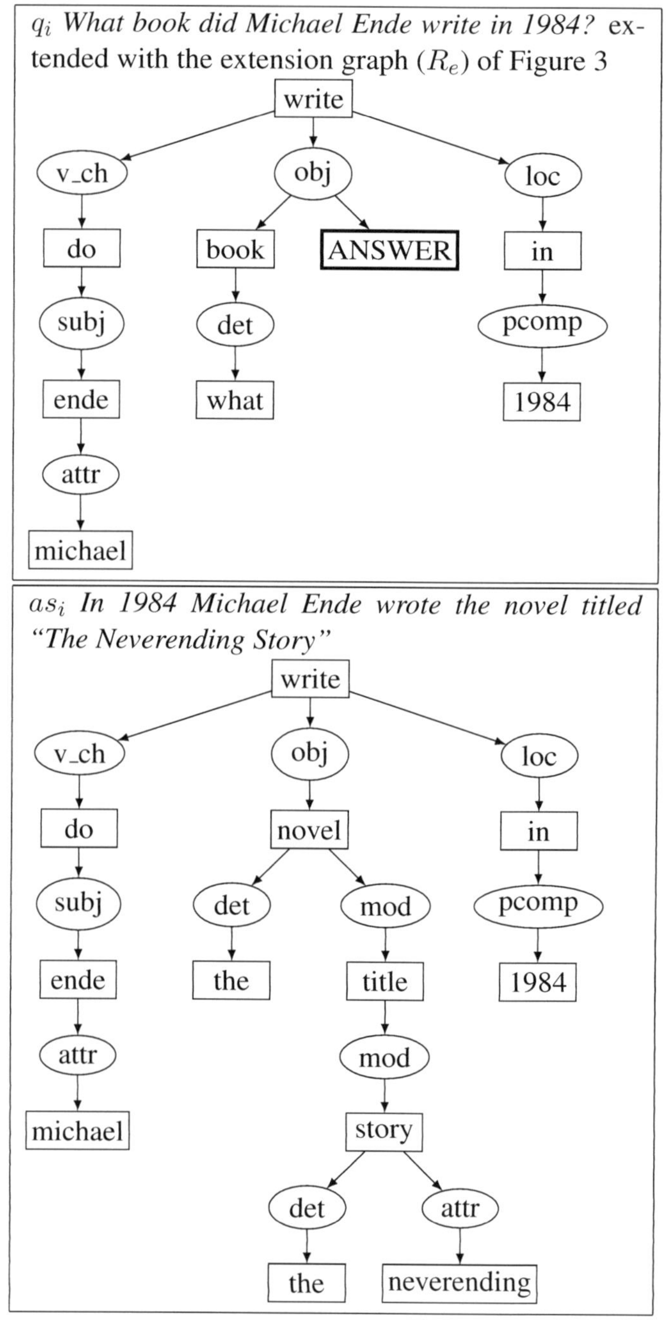


Figure 4: An extended graph of a question and a graph of an answer sentence

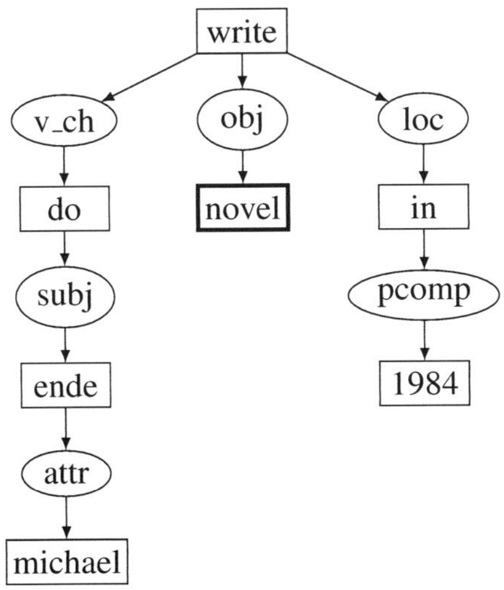


Figure 5: Overlap of the graphs of Figure 4

the answer. Part of the process is shown in Figures 4 and 5.

In Figure 5 the overlap between the extended question graph and the answer sentence graph contains the answer fragment *novel*. After expanding it we obtain the full answer *the novel titled "The Never Ending Story"*.[1]

## 3 Learning of Graph Rules

To learn a QA rule we need to determine the information that is common between a question and a sentence containing an answer. In terms of graphs, this is a variant of the well-known problem of finding the maximum common subgraph (MCS) of two graphs (Bunke et al., 2002).

The problem of finding the MCS of two graphs is known to be NP-complete, but there are implementations that are fast enough for practical uses, especially if the graphs are not particularly large (Bunke et al., 2002). Given that our graphs are used to represent sentences, their size would usually stay within a few tens of vertices. This size is acceptable.

There is an algorithm based on Conceptual Graphs (Myaeng and López-López, 1992) which is particularly efficient for our purposes.Their method follows the traditional procedure of building the association graph of the two input graphs. However, in contrast with the traditional approach, which finds the cliques of the association graph (and this is the part that is NP-complete), the method by Myaeng and López-López (1992) first simplifies the association graph by merging some of its vertices, and then it proceeds to searching the cliques. By so doing the algorithm is still exponential on the size of $n$, but now $n$ is smaller than with the traditional approach for the same input graphs.

The method presented by Myaeng and López-López (1992) finds connected graphs but we also need to find overlaps that form unconnected graphs. For example, Figure 6 shows two graphs and their MCS. The resulting MCS is an unconnected graph, though Myaeng and López-López (1992)'s algorithm returns the two parts of the graph as independent MCSs. It is easy to modify the original algorithm to obtain the desired output, as we did.

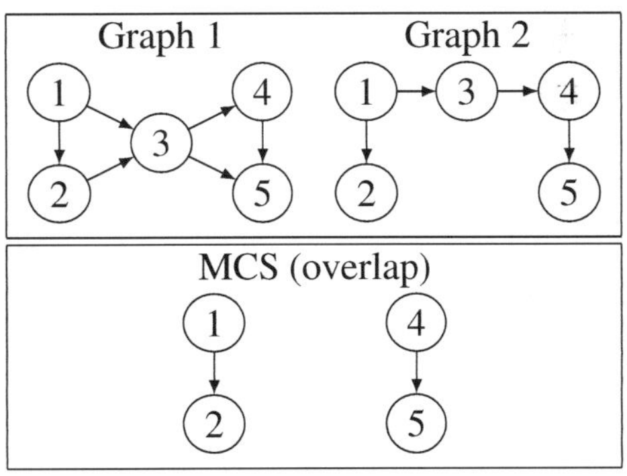


Figure 6: MCS of two graphs

Given two graphs $G_1$ and $G_2$, then their MCS is $MCS(G_1, G_2)$. To simplify the notation, we will often refer to the MCS of two sentences as $MCS(s_1, s_2)$. This is to be understood to be the MCS of the graphs of the two sentences $MCS(Gr(s_1), Gr(s_2))$.

Let us now assume that the graph rule $R$ is originated from a pair ($q$,$as$) in the training corpus, where $q$ is a question and $as$ a sentence containing the answer $a$. The rule components are built as follows:

$R_p$ is the MCS of $q$ and $as$, that is, $MCS(q, as)$.

$R_e$ is the path between the projection of $R_p$ in $Gr(as)$ and the actual answer $Gr(a)$.

$R_a$ is the graph representation of the exact answer.

[1] Note that this answer is not an exact answer according to the TREC definition since it contains the string *the novel titled*; one further step would be needed to extract the exact answer; this is work for further research.

Note that this process defines $R_p$ as the MCS of question and answer sentence. Consequently, $R_p$ is a subgraph of both the question and the answer sentence. This constraint is stronger than that of a typical QA rule, where the pattern needs to match the question only. The resulting question pattern is therefore more general than it could be had one manually built the rule. $R_p$ does not include question-only elements in the question pattern because it is difficult to determine what components of the question are to be added to the pattern, and what components are idiosyncratic to the specific question used in the training set.

Rules learnt this way need to be generalised in order to form generic patterns. We currently use a simple method of generalisation: convert a subset of the vertices into variables. To decide whether a vertex can be generalised a list of very common vertices is used. This is the list of "stop vertices", in analogy to the concept of stop words in methods to detect keywords in a string. Thus, if a vertex is not in the list of stop vertices, then the vertex can be generalised. The list of stop vertices is fixed and depends on the graph formalism used.

For the question answering process it is useful to associate a weight to every rule learnt. The rule weight is computed by testing the accuracy of the rule in the training corpus. This way, rules that over-generalise acquire a low weight. The weight $\mathcal{W}(r)$ of a rule $r$ is computed according to its precision on the training set:

$$\mathcal{W}(r) = \frac{\text{\# correct answers found}}{\text{\# answers found}}$$

## 4 Application: QA with Logical Graphs

The above method has been applied to graphs representing the logical contents of sentences. There has been a long tradition on the use of graphs for this kind of sentence representation, such as Sowa's Conceptual Graphs (Sowa, 1979), and Quillian's Semantic Nets (Quillian, 1968). In our particular experiment we have used a graph representation that can be built automatically and that can be used efficiently for QA (Mollá and van Zaanen, 2006).

A *Logical Graph* (LG) is a directed, bipartite graph with two types of vertices, concepts and relations.

**Concepts** Examples of concepts are objects *dog*, *table*, events and states *run*, *love*, and properties *red*, *quick*.

**Relations** Relations act as links between concepts. To facilitate the production of the LGs we have decided to use relation labels that represent verb argument positions. Thus, the relation *1* indicates the link to the first argument of a verb (that is, what is usually a subject). The relation *2* indicates the link to the second argument of a verb (usually the direct object), and so forth. Furthermore, relations introduced by prepositions are labelled with the prepositions themselves. Our relations are therefore close to the syntactic structure.

An example of a LG is shown in Figure 7, where the concepts are pictured in boxes and the relations are pictured in ovals.

The example in Figure 7 shows LG's ability to provide the graph representation of sentences with embedded clauses. In contrast, other theories (such as Sowa (1979)'s Conceptual Graphs) would represent the sentence as a graph containing vertices that are themselves graphs. This departs from the usual definition of a graph, and therefore standard Graph Theory algorithms would need to be adapted for Conceptual Graphs. An advantage of our LGs, therefore, is that they can be manipulated with standard Graph Theory algorithms such as the ones described in this paper.

Using the LG as the graph representation of questions and answer sentences, we implemented a proof-of-concept QA system. The implementation and examples of graphs are described by Mollá and van Zaanen (2005) and here we only describe the method to generalise rules and the decisions taken to choose the exact answer.

The process to generalise rules takes advantage of the two kinds of vertices. Basically, relation vertices represent names of relations and we considered these to be important in the rule. Consequently relations edges were left unmodified in the generalised rule. Concept vertices are generalised by replacing them with generic variables, except for a specific set of "stop concepts" which were not generalised. The list of stop concepts is very small:

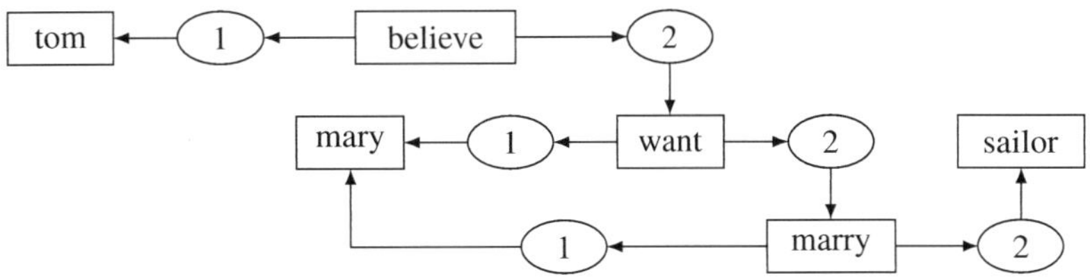


*Tom believes that Mary wants to marry a sailor*

Figure 7: Example of a Logical Graph

*and, or, not, nor, if, otherwise, have, be, become, do, make*

Every question/answer pair in the training corpus generates one rule (or more if we use a process of increasingly generalising the rules). Since the rule is based on deep linguistic information, it generalises over syntactic paraphrases. Consequently, a small training corpus suffices to produce a relatively large number of rules.

The QA system was trained with an annotated corpus of 560 pairs of TREC questions and answer sentences where the answers were manually annotated. We only tested the ability of the system to extract the exact answers. Thus, the system accepted pairs of question and answer sentences (where the sentence is guaranteed to contain an answer), and returned the exact answer. Given a question and answer sentence pair, the answer is found by applying all matching rules. All strings found as answers are ranked by multiplying the rule weights and the sizes of the overlaps. If an answer is found by several rules, its score is the sum of all scores of each individual sentence. Finally, if an answer occurs in the question it is ignored. The results of a five-fold cross validation on the annotated corpus gave an accuracy (percentage of questions where the correct answer was found) of 21.44%. Given that the QA system does not do any kind of question classification and it does not use any NE recogniser, the results are satisfactory.

## 5 Related Research

There have been other attempts to learn QA rules automatically. For example, Ravichandran and Hovy (2002) learns rules based on simple surface patterns. Given that surface patterns ignore much linguistic information, it becomes necessary to gather a large corpus of questions together with their answers and sentences containing the answers. To obtain such a corpus Ravichandran and Hovy (2002) mine the Web to gather the relevant data.

Other methods learn patterns based on syntactic information. For example, Shen et al. (2005) develop a method of extracting dependency paths connecting answers with words found in the question. However we are not aware of any method that attempts to learn patterns based on *logical* information, other than our own.

There is recent interest on the use of graph methods for Natural Language Processing, such as document summarisation (Mihalcea, 2004) document retrieval (Montes-y-Gómez et al., 2000; Mishne, 2004), and recognition of textual entailment (Pazienza et al., 2005). The present very workshop shows the current interest on the area. However, we are not aware of any significant research about the use of conceptual graphs (or any other form of graph representation) for question answering other than our own.

## 6 Conclusions

We have presented a method to learn question answering rules by applying graph manipulation methods on the representations of questions and answer sentences. The method is independent of the actual graph representation formalism.

We are studying to combine WordNet with a Named Entity Recogniser to produce generalised rules. This way it becomes possible to replace vertices with vertex types (e.g. "PERSON", "DATE", etc). We are also exploring the use of machine learning techniques to learn classes of vertices. In particular, grammar induction techniques (van Zaanen, 2002) could be applied to learn types of regularities in the strings.

Further research will also focus on developing methods to extend the question pattern $R_p$ with information found in the question only. A possibility is to keep a database of question subgraphs that are allowed to be added to $R_p$. This database could be built by hand, but ideally it should be learnt automatically.

Additional research efforts will be allocated to determine degrees of word similarity or paraphrasing, such as the connection between *was born in* and *'s birthplace is*. In particular, we will explore the use of nominalisations. We will also study paraphrasing methods to detect these connections.

Considering that text information as complex as syntactic information or even logic and semantic information can be expressed in graphs (Quillian, 1968; Schank, 1972; Sowa, 1979), we are convinced that the time is ripe to explore the use of graphs for question answering.

## References


H. Bunke, P. Foggia, C. Guidobaldi, C. Sansone, and M. Vento. 2002. A comparison of algorithms for maximum common subgraph on randomly connected graphs. In *Lecture Notes on Computer Science*, volume 2396, pages 123–132. Springer-Verlag, Heidelberg.

Noriko Kando. 2005. Overview of the fifth NTCIR workshop. In *Proceedings NTCIR 2005*.

Rada Mihalcea. 2004. Graph-based ranking algorithms for sentence extraction applied to text summarization. In *Proceedings of the 42nd Annual Meeting of the Association for Computational Linguistics, companion volume (ACL 2004)*.

Gilad Mishne. 2004. Source code retrieval using conceptual graphs. Master's thesis, University of Amsterdam.

Diego Mollá and Menno van Zaanen. 2005. Learning of graph rules for question answering. In *Proc. ALTW 2005*, Sydney.

Diego Mollá and Menno van Zaanen. 2006. Answerfinder at TREC 2005. In *Proceedings TREC 2005*. NIST.

Manuel Montes-y-Gómez, Aurelio López-López, and Alexander Gelbukh. 2000. Information retrieval with conceptual graph matching. In *Proc. DEXA-2000*, number 1873 in Lecture Notes in Computer Science, pages 312–321. Springer-Verlag.

Sung H. Myaeng and Aurelio López-López. 1992. Conceptual graph matching: a flexible algorithm and experiments. *Journal of Experimentation and Theoretical Artificial Intelligence*, 4:107–126.

Maria Teresa Pazienza, Marco Pennacchiotti, and Fabio Massimo Zanzotto. 2005. Textual entailment as syntactic graph distance: a rule based and a SVM based approach. In *Proceedings PASCAL RTE challenge 2005*.

Ross Quillian. 1968. Semantic memory. In *Semantic Information Processing*, pages 216–270. MIT Press.

Deepak Ravichandran and Eduard Hovy. 2002. Learning surface text patterns for a question answering system. In *Proc. ACL2002*.

Roger C. Schank. 1972. Conceptual dependency: A theory of natural language understanding. *Cognitive Psychology*, 3(4):532–631.

Dan Shen, Geert-Jan M. Kruijff, and Dietrich Klakow. 2005. Exploring syntactic relation patterns for question answering. In Robert Dale, Kam-Fai Wong, Jian Su, and Oi Yee Kwong, editors, *Natural Language Processing IJCNLP 2005: Second International Joint Conference, Jeju Island, Korea, October 11-13, 2005. Proceedings.* Springer-Verlag.

M. M. Soubbotin. 2001. Patterns of potential answer expression as clues to the right answers. In Voorhees and Harman (Voorhees and Harman, 2001).

John F. Sowa. 1979. Semantics of conceptual graphs. In *Proc. ACL 1979*, pages 39–44.

Pasi Tapanainen and Timo Järvinen. 1997. A non-projective dependency parser. In *Proc. ANLP-97*. ACL.

Alessandro Vallin, Bernardo Magnini, Danilo Giampiccolo, Lili Aunimo, Christelle Ayache, Petya Osenova, Anselmo Pe nas, Maarten de Rijke, Bogdan Sacaleanu, Diana Santos, and Richard Sutcliffe. 2005. Overview of the CLEF 2005 multilingual question answering track. In *Proceedings CLEF 2005*. Working note.

Menno van Zaanen. 2002. *Bootstrapping Structure into Language: Alignment-Based Learning*. Ph.D. thesis, University of Leeds, Leeds, UK.

Ellen M. Voorhees and Donna K. Harman, editors. 2001. *The Tenth Text REtrieval Conference (TREC 2001)*, number 500-250 in NIST Special Publication. NIST.

Ellen M. Voorhees. 2001a. Overview of the TREC 2001 question answering track. In Voorhees and Harman (Voorhees and Harman, 2001).

Ellen M. Voorhees. 2001b. The TREC question answering track. *Natural Language Engineering*, 7(4):361–378.

# Seeing stars when there aren't many stars: Graph-based semi-supervised learning for sentiment categorization

**Andrew B. Goldberg**
Computer Sciences Department
University of Wisconsin-Madison
Madison, W.I. 53706
goldberg@cs.wisc.edu

**Xiaojin Zhu**
Computer Sciences Department
University of Wisconsin-Madison
Madison, W.I. 53706
jerryzhu@cs.wisc.edu

## Abstract

We present a graph-based semi-supervised learning algorithm to address the sentiment analysis task of rating inference. Given a set of documents (e.g., movie reviews) and accompanying ratings (e.g., "4 stars"), the task calls for inferring numerical ratings for unlabeled documents based on the perceived sentiment expressed by their text. In particular, we are interested in the situation where labeled data is scarce. We place this task in the semi-supervised setting and demonstrate that considering unlabeled reviews in the learning process can improve rating-inference performance. We do so by creating a graph on both labeled and unlabeled data to encode certain assumptions for this task. We then solve an optimization problem to obtain a smooth rating function over the whole graph. When only limited labeled data is available, this method achieves significantly better predictive accuracy over other methods that ignore the unlabeled examples during training.

## 1 Introduction

Sentiment analysis of text documents has received considerable attention recently (Shanahan et al., 2005; Turney, 2002; Dave et al., 2003; Hu and Liu, 2004; Chaovalit and Zhou, 2005). Unlike traditional text categorization based on topics, sentiment analysis attempts to identify the subjective sentiment expressed (or implied) in documents, such as consumer product or movie reviews. In particular Pang and Lee proposed the rating-inference problem (2005). Rating inference is harder than binary positive / negative opinion classification. The goal is to infer a numerical rating from reviews, for example the number of "stars" that a critic gave to a movie. Pang and Lee showed that supervised machine learning techniques (classification and regression) work well for rating inference with large amounts of training data.

However, review documents often do not come with numerical ratings. We call such documents *unlabeled data*. Standard supervised machine learning algorithms cannot learn from unlabeled data. Assigning labels can be a slow and expensive process because manual inspection and domain expertise are needed. Often only a small portion of the documents can be labeled within resource constraints, so most documents remain unlabeled. Supervised learning algorithms trained on small labeled sets suffer in performance. Can one use the unlabeled reviews to improve rating-inference? Pang and Lee (2005) suggested that doing so should be useful.

We demonstrate that the answer is 'Yes.' Our approach is graph-based semi-supervised learning. Semi-supervised learning is an active research area in machine learning. It builds better classifiers or regressors using both labeled and unlabeled data, under appropriate assumptions (Zhu, 2005; Seeger, 2001). This paper contains three contributions:

- We present a novel adaptation of graph-based semi-supervised learning (Zhu et al., 2003)



*Workshop on TextGraphs, at HLT-NAACL 2006*, pages 45–52,
New York City, June 2006. 

to the sentiment analysis domain, extending past supervised learning work by Pang and Lee (2005);

- We design a special graph which encodes our assumptions for rating-inference problems (section 2), and present the associated optimization problem in section 3;
- We show the benefit of semi-supervised learning for rating inference with extensive experimental results in section 4.

## 2 A Graph for Sentiment Categorization

The semi-supervised rating-inference problem is formalized as follows. There are $n$ review documents $x_1 \dots x_n$, each represented by some standard feature representation (e.g., word-presence vectors). Without loss of generality, let the first $l \leq n$ documents be labeled with ratings $y_1 \dots y_l \in C$. The remaining documents are unlabeled. In our experiments, the unlabeled documents are also the test documents, a setting known as transduction. The set of numerical ratings are $C = \{c_1, \dots, c_C\}$, with $c_1 < \dots < c_C \in \mathbb{R}$. For example, a one-star to four-star movie rating system has $C = \{0, 1, 2, 3\}$. We seek a function $f : x \mapsto \mathbb{R}$ that gives a continuous rating $f(x)$ to a document $x$. Classification is done by mapping $f(x)$ to the nearest discrete rating in $C$. Note this is ordinal classification, which differs from standard multi-class classification in that $C$ is endowed with an order. In the following we use 'review' and 'document,' 'rating' and 'label' interchangeably.

We make two assumptions:

1. We are given a *similarity measure* $w_{ij} \geq 0$ between documents $x_i$ and $x_j$. $w_{ij}$ should be computable from features, so that we can measure similarities between any documents, including unlabeled ones. A large $w_{ij}$ implies that the two documents tend to express the same sentiment (i.e., rating). We experiment with *positive-sentence percentage* (PSP) based similarity which is proposed in (Pang and Lee, 2005), and mutual-information modulated word-vector cosine similarity. Details can be found in section 4.
2. Optionally, we are given numerical rating predictions $\hat{y}_{l+1}, \dots, \hat{y}_n$ on the unlabeled documents from a separate learner, for instance $\epsilon$-insensitive support vector regression (Joachims, 1999; Smola and Schölkopf, 2004) used by (Pang and Lee, 2005). This acts as an extra knowledge source for our semi-supervised learning framework to improve upon. We note our framework is general and works without the separate learner, too. (For this to work in practice, a reliable similarity measure is required.)

We now describe our graph for the semi-supervised rating-inference problem. We do this piece by piece with reference to Figure 1. Our undirected graph $G = (V, E)$ has $2n$ nodes $V$, and weighted edges $E$ among some of the nodes.

- Each document is a node in the graph (open circles, e.g., $x_i$ and $x_j$). The true ratings of these nodes $f(x)$ are unobserved. This is true even for the labeled documents because we allow for noisy labels. Our goal is to infer $f(x)$ for the unlabeled documents.
- Each labeled document (e.g., $x_j$) is connected to an observed node (dark circle) whose value is the given rating $y_j$. The observed node is a 'dongle' (Zhu et al., 2003) since it connects only to $x_j$. As we point out later, this serves to pull $f(x_j)$ towards $y_j$. The edge weight between a labeled document and its dongle is a large number $M$. $M$ represents the influence of $y_j$: if $M \to \infty$ then $f(x_j) = y_j$ becomes a hard constraint.
- Similarly each unlabeled document (e.g., $x_i$) is also connected to an observed dongle node $\hat{y}_i$, whose value is the prediction of the separate learner. Therefore we also require that $f(x_i)$ is close to $\hat{y}_i$. This is a way to incorporate multiple learners in general. We set the weight between an unlabeled node and its dongle arbitrarily to 1 (the weights are scale-invariant otherwise). As noted earlier, the separate learner is optional: we can remove it and still carry out graph-based semi-supervised learning.

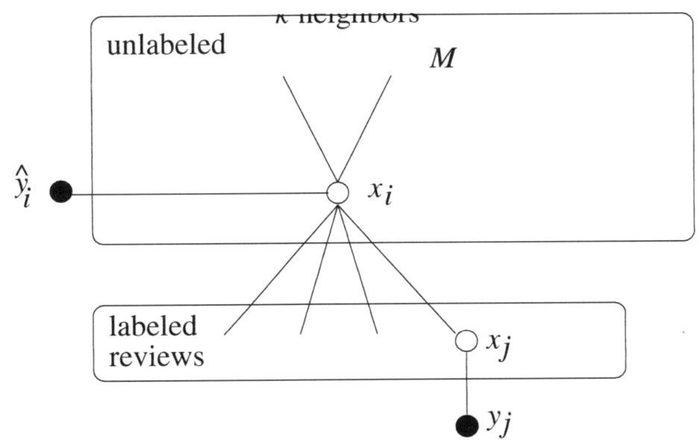


Figure 1: The graph for semi-supervised rating inference.

- Each unlabeled document $x_i$ is connected to $kNN_L(i)$, its $k$ nearest *labeled documents*. Distance is measured by the given similarity measure $w$. We want $f(x_i)$ to be consistent with its similar labeled documents. The weight between $x_i$ and $x_j \in kNN_L(i)$ is $a \cdot w_{ij}$.
- Each unlabeled document is also connected to $k'NN_U(i)$, its $k'$ nearest *unlabeled documents* (excluding itself). The weight between $x_i$ and $x_j \in k'NN_U(i)$ is $b \cdot w_{ij}$. We also want $f(x_i)$ to be consistent with its similar unlabeled neighbors. We allow potentially different numbers of neighbors ($k$ and $k'$), and different weight coefficients ($a$ and $b$). These parameters are set by cross validation in experiments.

The last two kinds of edges are the key to semi-supervised learning: They connect unobserved nodes and force ratings to be smooth throughout the graph, as we discuss in the next section.

## 3 Graph-Based Semi-Supervised Learning

With the graph defined, there are several algorithms one can use to carry out semi-supervised learning (Zhu et al., 2003; Delalleau et al., 2005; Joachims, 2003; Blum and Chawla, 2001; Belkin et al., 2005). The basic idea is the same and is what we use in this paper. That is, our rating function $f(x)$ should be *smooth* with respect to the graph. $f(x)$ is not smooth if there is an edge with large weight $w$ between nodes $x_i$ and $x_j$, *and* the difference between $f(x_i)$ and $f(x_j)$ is large. The (un)smoothness over the particular edge can be defined as $w\big(f(x_i) - f(x_j)\big)^2$. Summing over all edges in the graph, we obtain the (un)smoothness $\mathcal{L}(f)$ over the whole graph. We call $\mathcal{L}(f)$ the *energy* or *loss*, which should be minimized. Let $L = 1 \ldots l$ and $U = l+1 \ldots n$ be labeled and unlabeled review indices, respectively. With the graph in Figure 1, the loss $\mathcal{L}(f)$ can be written as

$$\sum_{i \in L} M(f(x_i) - y_i)^2 + \sum_{i \in U} (f(x_i) - \hat{y}_i)^2 + \sum_{i \in U} \sum_{j \in kNN_L(i)} a w_{ij} (f(x_i) - f(x_j))^2 + \sum_{i \in U} \sum_{j \in k'NN_U(i)} b w_{ij} (f(x_i) - f(x_j))^2. \quad (1)$$

A small loss implies that the rating of an unlabeled review is close to its labeled peers as well as its unlabeled peers. This is how unlabeled data can participate in learning. The optimization problem is $\min_f \mathcal{L}(f)$. To understand the role of the parameters, we define $\alpha = ak + bk'$ and $\beta = \frac{b}{a}$, so that $\mathcal{L}(f)$ can be written as

$$\sum_{i \in L} M(f(x_i) - y_i)^2 + \sum_{i \in U} \Big[ (f(x_i) - \hat{y}_i)^2 + \frac{\alpha}{k + \beta k'} \Big( \sum_{j \in kNN_L(i)} w_{ij} (f(x_i) - f(x_j))^2 + \sum_{j \in k'NN_U(i)} \beta w_{ij} (f(x_i) - f(x_j))^2 \Big) \Big]. \quad (2)$$

Thus $\beta$ controls the relative weight between labeled neighbors and unlabeled neighbors; $\alpha$ is roughly the relative weight given to semi-supervised (non-dongle) edges.

We can find the closed-form solution to the optimization problem. Defining an $n \times n$ matrix $\bar{W}$,

$$\bar{W}_{ij} = \begin{cases} 0, & i \in L \\ w_{ij}, & j \in kNN_L(i) \\ \beta w_{ij}, & j \in k'NN_U(i). \end{cases} \quad (3)$$

Let $W = \max(\bar{W}, \bar{W}^\top)$ be a symmetrized version of this matrix. Let $D$ be a diagonal *degree* matrix with

$$D_{ii} = \sum_{j=1}^{n} W_{ij}. \quad (4)$$

Note that we define a node's degree to be the sum of its edge weights. Let $\Delta = D - W$ be the combinatorial *Laplacian* matrix. Let $C$ be a diagonal dongle weight matrix with

$$C_{ii} = \begin{cases} M, & i \in L \\ 1, & i \in U \end{cases}. \quad (5)$$

Let $\mathbf{f} = (f(x_1), \ldots, f(x_n))^\top$ and $\mathbf{y} = (y_1, \ldots, y_l, \hat{y}_{l+1}, \ldots, \hat{y}_n)^\top$. We can rewrite $\mathcal{L}(f)$ as

$$(\mathbf{f} - \mathbf{y})^\top C(\mathbf{f} - \mathbf{y}) + \frac{\alpha}{k + \beta k'} \mathbf{f}^\top \Delta \mathbf{f}. \quad (6)$$

This is a quadratic function in $\mathbf{f}$. Setting the gradient to zero, $\partial \mathcal{L}(f)/\partial \mathbf{f} = 0$ , we find the minimum loss function

$$\mathbf{f} = \left( C + \frac{\alpha}{k + \beta k'} \Delta \right)^{-1} C\mathbf{y}. \quad (7)$$

Because $C$ has strictly positive eigenvalues, the inverse is well defined. All our semi-supervised learning experiments use (7) in what follows.

Before moving on to experiments, we note an interesting connection to the supervised learning method in (Pang and Lee, 2005), which formulates rating inference as a *metric labeling* problem (Kleinberg and Tardos, 2002). Consider a special case of our loss function (1) when $b = 0$ and $M \to \infty$. It is easy to show for labeled nodes $j \in L$, the optimal value is the given label: $f(x_j) = y_j$. Then the optimization problem decouples into a set of one-dimensional problems, one for each unlabeled node $i \in U$: $\mathcal{L}_{b=0,M\to\infty}(f(x_i)) =$

$$(f(x_i) - \hat{y}_i)^2 + \sum_{j \in kNN_L(i)} a w_{ij} (f(x_i) - y_j)^2. \quad (8)$$

The above problem is easy to solve. It corresponds exactly to the supervised, non-transductive version of metric labeling, except we use squared difference while (Pang and Lee, 2005) used absolute difference. Indeed in experiments comparing the two (not reported here), their differences are not statistically significant. From this perspective, our semi-supervised learning method is an extension with interacting terms among unlabeled data.

## 4 Experiments

We performed experiments using the movie review documents and accompanying 4-class ($C = \{0, 1, 2, 3\}$) labels found in the "scale dataset v1.0" available at http://www.cs.cornell.edu/people/pabo/movie-review-data/ and first used in (Pang and Lee, 2005). We chose 4-class instead of 3-class labeling because it is harder. The dataset is divided into four author-specific corpora, containing 1770, 902, 1307, and 1027 documents. We ran experiments individually for each author. Each document is represented as a $\{0, 1\}$ word-presence vector, normalized to sum to 1.

We systematically vary labeled set size $|L| \in \{0.9n, 800, 400, 200, 100, 50, 25, 12, 6\}$ to observe the effect of semi-supervised learning. $|L| = 0.9n$ is included to match 10-fold cross validation used by (Pang and Lee, 2005). For each $|L|$ we run 20 trials where we randomly split the corpus into labeled and test (unlabeled) sets. We ensure that all four classes are represented in each labeled set. The same random splits are used for all methods, allowing paired $t$-tests for statistical significance. All reported results are average test set accuracy.

We compare our graph-based semi-supervised method with two previously studied methods: regression and metric labeling as in (Pang and Lee, 2005).

### 4.1 Regression

We ran linear $\epsilon$-insensitive support vector regression using Joachims' SVM$^{light}$ package (1999) with all default parameters. The continuous prediction on a test document is discretized for classification. Regression results are reported under the heading 'reg.' Note this method does not use unlabeled data for training.

### 4.2 Metric labeling

We ran Pang and Lee's method based on metric labeling, using SVM regression as the initial label preference function. The method requires an item-similarity function, which is equivalent to our similarity measure $w_{ij}$. Among others, we experimented with PSP-based similarity. For consistency with (Pang and Lee, 2005), supervised metric labeling results with this measure are reported under 'reg+PSP.' Note this method does not use unlabeled data for training either.

PSP$_i$ is defined in (Pang and Lee, 2005) as the percentage of positive sentences in review $x_i$. The similarity between reviews $x_i, x_j$ is the cosine angle

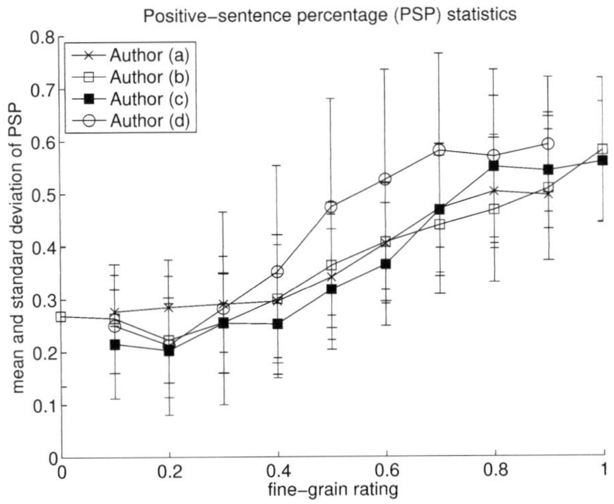


Figure 2: PSP for reviews expressing each fine-grain rating. We identified positive sentences using SVM instead of Naïve Bayes, but the trend is qualitatively the same as in (Pang and Lee, 2005).

between the vectors $(\text{PSP}_i, 1-\text{PSP}_i)$ and $(\text{PSP}_j, 1-\text{PSP}_j)$. Positive sentences are identified using a binary classifier trained on a separate "snippet data set" located at the same URL as above. The snippet data set contains 10662 short quotations taken from movie reviews appearing on the rottentomatoes.com Web site. Each snippet is labeled positive or negative based on the rating of the originating review. Pang and Lee (2005) trained a Naïve Bayes classifier. They showed that PSP is a (noisy) measure for comparing reviews—reviews with low ratings tend to receive low PSP scores, and those with higher ratings tend to get high PSP scores. Thus, two reviews with a high PSP-based similarity are expected to have similar ratings. For our experiments we derived PSP measurements in a similar manner, but using a linear SVM classifier. We observed the same relationship between PSP and ratings (Figure 2).

The metric labeling method has parameters (the equivalent of $k, \alpha$ in our model). Pang and Lee tuned them on a per-author basis using cross validation but did not report the optimal parameters. We were interested in learning a single set of parameters for use with all authors. In addition, since we varied labeled set size, it is convenient to tune $c = k/|L|$, the fraction of labeled reviews used as neighbors, instead of $k$. We then used the same $c, \alpha$ for all authors at all labeled set sizes in experiments involving PSP. Because $c$ is fixed, $k$ varies directly with $|L|$ (i.e., when less labeled data is available, our algorithm considers fewer nearby labeled examples). In an attempt to reproduce the findings in (Pang and Lee, 2005), we tuned $c, \alpha$ with cross validation. Tuning ranges are $c \in \{0.05, 0.1, 0.15, 0.2, 0.25, 0.3\}$ and $\alpha \in \{0.01, 0.1, 0.5, 1.0, 1.5, 2.0, 2.5, 3.0, 3.5, 4.0, 5.0\}$. The optimal parameters we found are $c = 0.2$ and $\alpha = 1.5$. (In section 4.4, we discuss an alternative similarity measure, for which we re-tuned these parameters.)

Note that we learned a single set of shared parameters for all authors, whereas (Pang and Lee, 2005) tuned $k$ and $\alpha$ on a per-author basis. To demonstrate that our implementation of metric labeling produces comparable results, we also determined the optimal author-specific parameters. Table 1 shows the accuracy obtained over 20 trials with $|L| = 0.9n$ for each author, using SVM regression, reg+PSP using shared $c, \alpha$ parameters, and reg+PSP using author-specific $c, \alpha$ parameters (listed in parentheses). The best result in each row of the table is highlighted in bold. We also show in bold any results that cannot be distinguished from the best result using a paired $t$-test at the 0.05 level.

(Pang and Lee, 2005) found that their metric labeling method, when applied to the 4-class data we are using, was not statistically better than regression, though they observed some improvement for authors (c) and (d). Using author-specific parameters, we obtained the same qualitative result, but the improvement for (c) and (d) appears even less significant in our results. Possible explanations for this difference are the fact that we derived our PSP measurements using an SVM classifier instead of an NB classifier, and that we did not use the same range of parameters for tuning. The optimal shared parameters produced almost the same results as the optimal author-specific parameters, and were used in subsequent experiments.

### 4.3 Semi-Supervised Learning

We used the same PSP-based similarity measure and the same shared parameters $c = 0.2, \alpha = 1.5$ from our metric labeling experiments to perform graph-based semi-supervised learning. The results are reported as 'SSL+PSP.' SSL has three

| Author | reg | reg+PSP (shared) | reg+PSP (specific) |
|---|---|---|---|
| (a) | **0.592** | **0.592** | **0.592** (0.05, 0.01) |
| (b) | **0.501** | **0.498** | **0.496** (0.05, 3.50) |
| (c) | **0.592** | 0.589 | **0.593** (0.15, 1.50) |
| (d) | **0.496** | **0.498** | **0.500** (0.05, 3.00) |

Table 1: Accuracy using shared ($c = 0.2$, $\alpha = 1.5$) vs. author-specific parameters, with $|L| = 0.9n$.

additional parameters $k'$, $\beta$, and $M$. Again we tuned $k', \beta$ with cross validation. Tuning ranges are $k' \in \{2, 3, 5, 10, 20\}$ and $\beta \in \{0.001, 0.01, 0.1, 1.0, 10.0\}$. The optimal parameters are $k' = 5$ and $\beta = 1.0$. These were used for all authors and for all labeled set sizes. Note that unlike $k = c|L|$, which decreases as the labeled set size decreases, we let $k'$ remain fixed for all $|L|$. We set $M$ arbitrarily to a large number $10^8$ to ensure that the ratings of labeled reviews are respected.

### 4.4 Alternate Similarity Measures

In addition to using PSP as a similarity measure between reviews, we investigated several alternative similarity measures based on the cosine of word vectors. Among these options were the cosine between the word vectors used to train the SVM regressor, and the cosine between word vectors containing only words with high (top 1000 or top 5000) mutual information values. The mutual information is computed with respect to the positive and negative classes in the 10662-document "snippet data set." Finally, we experimented with using as a similarity measure the cosine between word vectors containing all words, each weighted by its mutual information. We found this measure to be the best among the options tested in pilot trial runs using the metric labeling algorithm. Specifically, we scaled the mutual information values such that the maximum value was one. Then, we used these values as weights for the corresponding words in the word vectors. For words in the movie review data set that did not appear in the snippet data set, we used a default weight of zero (i.e., we excluded them. We experimented with setting the default weight to one, but found this led to inferior performance.)

We repeated the experiments described in sections 4.2 and 4.3 with the only difference being that we used the mutual-information weighted word vector similarity instead of PSP whenever a similarity measure was required. We repeated the tuning procedures described in the previous sections. Using this new similarity measure led to the optimal parameters $c = 0.1$, $\alpha = 1.5$, $k' = 5$, and $\beta = 10.0$. The results are reported under 'reg+WV' and 'SSL+WV,' respectively.

### 4.5 Results

We tested the five algorithms for all four authors using each of the nine labeled set sizes. The results are presented in table 2. Each entry in the table represents the average accuracy across 20 trials for an author, a labeled set size, and an algorithm. The best result in each row is highlighted in bold. Any results on the same row that cannot be distinguished from the best result using a paired $t$-test at the 0.05 level are also bold.

The results indicate that the graph-based semi-supervised learning algorithm based on PSP similarity (SSL+PSP) achieved better performance than all other methods in all four author corpora when only 200, 100, 50, 25, or 12 labeled documents were available. In 19 out of these 20 learning scenarios, the unlabeled set accuracy by the SSL+PSP algorithm was significantly higher than all other methods. While accuracy generally degraded as we trained on less labeled data, the decrease for the SSL approach was less severe through the mid-range labeled set sizes. SSL+PSP remains among the best methods with only 6 labeled examples.

Note that the SSL algorithm appears to be quite sensitive to the similarity measure used to form the graph on which it is based. In the experiments where we used mutual-information weighted word vector similarity (reg+WV and SSL+WV), we notice that reg+WV remained on par with reg+PSP at high labeled set sizes, whereas SSL+WV appears significantly worse in most of these cases. It is clear that PSP is the more reliable similarity measure. SSL uses the similarity measure in more ways than the metric labeling approaches (i.e., SSL's graph is denser), so it is not surprising that SSL's accuracy would suffer more with an inferior similarity measure.

Unfortunately, our SSL approach did not do as well with large labeled set sizes. We believe this

| | $\|L\|$ | regression | PSP | | word vector | |
|---|---|---|---|---|---|---|
| | | | reg+PSP | SSL+PSP | reg+WV | SSL+WV |
| Author (a) | 1593 | **0.592** | **0.592** | 0.546 | **0.592** | 0.544 |
| | 800 | **0.553** | **0.554** | 0.534 | **0.553** | 0.517 |
| | 400 | **0.522** | **0.525** | **0.526** | **0.522** | 0.497 |
| | 200 | 0.494 | 0.498 | **0.521** | 0.494 | 0.472 |
| | 100 | 0.463 | 0.477 | **0.511** | 0.462 | 0.450 |
| | 50 | 0.439 | 0.458 | **0.499** | 0.438 | 0.429 |
| | 25 | 0.408 | 0.421 | **0.465** | 0.400 | 0.404 |
| | 12 | 0.401 | 0.378 | **0.451** | 0.335 | 0.398 |
| | 6 | 0.390 | 0.359 | **0.422** | 0.314 | 0.389 |
| Author (b) | 811 | 0.501 | 0.498 | 0.481 | **0.503** | 0.473 |
| | 800 | 0.501 | 0.497 | 0.478 | **0.503** | 0.474 |
| | 400 | **0.471** | **0.471** | **0.465** | **0.471** | 0.450 |
| | 200 | **0.447** | **0.449** | **0.452** | **0.447** | 0.429 |
| | 100 | 0.415 | 0.423 | **0.443** | 0.415 | 0.397 |
| | 50 | 0.388 | 0.396 | **0.434** | 0.387 | 0.376 |
| | 25 | 0.373 | 0.380 | **0.418** | 0.364 | 0.367 |
| | 12 | 0.354 | 0.360 | **0.399** | 0.313 | 0.353 |
| | 6 | 0.348 | **0.352** | **0.380** | 0.302 | 0.347 |
| Author (c) | 1176 | **0.592** | **0.589** | 0.566 | **0.594** | 0.514 |
| | 800 | 0.579 | **0.585** | 0.559 | 0.579 | 0.509 |
| | 400 | 0.550 | **0.556** | 0.544 | 0.551 | 0.491 |
| | 200 | 0.513 | 0.519 | **0.532** | 0.513 | 0.479 |
| | 100 | 0.484 | 0.495 | **0.521** | 0.484 | 0.466 |
| | 50 | 0.462 | 0.476 | **0.504** | 0.461 | 0.456 |
| | 25 | 0.459 | 0.472 | **0.484** | 0.439 | 0.454 |
| | 12 | 0.420 | 0.405 | **0.477** | 0.356 | 0.414 |
| | 6 | 0.320 | **0.382** | **0.366** | 0.334 | **0.322** |
| Author (d) | 924 | **0.496** | **0.498** | **0.495** | **0.499** | **0.490** |
| | 800 | 0.500 | **0.501** | **0.495** | **0.504** | 0.483 |
| | 400 | 0.474 | 0.478 | **0.486** | 0.477 | 0.463 |
| | 200 | 0.459 | 0.459 | **0.468** | 0.459 | 0.445 |
| | 100 | 0.444 | 0.445 | **0.460** | 0.444 | 0.437 |
| | 50 | 0.429 | 0.431 | **0.445** | 0.429 | 0.428 |
| | 25 | 0.411 | 0.411 | **0.425** | 0.400 | 0.409 |
| | 12 | 0.393 | 0.362 | **0.405** | 0.335 | 0.391 |
| | 6 | **0.393** | 0.357 | **0.403** | 0.312 | **0.393** |

Table 2: 20-trial average unlabeled set accuracy for each author across different labeled set sizes and methods. In each row, we list in bold the best result and any results that cannot be distinguished from it with a paired $t$-test at the 0.05 level.

is due to two factors: a) the baseline SVM regressor trained on a large labeled set can achieve fairly high accuracy for this difficult task without considering pairwise relationships between examples; b) PSP similarity is not accurate enough. Gain in variance reduction achieved by the SSL graph is offset by its bias when labeled data is abundant.

## 5 Discussion

We have demonstrated the benefit of using unlabeled data for rating inference. There are several directions to improve the work: 1. We will investigate better document representations and similarity measures based on parsing and other linguistic knowledge, as well as reviews' sentiment patterns. For example, several positive sentences followed by a few concluding negative sentences could indicate an overall negative review, as observed in prior work (Pang and Lee, 2005). 2. Our method is transductive: new reviews must be added to the graph before they can be classified. We will extend it to the inductive learning setting based on (Sindhwani et al., 2005). 3. We plan to experiment with cross-reviewer and cross-domain analysis, such as using a model learned on movie reviews to help classify product reviews.

## Acknowledgment

We thank Bo Pang, Lillian Lee and anonymous reviewers for helpful comments.

## References

Mikhail Belkin, Partha Niyogi, and Vikas Sindhwani. 2005. On manifold regularization. In *Proceedings of the Tenth International Workshop on Artificial Intelligence and Statistics (AISTAT 2005)*.

A. Blum and S. Chawla. 2001. Learning from labeled and unlabeled data using graph mincuts. In *Proc. 18th International Conf. on Machine Learning*.

Pimwadee Chaovalit and Lina Zhou. 2005. Movie review mining: a comparison between supervised and unsupervised classification approaches. In *HICSS*. IEEE Computer Society.

Kushal Dave, Steve Lawrence, and David M. Pennock. 2003. Mining the peanut gallery: opinion extraction and semantic classification of product reviews. In *WWW '03: Proceedings of the 12th international conference on World Wide Web*, pages 519–528.

Olivier Delalleau, Yoshua Bengio, and Nicolas Le Roux. 2005. Efficient non-parametric function induction in semi-supervised learning. In *Proceedings of the Tenth International Workshop on Artificial Intelligence and Statistics (AISTAT 2005)*.

Minqing Hu and Bing Liu. 2004. Mining and summarizing customer reviews. In *Proceedings of KDD '04, the ACM SIGKDD international conference on Knowledge discovery and data mining*, pages 168–177. ACM Press.

T. Joachims. 1999. Making large-scale svm learning practical. In B. Schölkopf, C. Burges, and A. Smola, editors, *Advances in Kernel Methods - Support Vector Learning*. MIT Press.

T. Joachims. 2003. Transductive learning via spectral graph partitioning. In *Proceedings of ICML-03, 20th International Conference on Machine Learning*.

Jon M. Kleinberg and Éva Tardos. 2002. Approximation algorithms for classification problems with pairwise relationships: metric labeling and markov random fields. *J. ACM*, 49(5):616–639.

Bo Pang and Lillian Lee. 2005. Seeing stars: exploiting class relationships for sentiment categorization with respect to rating scales. In *Proceedings of the ACL*.

Matthias Seeger. 2001. Learning with labeled and unlabeled data. Technical report, University of Edinburgh.

James Shanahan, Yan Qu, and Janyce Wiebe, editors. 2005. *Computing attitude and affect in text*. Springer, Dordrecht, The Netherlands.

Vikas Sindhwani, Partha Niyogi, and Mikhail Belkin. 2005. Beyond the point cloud: from transductive to semi-supervised learning. In *ICML05, 22nd International Conference on Machine Learning*, Bonn, Germany.

A. J. Smola and B. Schölkopf. 2004. A tutorial on support vector regression. *Statistics and Computing*, 14:199–222.

Peter Turney. 2002. Thumbs up or thumbs down? Semantic orientation applied to unsupervised classification of reviews. In *Proceedings of ACL-02, 40th Annual Meeting of the Association for Computational Linguistics*, pages 417–424.

Xiaojin Zhu, Zoubin Ghahramani, and John Lafferty. 2003. Semi-supervised learning using Gaussian fields and harmonic functions. In *ICML-03, 20th International Conference on Machine Learning*.

Xiaojin Zhu. 2005. Semi-supervised learning literature survey. Technical Report 1530, Computer Sciences, University of Wisconsin-Madison. http://www.cs.wisc.edu/~jerryzhu/pub/ssl_survey.pdf.

# Random-Walk Term Weighting for Improved Text Classification

**Samer Hassan** and **Carmen Banea**
Department of Computer Science
University of North Texas
Denton, TX 76203
samer@unt.edu, carmen@unt.edu

## Abstract

This paper describes a new approach for estimating term weights in a text classification task. The approach uses term co-occurrence as a measure of dependency between word features. A random walk model is applied on a graph encoding words and co-occurrence dependencies, resulting in scores that represent a quantification of how a particular word feature contributes to a given context. We argue that by modeling feature weights using these scores, as opposed to the traditional frequency-based scores, we can achieve better results in a text classification task. Experiments performed on four standard classification datasets show that the new random-walk based approach outperforms the traditional term frequency approach to feature weighting.

## 1 Introduction

Term frequency has long been adapted as a measure of term significance in a specific context (Robertson and Jones, 1997). The logic behind it is that the more a certain term is encountered in a certain context, the more it carries or contributes to the meaning of the context. Due to this belief, term frequency has been a major factor in estimating the probabilistic distribution of features using maximum likelihood estimates and hence has been incorporated in a broad spectrum of tasks ranging from feature selection techniques (Yang and Pedersen, 1997; Schutze et al., 1995) to language models (Bahl et al., 1983).

In this paper we introduce a new measure of term weighting, which integrates the locality of a term and its relation to the surrounding context. We model this local contribution using a co-occurrence relation in which terms that co-occur in a certain context are likely to share between them some of their importance (or significance). Note that in this model the relation between a given term and its context is not linear, since the context itself consists of a collection of other terms, which in turn have a dependency relation with their own context, which might include the original given term. In order to model this recursive relation we use a graph-based ranking algorithm, namely the PageRank random-walk algorithms (Brin and Page, 1998), and its TextRank adaption to text processing applications (Mihalcea and Tarau, 2004). TextRank takes as input a set of textual entities and relations between them, and uses a graph-based ranking algorithm (also known as random walk algorithm) to produce a set of scores that represent the accumulated weight or rank for each textual entity in their context. The TextRank model was so far evaluated on three natural language processing tasks: document summarization, word sense disambiguation, and keyword extraction, and despite being fully unsupervised, it has been shown to be competitive with other sometime supervised state-of-the-art algorithms.

In this paper, we show how TextRank can be used to model the probabilistic distribution of word features in a document, by making further use of the scores produced by the random-walk model.



*Workshop on TextGraphs, at HLT-NAACL 2006*, pages 53–60,
New York City, June 2006. 

Through experiments performed on a text classification task, we show that these random walk scores outperform the traditional term frequencies typically used to model the feature weights for this task.

## 2 Graph-based Ranking Algorithms

The basic idea implemented by an iterative graph-based ranking algorithm is that of "voting" or "recommendation". When one vertex links to another one, it is basically casting a vote for that other vertex. The higher the number of votes that are cast for a vertex, the higher the importance of the vertex. Moreover, the importance of the vertex casting a vote determines how important the vote itself is, and this information is also taken into account by the ranking algorithm. Hence, the score associated with a vertex is determined based on the votes that are cast for it, and the scores of the vertices casting these votes.

While there are several graph-based ranking algorithms previously proposed in the literature (Herings et al., 2001), we focus on only one such algorithm, namely PageRank (Brin and Page, 1998), as it was previously found successful in a number of applications, including Web link analysis (Brin and Page, 1998), social networks (Dom et al., 2003), citation analysis, and more recently in several text processing applications (Mihalcea and Tarau, 2004), (Erkan and Radev, 2004).

Given a graph $G = (V, E)$, let $In(V_a)$ be the set of vertices that point to vertex $V_a$ (predecessors), and let $Out(V_a)$ be the set of vertices that vertex $V_a$ points to (successors). The PageRank score associated with the vertex $V_a$ is then defined using a recursive function that integrates the scores of its predecessors:

$$S(V_a) = (1 - d) + d * \sum_{V_b \in In(V_a)} \frac{S(V_b)}{|Out(V_b)|} \quad (1)$$

where $d$ is a parameter that is set between 0 and 1[1].

The score of each vertex is recalculated upon each iteration based on the new weights that the neighboring vertices have accumulated. The algorithm terminates when the convergence point is reached for all the vertices, meaning that the error rate for each vertex falls below a pre-defined threshold. Formally, for a vertex $V_i$ let $S^k(V_i)$ be the rank or the score at iteration $k$ and $S^{k+1}(V_i)$ be the score at iteration $k + 1$. The error rate $ER$ is defined as:

$$ER = S^{k+1}(V_i) - S^k(V_i) \quad (2)$$

This vertex scoring scheme is based on a random walk model, where a walker takes random steps on the graph $G$, with the walk being modeled as a Markov process – that is, the decision on what edge to follow is solely based on the vertex where the walker is currently located. Under certain conditions, this model converges to a stationary distribution of probabilities, associated with vertices in the graph. Based on the Ergodic theorem for Markov chains (Grimmett and Stirzaker, 1989), the algorithm is guaranteed to converge if the graph is both aperiodic and irreducible. The first condition is achieved for any graph that is a non-bipartite graph, while the second condition holds for any strongly connected graph – property achieved by PageRank through the random jumps introduced by the $(1-d)$ factor. In matrix notation, the PageRank vector of stationary probabilities is the principal eigenvector for the matrix $A_{row}$, which is obtained from the adjacency matrix $A$ representing the graph, with all rows normalized to sum to 1: $(P = A_{row}^T P)$.

Intuitively, the stationary probability associated with a vertex in the graph represents the probability of finding the walker at that vertex during the random walk, and thus it represents the importance of the vertex within the graph. In the context of sequence data labeling, the random walk is performed on the label graph associated with a sequence of words, and thus the resulting stationary distribution of probabilities can be used to decide on the most probable set of labels for the given sequence.

### 2.1 TextRank

Given a natural language processing task, the TextRank model includes four general steps for the application of a graph-based ranking algorithm to graph structures derived from natural language texts:

1. Identify text units that best define the proposed task and add them as vertices in the graph.

2. Identify relations that connect such test units, and use these relations to draw edges between

[1] The typical value for $d$ is 0.85 (Brin and Page, 1998), and this is the value we are also using in our implementation.

vertices in the graph. Edges can be directed or undirected, weighted or un-weighted.

3. Iterate the graph ranking algorithm to convergence.

4. Sort vertices based on their final score. Use the values attached to each vertex for ranking.

The strength of this model lies in the global representation of the context and its ability to model how the co-occurrence between features might propagate across the context and affect other distant features.

While TextRank has already been applied to several language processing tasks, we focus here on the keyword extraction task, since it best relates to our approach. The goal of a keyword extraction tool is to find a set of words or phrases that best describe a given document. The co-occurrence relation within a specific window is used to portray the correlation between words, which are represented as vertices in the graph. Two vertices are connected if their corresponding lexical units co-occur within a window of at most $N$ words, where $N$ can be set to any value greater than two. The TextRank application to keyword extraction has also used different syntactic filters for vertex selection, including all open class words, nouns and verbs, nouns and adjectives, and others. The algorithm was found to provide the best results using nouns and adjectives with a window size of two.

Our approach follows the same main steps as used in the TextRank keyword extraction application. We are however incorporating a larger number of lexical units, and we use different window sizes, as we will show in the following section.

## 3 TextRank for Term Weighting

The goal of the work reported in this paper is to study the ranking scores obtained using TextRank, and evaluate their potential usefulness as a new measure of term weighting.

To understand how the random-walk weights ($rw$) might be a good replacement for the traditional term frequency weights ($tf$), consider the example in Figure 1. The example represents a sample document from the Reuters collection. A graph is constructed as follows. If a term has not been previously seen, then a node is added to the graph to represent this term. A term can only be represented by one node in the graph. An undirected edge is drawn between two nodes if they co-occur within a certain window size. This example assumes a window size of two, corresponding to two consecutive terms in the text (e.g. *London* is linked to *based*).

> *London-based sugar operator Kaines Ltd confirmed it sold two cargoes of white sugar to India out of an estimated overall sales total of four or five cargoes in which other brokers participated. The sugar, for April/May and April/June shipment, was sold at between 214 and 218 dlrs a tonne cif, it said.*

Figure 1: Sample Reuters document

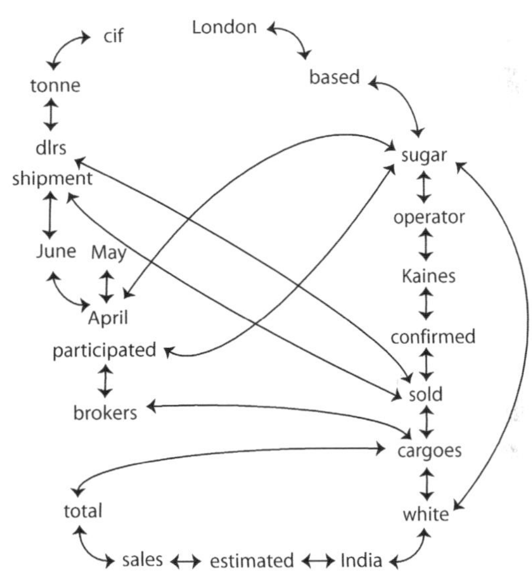


Figure 2: Sample graph

Table 1 shows the $tf$ and $rw$ weights, also plotted in Figure 3. By analyzing the $rw$ weights, we can observe a non-linear correlation with the $tf$ weights, with an emphasis given to terms surrounding important key term like e.g. "sugar" or "cargoes." This spatial locality has resulted in higher ranks for terms like "operator" compared to other terms like "london"[2].

[2]All the missing words (e.g. "Ltd," "it") that are not shown in the graph are common-words that were eliminated in the preprocessing phase.

| Term | $rw$ | $tf$ |
|---|---|---|
| sugar | 2.248 | 3 |
| sold | 1.594 | 2 |
| april | 1.407 | 2 |
| cargoes | 1.542 | 2 |
| cif | 0.600 | 1 |
| sales | 0.891 | 1 |
| london | 0.546 | 1 |
| tonne | 1.059 | 1 |
| shipment | 0.829 | 1 |
| based | 0.933 | 1 |
| estimated | 0.888 | 1 |
| dlrs | 0.938 | 1 |
| kaines | 0.871 | 1 |
| confirmed | 0.859 | 1 |
| total | 0.856 | 1 |
| white | 0.796 | 1 |
| india | 0.846 | 1 |
| operator | 0.839 | 1 |
| brokers | 0.826 | 1 |
| june | 0.801 | 1 |
| participated | 0.819 | 1 |

Table 1: $tf$ & $rw$ scores

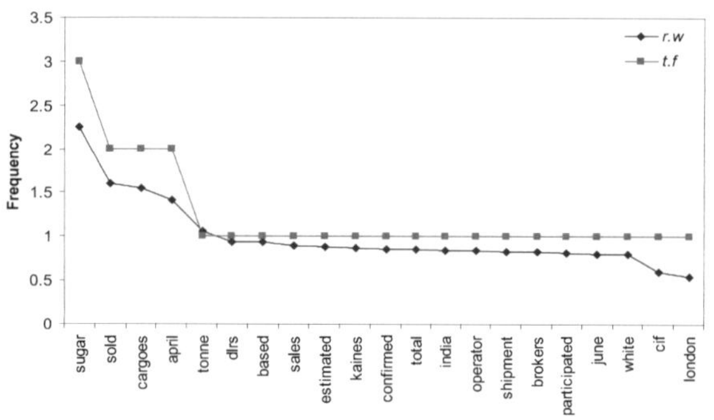


Figure 3: $tf$ & $rw$ plots

## 4 Experimental Setup

To evaluate our random-walk based approach to feature weighting, we integrate it in a text classification algorithm, and evaluate its performance on several standard text classification data sets.

### 4.1 Random-Walk Term Weighting

Starting with a given document, we determine a ranking over the words in the document by using the approach described in Section 3.

First, we tokenize the document for punctuation, special symbols, word abbreviations. We also remove the common words, using a list of approximately 500 frequently used words as used in the Smart retrieval system [3].

Next, the resulting text is processed to extract both $tf$ and $rw$ weights for each term in the document. Note that we do not apply any syntactic filters, as it was previously done in applications of TextRank. Instead, we consider each word as a potential feature. To determine $tf$ we simply count the frequencies of each word in the document. To determine $rw$, all the terms are added as vertices in a graph representing the document. A co-occurrence scanner is then applied to the text to relate the terms that co-occur within a given window size . For a given term, all the terms that fall in the vicinity of this term are considered dependent terms. This is represented by a set of edges that connect this term to all the other terms in the window. Experiments are performed for window sizes of 2, 4, 6, and 8. Once the graph is constructed and the edges are in place, the TextRank algorithm is applied[4]. The result of the ranking process is a list of all input terms and their corresponding $rw$ scores.

We then calculate $tf.idf$ and $rw.idf$ as follows:

$$tf.idf = tf * log\frac{N_D}{n}$$

where $N_D$ represent the total number of documents in the collection and $n$ is the number of documents in which the target term appeared at least once.

Similarly,

$$rw.idf = rw * log\frac{N_D}{n}$$

These term weights ($tf.idf$ or $rw.idf$) are then used to create a feature vector for each document. The vectors are fed to a traditional text classification system, using one of the learning algorithms described below. The results obtained using $tf.idf$ will act as a baseline in our evaluation.

### 4.2 Text Classification

Text classification is a problem typically formulated as a machine learning task, where a classifier learns how to distinguish between categories in a given set

[3]ftp://ftp.cs.cornell.edu/pub/smart.

[4]We use an implementation where the maximum number of iterations is limited to 100, the damping factor is set to 0.85, and convergence threshold to 0.0001. Each graph node is assigned with an initial weight of 0.25.

using features automatically extracted from a collection of training documents. There is a large body of algorithms previously tested on text classification problems, due also to the fact that this task is one of the testbeds of choice for machine learning algorithms. In the experiments reported here, we compare results obtained with four frequently used text classifiers – Rocchio, Naïve Bayes, Nearest Neighbor, and Support Vector Machines, selected based on their diversity of learning methodologies.

**Naïve Bayes.** The basic idea in a Naïve Bayes text classifier is to estimate the probability of a category given a document using joint probabilities of words and documents. Naïve Bayes assumes word independence, which means that the conditional probability of a word given a category is assumed to be independent of the conditional probability of other words given the same category. Despite this simplification, Naïve Bayes classifiers were shown to perform surprisingly well on text classification (Joachims, 1997), (Schneider, 2004). While there are several versions of Naïve Bayes classifiers (variations of multinomial and multivariate Bernoulli), we use the multinomial model (McCallum and Nigam, 1998), which was shown to be more effective.

**Rocchio.** This is an adaptation of the relevance feedback method developed in information retrieval (Rocchio, 1971). It uses standard $tf.idf$ weighted vectors to represent documents, and builds a prototype vector for each category by summing up the vectors of the training documents in each category. Test documents are then assigned to the category that has the closest prototype vector, based on a cosine similarity. Text classification experiments with different versions of the Rocchio algorithm showed competitive results on standard benchmarks (Joachims, 1997), (Moschitti, 2003).

**KNN.** K-Nearest Neighbor is one of the earliest text categorization approaches (Makoto and Takenobu, 1995; Masand et al., 1992). The algorithm classifies a test document based on the best class label identified for the nearest K-neighbors in the training documents. The best class label is chosen by weighting the class of each similar training document with its similarity to the target test document.

**SVM.** Support Vector Machines (Vapnik, 1995) is a state-of-the-art machine learning approach based on decision plans. The algorithm defines the best hyper-plan which separates set of points associated with different class labels with a maximum-margin. The unlabeled examples are then classified by deciding in which side of the hyper-surface they reside. The hyper-plan can be a simple linear plan as first proposed by Vapnik, or a non-linear plan such as e.g. polynomial, radial, or sigmoid. In our evaluation we used the linear kernel since it was proved to be as powerful as the other kernels when tested on text classification data sets (Yang and Liu, 1999).

### 4.3 Data Sets

In our experiments we use $Reuters\text{-}21578$, $WebKB$, $20Newsgroups$, and $LingSpam$ datasets. These datasets are commonly used for text classification evaluations (Joachims, 1996; Craven et al., 1998; Androutsopoulos et al., 2000; Mihalcea and Hassan, 2005).

**Reuter-21578.** This is a publicly available subset of the Reuters news, containing about 120 categories. We use the standard ModApte data split (Apte et al., 1994). The unlabeled documents were discarded and only the documents with one or more class labels were used in the classification experiments.

**WebKB.** This is a data set collected from computer science departments of various universities by the CMU text learning group. The dataset contains seven class labels which are Project, Student, Department, Faculty, Staff, Course, and Other. The Other label was removed from the dataset for evaluation purposes. Most of the evaluations in the literature have been performed on only four of the categories (Project, Student, Faculty, and Course) since they represent the largest categories. However, since we wanted to see how our system behaves when only a few training examples were available as e.g. in the Staff and the Department classes, we performed our evaluations on two versions of $WebKB$: one with the four categories version ($WebKB_4$) and one with the six categories ($WebKB_6$).

**20-Newsgroups.** This is a collection of 20,000 messages from 20 different newsgroups, corresponding to different topics or subjects. Each newsgroup has about 1000 message split into 400 test and 600 train documents.

**LingSpam.** This is a spam corpus, consisting of email messages organized in 10 collections to allow for 10-fold cross validation. Each collection has roughly 300 spam and legitimate messages. There are four versions of the corpus standing for bare, stop-word filtered, lemmatized, and stop-word and lemmatized. We use the bare collection with a standard 10-fold cross validation.

### 4.4 Performance Measures

To evaluate the classification system we used the traditional accuracy measure defined as the number of correct predictions divided with the number of evaluated examples.

We also use the correlation coefficient ($\rho$) as a diversity measure to evaluate the dissimilarity between the weighting models. Pairwise diversity measures have been traditionally used to measure the statistical independence among ensemble of classifiers (Kuncheva and Whitaker, 2003). Here, we use them to measure the correlation between our random-walk approach and the traditional term frequency approach. The typical setting in which the pairwise diversity measures are used is a set of different classifiers which are used to classify the same set of feature vectors or documents over a given dataset. In our evaluation we use the same classifier to evaluate two different sets of feature vectors that are produced by different weighting features: the $rw$ random walk weighting, and the $tf$ term frequency weighting. Since the two feature vector collections are evaluated by one classifier at a time, the resulted diversity scores will reflect the diversity of the two systems.

Let $D_i$ and $D_j$ be two feature weighting models with the following contingency table.

| | $D_{j\ correct=Y}$ | $D_{j\ correct=N}$ |
|---|---|---|
| $D_{i\ correct=Y}$ | $a$ | b |
| $D_{i\ correct=N}$ | $c$ | d |

Table 2: $D_i$ & $D_j$ Contingency table

The correlation coefficient ($\rho$) is defined as:

$$\rho_{ij} = \frac{ad - bc}{\sqrt{(a+b)(c+d)(a+c)(b+d)}}$$

[5]The symbol †indicates a statistically significant result using a paired t-test, with $p < 0.05$. The result is marked by ‡ when $p < 0.001$.

Table 3: Naive Bayes Results[5]

| $N.B.$ | $tf$ | $rw_2$ | $rw_4$ | $rw_6$ | $rw_8$ |
|---|---|---|---|---|---|
| $WebKB_4$ | 81.9 | 81.9 | **82.8** | 82.7 | 81.2 |
| $WebKB_6$ | 71.7 | 73.0 | 74.2† | **74.4**† | 73.5 |
| $Reuter$ | **83.2** | 82.5 | 82.9 | 83.0 | 82.8 |
| $20NG$ | 81.7 | 82.0 | **82.3**‡ | 82.3‡ | 82.1† |
| $LSpam$ | 99.3 | **99.4** | 99.3 | 99.3 | 99.3 |

Table 4: Rocchio Results

| $ROC$ | $tf$ | $rw_2$ | $rw_4$ | $rw_6$ | $rw_8$ |
|---|---|---|---|---|---|
| $WebKB_4$ | 71.9 | 77.5‡ | **78.6**‡ | 80.8‡ | 80.9‡ |
| $WebKB_6$ | 58.3 | 69.6‡ | 72.0‡ | **76.5**‡ | 76.2‡ |
| $Reuter$ | 78.2 | 80.8‡ | 81.1‡ | 81.0‡ | **81.4**‡ |
| $20NG$ | 76.2 | 77.3‡ | 77.1‡ | 77.2‡ | **77.4**‡ |
| $LSpam$ | 97.5 | **97.8** | 97.8 | 97.7 | 97.8 |

## 5 Evaluation and Discussion

Tables 3, 4, 5, 6 show the classification results for $WebKB_4$, $WebKB_6$, $LingSpam$, $Reuter$, and $20Newsgroups$ respectively. The $rw_2$, $rw_4$, $rw_6$, and $rw_8$ represent the accuracies achieved using random-walk weighting under window sizes of 2, 4, 6, and 8 respectively. The $tf$ column represents the results obtained with a term frequency weighting scheme.

By examining the results we can see that the $rw.idf$ model outperforms the $tf.idf$ model on all the classifiers and datasets with only one exception in the case of a Naïve Bayes classifier under $Reuter$. The error reductions range from 3.5% as in $\{20Newsgroups, NaiveBayes, rw_4\}$ to 44% as in the case of $\{WebKB_6, Rocchio, rw_6\}$. The system gives, in its worst performance, a comparable result to the $tf.idf$ baseline. The system shows a consistent performance with different window sizes, with no clear cut window size that would give the best result. By further analyzing the results using statistical paired t-tests we can see that windows of size 4 and 6 supply the most significant results across all the classifiers as well as the datasets.

Comparing $WebKB_4$ and $WebKB_6$ fine-grained results, we found that both systems failed to predict the class Staff; however the significant improve-

Table 5: KNN Results

| *KNN* | *tf* | $rw_2$ | $rw_4$ | $rw_6$ | $rw_8$ |
|---|---|---|---|---|---|
| $WebKB_4$ | 59.2 | **68.6**‡ | 67.0‡ | 64.6‡ | 66.6‡ |
| $WebKB_6$ | 55.8 | **63.7**‡ | 55.8 | 59.9† | 61.0‡ |
| *Reuter* | 73.6 | 76.9‡ | 78.1‡ | **78.5**‡ | 78.5‡ |
| 20*NG* | 70.3 | 76.1‡ | 76.5‡ | 77.2‡ | **77.8**‡ |
| *LSpam* | 97.5 | 97.8 | 97.8 | **98.1**† | 97.9 |

Table 6: SVM Results

| *SVM* | *tf* | $rw_2$ | $rw_4$ | $rw_6$ | $rw_8$ |
|---|---|---|---|---|---|
| $WebKB_4$ | 87.7 | 87.9 | 87.9 | **89**† | 88.5 |
| $WebKB_6$ | 82.5 | 84.5‡ | **85.2**‡ | 85.2‡ | 84.6‡ |
| *Reuter* | 83.2 | 84.5‡ | 84.4‡ | **84.6**‡ | 84.1† |
| 20*NG* | 95.2 | 95.5‡ | **95.6**‡ | 95.6‡ | 95.4† |
| *LSpam* | 95.6 | 96.4‡ | **96.4**‡ | 96.2‡ | 96.3‡ |

ment was over the class Department, in which our *rw* model scores an accuracy of 47% compared to 4% in using *tf.idf*. This indicates how successful *rw.idf* model is in cases where there are few training examples. This could be due to the ability of the model to extract more realistic and smoother distribution of terms as seen in the *rw* curve plotted in Figure 3, hence reducing the feature bias imposed by the limited number of training examples.

Table 7: Naive Bayes Correlation $\rho$

| *N.B.* | $rw_2$ | $rw_4$ | $rw_6$ | $rw_8$ |
|---|---|---|---|---|
| $WebKB_4$ | 0.68 | 0.70 | 0.70 | **0.66** |
| $WebKB_6$ | 0.71 | 0.71 | 0.71 | **0.65** |
| *Reuter* | 0.86 | 0.87 | 0.87 | **0.85** |
| 20*NG* | **0.82** | 0.84 | 0.83 | 0.82 |
| *LSpam* | **0.89** | 0.89 | 0.92 | 0.92 |

By also examining the *diversity* of the classification systems based on *rw* and *tf* weighting, as shown in Table 7, 8, 9, 10, we can see an interesting property of the system. The two models are generally more diverse and less correlated when using windows of size 6 and 8 than using windows of size 2 and 4. This could be due to the increasing drift from the feature independence assumption that is implied by *tf.idf*. However increasing the dependency is not always desirable as seen in the reported accuracies. We expect that at a certain window size the system performance will degrade to *tf.idf*. This

Table 8: Rocchio Correlation $\rho$

| *ROC* | $rw_2$ | $rw_4$ | $rw_6$ | $rw_8$ |
|---|---|---|---|---|
| $WebKB_4$ | **0.49** | 0.51 | 0.53 | 0.54 |
| $WebKB_6$ | **0.40** | 0.40 | 0.41 | 0.42 |
| *Reuter* | 0.75 | 0.77 | 0.75 | **0.71** |
| 20*NG* | 0.77 | 0.77 | 0.77 | **0.77** |
| *LSpam* | 0.82 | 0.85 | 0.81 | **0.78** |

Table 9: KNN Correlation $\rho$

| *KNN* | $rw_2$ | $rw_4$ | $rw_6$ | $rw_8$ |
|---|---|---|---|---|
| $WebKB_4$ | 0.35 | **0.32** | 0.36 | 0.37 |
| $WebKB_6$ | **0.35** | 0.35 | 0.37 | 0.37 |
| *Reuter* | 0.74 | 0.70 | 0.68 | **0.67** |
| 20*NG* | 0.62 | 0.64 | 0.63 | **0.59** |
| *LSpam* | 0.66 | 0.69 | 0.63 | **0.57** |

threshold window size will be equal to the document size. In such a case each term will depend on all the remaining terms resulting in an almost completely connected graph. Consequently, each feature contribution to the surrounding will be equal resulting in similar *rw* scores to all the features.

## 6 Conclusions and Future Work

Based on results obtained in text classification experiments, the TextRank random-walk model to term weighting was found to achieve error rate reductions of 3.5–44% as compared to the traditional frequency-based approach. The evaluation results have shown that the system performance varies depending on window size, dataset, as well as classifier, with the greatest boost in performance recorded for KNN ,Rocchio, and SVM. We believe that these results support our claim that random-walk models can accurately estimate term weights, and can be used as a technique to model the probabilistic distribution of features in a document.

The evaluations reported in this paper has shown that the TextRank model can accurately provide *unigram* probabilities for a sequence of words. In future work we will try to extend the TextRank model and use it to define a formal language model in which we can estimate the probability of entire sequences of words (*n-grams*).

Table 10: SVM Correlation $\rho$

| $SVM$ | $rw_2$ | $rw_4$ | $rw_6$ | $rw_8$ |
|---|---|---|---|---|
| $WebKB_4$ | **0.73** | 0.77 | 0.78 | 0.82 |
| $WebKB_6$ | **0.73** | 0.76 | 0.78 | 0.80 |
| $Reuter$ | **0.80** | 0.83 | 0.82 | 0.82 |
| $20NG$ | 0.80 | **0.78** | 0.82 | 0.83 |
| $LSpam$ | **0.86** | 0.88 | 0.88 | 0.89 |

## References


I. Androutsopoulos, J. Koutsias, K. V. Chandrinos, G. Paliouras, and C. D. Spyropoulos. 2000. An evaluation of naive bayesian anti-spam filtering. In *Proceedings of the workshop on Machine Learning in the New Information Age*.

C. Apte, F. Damerau, and S. M. Weiss. 1994. Towards language independent automated learning of text categorisation models. In *Proceedings of the 17th ACM SIGIR Conference on Research and Development in Information Retrieval*.

L. Bahl, F. Jelinek, and R. Mercer. 1983. A maximum likelihood approach to continuous speech recognition. *IEEE Transactions on Pattern Analysis and Machine Intelligence*, 5(2).

S. Brin and L. Page. 1998. The anatomy of a large-scale hypertextual Web search engine. *Computer Networks and ISDN Systems*, 30(1–7).

M. Craven, D. DiPasquo, D. Freitag, A. McCallum, T. Mitchell, K. Nigam, and S. Slattery. 1998. Learning to extract symbolic knowledge from the World Wide Web. In *Proceedings of the 15th Conference of the American Association for Artificial Intelligence*.

B. Dom, I. Eiron, A. Cozzi, and Y. Shang. 2003. Graph-based ranking algorithms for e-mail expertise analysis. In *Proceedings of the 8th ACM SIGMOD workshop on Research issues in data mining and knowledge discovery*, San Diego, California.

G. Erkan and D. Radev. 2004. Lexpagerank: Prestige in multi-document text summarization. In *Proceedings of the Conference on Empirical Methods in Natural Language Processing*, Barcelona, Spain, July.

G. Grimmett and D. Stirzaker. 1989. *Probability and Random Processes*. Oxford University Press.

P.J. Herings, G. van der Laan, and D. Talman. 2001. Measuring the power of nodes in digraphs. Technical report, Tinbergen Institute.

T. Joachims. 1996. A probabilistic analysis of the rocchio algorithm with tf.idf for text categorization. In *Proceedings of the 14th International Conference on Machine Learning*.

T. Joachims. 1997. A probabilistic analysis of the Rocchio algorithm with TFIDF for text categorization. In *Proceedings of ICML-97, 14th International Conference on Machine Learning*, Nashville, US.

L. Kuncheva and C. Whitaker. 2003. Measures of diversity in classifier ensembles and their relationship with the ensemble accuracy. *Machine Learning*, 51.

I. Makoto and T. Takenobu. 1995. Cluster-based text categorization: A comparison of category search startegies. In *Proceedings of the 18th ACM International Conference on Research and Development in Information Retrieval*.

B. Masand, G. Linoff, and D. Waltz. 1992. Classifying news stories using memory based reasoning. In *Proceedings of the 15th International Conference on Research and Development in information Retrieval*.

A. McCallum and K. Nigam. 1998. A comparison of event models for Naive Bayes text classification. In *Proceedings of AAAI-98 Workshop on Learning for Text Categorization*.

R. Mihalcea and S. Hassan. 2005. Using the essence of texts to improve document classification. In *Proceedings of the Conference on Recent Advances in Natural Language Processing (RANLP)*, Borovetz, Bulgaria.

R. Mihalcea and P. Tarau. 2004. TextRank – bringing order into texts. In *Proceedings of the Conference on Empirical Methods in Natural Language Processing (EMNLP 2004)*, Barcelona, Spain.

A. Moschitti. 2003. A study on optimal paramter tuning for Rocchio text classifier. In *Proceedings of the European Conference on Information Retrieval*, Pisa, Italy.

R. Robertson and K. Sparck Jones. 1997. Simple, proven approaches to text retrieval. Technical report.

J. Rocchio, 1971. *Relevance feedback in information retrieval*. Prentice Hall, Ing. Englewood Cliffs, New Jersey.

K. Schneider. 2004. A new feature selection score for multinomial naive bayes text classification based on kl-divergence. In *The Companion Volume to the Proceedings of 42st Annual Meeting of the Association for Computational Linguistics*, Barcelona, Spain, July.

H. Schutze, D. A. Hull, and J. O. Pedersen. 1995. A comparison of classifiers and document representations for the routing problem. In *Proceedings of the 18th annual international ACM SIGIR conference on Research and development in information retrieval*, Seattle, Washington.

V. Vapnik. 1995. *The Nature of Statistical Learning Theory*. Springer, New York.

Y. Yang and X. Liu. 1999. A reexamination of text categorization methods. In *Proceedings of the 22nd ACM SIGIR Conference on Research and Development in Information Retrieval*.

Y. Yang and J. O. Pedersen. 1997. A comparative study on feature selection in text categorization. In *Proceedings of the 14th International Conference on Machine Learning*, Nashville, US.

# Graph-based Generalized Latent Semantic Analysis for Document Representation

**Irina Matveeva**
Dept. of Computer Science
University of Chicago
Chicago, IL 60637
matveeva@cs.uchicago.edu

**Gina-Anne Levow**
Dept. of Computer Science
University of Chicago
Chicago, IL 60637
levow@cs.uchicago.edu

## Abstract

Document indexing and representation of term-document relations are very important for document clustering and retrieval. In this paper, we combine a graph-based dimensionality reduction method with a corpus-based association measure within the Generalized Latent Semantic Analysis framework. We evaluate the graph-based GLSA on the document clustering task.

## 1 Introduction

Document indexing and representation of term-document relations are very important issues for document clustering and retrieval. Although the vocabulary space is very large, content bearing words are often combined into semantic classes that contain synonyms and semantically related words. Hence there has been a considerable interest in low-dimensional term and document representations.

Latent Semantic Analysis (LSA) (Deerwester et al., 1990) is one of the best known dimensionality reduction algorithms. The dimensions of the LSA vector space can be interpreted as latent semantic concepts. The cosine similarity between the LSA document vectors corresponds to documents' similarity in the input space. LSA preserves the documents similarities which are based on the inner products of the input bag-of-word documents and it preserves these similarities globally.

More recently, a number of graph-based dimensionality reduction techniques were successfully applied to document clustering and retrieval (Belkin and Niyogi, 2003; He et al., 2004). The main advantage of the graph-based approaches over LSA is the notion of locality. Laplacian Eigenmaps Embedding (Belkin and Niyogi, 2003) and Locality Preserving Indexing (LPI) (He et al., 2004) discover the local structure of the term and document space and compute a semantic subspace with a stronger discriminative power. Laplacian Eigenmaps Embedding and LPI preserve the input similarities only locally, because this information is most reliable. Laplacian Eigenmaps Embedding does not provide a fold-in procedure for unseen documents. LPI is a linear approximation to Laplacian Eigenmaps Embedding that eliminates this problem. Similar to LSA, the input similarities to LPI are based on the inner products of the bag-of-word documents. Laplacian Eigenmaps Embedding can use any kind of similarity in the original space.

Generalized Latent Semantic Analysis (GLSA) (Matveeva et al., 2005) is a framework for computing semantically motivated term and document vectors. It extends the LSA approach by focusing on term vectors instead of the dual document-term representation. GLSA requires a measure of semantic association between terms and a method of dimensionality reduction.

In this paper, we use GLSA with point-wise mutual information as a term association measure. We introduce the notion of locality into this framework and propose to use Laplacian Eigenmaps Embedding as a dimensionality reduction algorithm. We evaluate the importance of locality for document representation in document clustering experiments.

The rest of the paper is organized as follows. Sec-



*Workshop on TextGraphs, at HLT-NAACL 2006*, pages 61–64,
New York City, June 2006. 

tion 2 contains the outline of the graph-based GLSA algorithm. Section 3 presents our experiments, followed by conclusion in section 4.

## 2 Graph-based GLSA

### 2.1 GLSA Framework

The GLSA algorithm (Matveeva et al., 2005) has the following setup. The input is a document collection $C$ with vocabulary $V$ and a large corpus $W$.

1. For the vocabulary in $V$, obtain a matrix of pair-wise similarities, $S$, using the corpus $W$
2. Obtain the matrix $U^T$ of a low dimensional vector space representation of terms that preserves the similarities in $S$, $U^T \in R^{k \times |V|}$
3. Construct the term document matrix $D$ for $C$
4. Compute document vectors by taking linear combinations of term vectors $\hat{D} = U^T D$

The columns of $\hat{D}$ are documents in the $k$-dimensional space.

GLSA approach can combine any kind of similarity measure on the space of terms with any suitable method of dimensionality reduction. The inner product between the term and document vectors in the GLSA space preserves the semantic association in the input space. The traditional term-document matrix is used in the last step to provide the weights in the linear combination of term vectors. LSA is a special case of GLSA that uses inner product in step 1 and singular value decomposition in step 2, see (Bartell et al., 1992).

### 2.2 Singular Value Decomposition

Given any matrix $S$, its singular value decomposition (SVD) is $S = U\Sigma V^T$. The matrix $S_k = U\Sigma_k V^T$ is obtained by setting all but the first $k$ diagonal elements in $\Sigma$ to zero. If $S$ is symmetric, as in the GLSA case, $U = V$ and $S_k = U\Sigma_k U^T$. The inner product between the GLSA term vectors computed as $U\Sigma_k^{1/2}$ optimally preserves the similarities in $S$ wrt square loss.

The basic GLSA computes the SVD of $S$ and uses $k$ eigenvectors corresponding to the largest eigenvalues as a representation for term vectors. We will refer to this approach as *GLSA*. As for LSA, the similarities are preserved globally.

### 2.3 Laplacian Eigenmaps Embedding

We used the Laplacian Embedding algorithm (Belkin and Niyogi, 2003) in step 2 of the GLSA algorithm to compute low-dimensional term vectors. Laplacian Eigenmaps Embedding preserves the similarities in $S$ only locally since local information is often more reliable. We will refer to this variant of GLSA as *GLSA*$_\mathrm{L}$.

The Laplacian Eigenmaps Embedding algorithm computes the low dimensional vectors $y$ to minimize under certain constraints

$$\sum_{ij} ||y_i - y_j||^2 W_{ij}.$$

$W$ is the weight matrix based on the graph adjacency matrix. $W_{ij}$ is large if terms $i$ and $j$ are similar according to $S$. $W_{ij}$ can be interpreted as the penalty of mapping similar terms far apart in the Laplacian Embedding space, see (Belkin and Niyogi, 2003) for details. In our experiments we used a binary adjacency matrix $W$. $W_{ij} = 1$ if terms $i$ and $j$ are among the k nearest neighbors of each other and is zero otherwise.

### 2.4 Measure of Semantic Association

Following (Matveeva et al., 2005), we primarily used point-wise mutual information (PMI) as a measures of semantic association in step 1 of GLSA. PMI between random variables representing two words, $w_1$ and $w_2$, is computed as

$$PMI(w_1, w_2) = \log \frac{P(W_1 = 1, W_2 = 1)}{P(W_1 = 1)P(W_2 = 1)}.$$

### 2.5 GLSA Space

GLSA offers a greater flexibility in exploring the notion of semantic relatedness between terms. In our preliminary experiments, we obtained the matrix of semantic associations in step 1 of GLSA using point-wise mutual information (PMI), likelihood ratio and $\chi^2$ test. Although PMI showed the best performance, other measures are particularly interesting in combination with the Laplacian Embedding.

Related approaches, such as LSA, the Word Space Model (WS) (Schütze, 1998) and Latent Relational Analysis (LRA) (Turney, 2004) are limited to only one measure of semantic association and preserve the similarities globally.

Assuming that the vocabulary space has some underlying low dimensional semantic manifold. Laplacian Embedding algorithm tries to approximate this manifold by relying only on the local similarity information. It uses the nearest neighbors graph constructed using the pair-wise term similarities. The computations of the Laplacian Embedding uses the graph adjacency matrix $W$. This matrix can be binary or use weighted similarities. The advantage of the binary adjacency matrix is that it conveys the neighborhood information without relying on individual similarity values. It is important for co-occurrence based similarity measures, see discussion in (Manning and Schütze, 1999).

The Locality Preserving Indexing (He et al., 2004) has a similar notion of locality but has to use bag-of-words document vectors.

## 3 Document Clustering Experiments

We conducted a document clustering experiment for the Reuters-21578 collection. To collect the co-occurrence statistics for the similarities matrix $S$ we used a subset of the English Gigaword collection (LDC), containing New York Times articles labeled as "story". We had 1,119,364 documents with 771,451 terms. We used the Lemur toolkit[1] to tokenize and index all document collections used in our experiments, with stemming and a list of stop words.

Since Locality Preserving Indexing algorithm (LPI) is most related to the graph-based GLSA$_L$, we ran experiments similar to those reported in (He et al., 2004). We computed the GLSA document vectors for the 20 largest categories from the Reuters-21578 document collection. We had 8564 documents and 7173 terms. We used the same list of 30 TREC words as in (He et al., 2004) which are listed in table 1[2]. For each word on this list, we generated a cluster as a subset of Reuters documents that contained this word. Clusters are not disjoint and contain documents from different Reuters categories.

We computed *GLSA*, *GLSA*$_{\mathrm{L}}$, LSA and LPI representations. We report the results for $k = 5$ for the $k$ nearest neighbors graph for LPI and Laplacian Embedding, and binary weights for the adjacency matrix. We report results for 300 embedding dimensions for GLSA, LPI and LSA and 500 dimensions for *GLSA*$_{\mathrm{L}}$.

We evaluate these representations in terms of how well the cosine similarity between the document vectors within each cluster corresponds to the true semantic similarity. We expect documents from the same Reuters category to have higher similarity.

For each cluster we computed all pair-wise document similarities. All pair-wise similarities were sorted in decreasing order. The term "inter-pair" describes a pair of documents that have the same label. For the k$^{th}$ inter-pair, we computed precision at $k$ as:

$$\mathrm{precision}(\mathrm{p_k}) = \frac{\#\mathrm{inter-pairs}\ p_j, \mathrm{s.t.}\ j < k}{k},$$

where $p_j$ refers to the $j^{th}$ inter-pair. The average of the precision values for each of the inter-pairs was used as the average precision for the particular document cluster.

Table 1 summarizes the results. The first column shows the words according to which document clusters were generated and the entropy of the category distribution within that cluster. The baseline was to use the *tf* document vectors. We report results for *GLSA*, *GLSA*$_{\mathrm{L}}$, LSA and LPI. The LSA and LPI computations were based solely on the Reuters collection. For *GLSA* and *GLSA*$_{\mathrm{L}}$we used the term associations computed for the Gigaword collection, as described above. Therefore, the similarities that are preserved are quite different. For LSA and LPI they reflect the term distribution specific for the Reuters collection whereas for GLSA they are more general. By paired 2-tailed t-test, at $p \leq 0.05$, *GLSA* outperformed all other approaches. There was no significant difference in performance of *GLSA*$_{\mathrm{L}}$, LSA and the baseline. Disappointingly, we could not achieve good performance with LPI. Its performance varies over clusters similar to that of other approaches but the average is significantly lower. We would like to stress that the comparison of our results to those presented in (He et al., 2004) are only suggestive since (He et al., 2004) applied LPI to each cluster separately and used PCA as preprocessing. We computed the LPI representation for the full collection and did not use PCA.

[1] http://www.lemurproject.org/

[2] We used 28 words because we used stemming whereas (He et al., 2004) did not, so that in two cases, two words were reduces to the same stem.

| word | tf | glsa | glsaL | lsa | lpi |
|---|---|---|---|---|---|
| agreement(1) | 0.74 | 0.73 | 0.73 | 0.75 | 0.46 |
| american(0.8) | 0.63 | 0.72 | 0.59 | 0.64 | 0.36 |
| bank(1.4) | 0.45 | 0.52 | 0.40 | 0.48 | 0.28 |
| control(0.7) | 0.78 | 0.82 | 0.80 | 0.80 | 0.58 |
| domestic(0.8) | 0.64 | 0.68 | 0.66 | 0.68 | 0.35 |
| export(0.8) | 0.64 | 0.65 | 0.70 | 0.67 | 0.37 |
| five(1.3) | 0.74 | 0.77 | 0.71 | 0.70 | 0.40 |
| foreign(1.2) | 0.51 | 0.58 | 0.55 | 0.56 | 0.28 |
| growth(1) | 0.51 | 0.58 | 0.48 | 0.54 | 0.32 |
| income(0.5) | 0.84 | 0.86 | 0.83 | 0.80 | 0.69 |
| increase(1.3) | 0.51 | 0.61 | 0.53 | 0.53 | 0.29 |
| industrial(1.2) | 0.59 | 0.66 | 0.58 | 0.61 | 0.34 |
| internat.(1.1) | 0.58 | 0.59 | 0.54 | 0.61 | 0.34 |
| investment(1) | 0.68 | 0.77 | 0.70 | 0.72 | 0.46 |
| loss(0.3) | 0.98 | 0.99 | 0.98 | 0.98 | 0.88 |
| money(1.1) | 0.70 | 0.62 | 0.71 | 0.65 | 0.38 |
| national(1.3) | 0.49 | 0.58 | 0.49 | 0.55 | 0.27 |
| price(1.2) | 0.53 | 0.63 | 0.57 | 0.57 | 0.29 |
| production(1) | 0.56 | 0.66 | 0.58 | 0.59 | 0.29 |
| public(1.2) | 0.58 | 0.60 | 0.57 | 0.57 | 0.31 |
| rate(1.1) | 0.61 | 0.62 | 0.64 | 0.60 | 0.35 |
| report(1.2) | 0.66 | 0.72 | 0.62 | 0.65 | 0.35 |
| service(0.9) | 0.59 | 0.66 | 0.56 | 0.61 | 0.39 |
| source(1.2) | 0.56 | 0.54 | 0.59 | 0.60 | 0.27 |
| talk(0.9) | 0.74 | 0.67 | 0.73 | 0.74 | 0.39 |
| tax(0.7) | 0.91 | 0.93 | 0.90 | 0.89 | 0.67 |
| trade(1) | 0.85 | 0.74 | 0.82 | 0.60 | 0.33 |
| world(1.1) | 0.63 | 0.65 | 0.68 | 0.66 | 0.33 |
| Av. Acc | 0.65 | 0.68 | 0.65 | 0.66 | 0.40 |

Table 1: Average inter-pairs accuracy.

The inter-pair accuracy depended on the categories distribution within clusters. For more homogeneous clusters, e.g. "loss", all methods (except LPI) achieve similar precision. For less homogeneous clusters, e.g. "national", "industrial", "bank", GLSA and LSA outperformed the *tf* document vectors more significantly.

## 4 Conclusion and Future Work

We introduced a graph-based method of dimensionality reduction into the GLSA framework. Laplacian Eigenmaps Embedding preserves the similarities only locally, thus providing a potentially better approximation to the low dimensional semantic space. We explored the role of locality in the GLSA representation and used binary adjacency matrix as similarity which was preserved and compared it to GLSA with unnormalized PMI scores.

Our results did not show an advantage of $GLSA_L$. $GLSA_L$ and LPI seem to be very sensitive to the parameters of the neighborhood graph. We tried different parameter settings but more experiments are required for a thorough analysis. We are also planning to use a different document collection to eliminate the possible effect of the specific term distribution in the Reuters collection. Further experiments are needed to make conclusions about the geometry of the vocabulary space and the appropriateness of these methods for term and document embedding.

## References


Brian T. Bartell, Garrison W. Cottrell, and Richard K. Belew. 1992. Latent semantic indexing is an optimal special case of multidimensional scaling. In *Proc. of the 15th ACM SIGIR*, pages 161–167. ACM Press.

Mikhail Belkin and Partha Niyogi. 2003. Laplacian eigenmaps for dimensionality reduction and data representation. *Neural Computation*, 15(6):1373–1396.

Scott C. Deerwester, Susan T. Dumais, Thomas K. Landauer, George W. Furnas, and Richard A. Harshman. 1990. Indexing by latent semantic analysis. *Journal of the American Society of Information Science*, 41(6):391–407.

Xiaofei He, Deng Cai, Haifeng Liu, and Wei-Ying Ma. 2004. Locality preserving indexing for document representation. In *Proc. of the 27rd ACM SIGIR*, pages 96–103. ACM Press.

Chris Manning and Hinrich Schütze. 1999. *Foundations of Statistical Natural Language Processing*. MIT Press. Cambridge, MA.

Irina Matveeva, Gina-Anne Levow, Ayman Farahat, and Christian Royer. 2005. Generalized latent semantic analysis for term representation. In *Proc. of RANLP*.

Hinrich Schütze. 1998. Automatic word sense discrimination. *Computational Linguistics*, 24(21):97–124.

Peter D. Turney. 2004. Human-level performance on word analogy questions by latent relational analysis. Technical report, Technical Report ERB-1118, NRC-47422.

# Synonym Extraction Using a Semantic Distance on a Dictionary

**Philippe Muller**
IRIT – CNRS, UPS & INPT
Toulouse, France
muller@irit.fr

**Nabil Hathout**
ERSS – CNRS & UTM
Toulouse, France
hathout@univ-tlse2.fr

**Bruno Gaume**
IRIT – CNRS, UPS & INPT
Toulouse, France
gaume@irit.fr

## Abstract

Synonyms extraction is a difficult task to achieve and evaluate. Some studies have tried to exploit general dictionaries for that purpose, seeing them as graphs where words are related by the definition they appear in, in a complex network of an arguably semantic nature. The advantage of using a general dictionary lies in the coverage, and the availability of such resources, in general and also in specialised domains. We present here a method exploiting such a graph structure to compute a distance between words. This distance is used to isolate candidate synonyms for a given word. We present an evaluation of the relevance of the candidates on a sample of the lexicon.

## 1 Introduction

Thesaurus are an important resource in many natural language processing tasks. They are used to help information retrieval (Zukerman et al., 2003), machine or semi-automated translation, (Ploux and Ji, 2003; Barzilay and McKeown, 2001; Edmonds and Hirst, 2002) or generation (Langkilde and Knight, 1998). Since the gathering of such lexical information is a delicate and time-consuming endeavour, some effort has been devoted to the automatic building of sets of synonyms words or expressions.

Synonym extraction suffers from a variety of methodological problems, however. Synonymy itself is not an easily definable notion. Totally equivalent words (in meaning and use) arguably do not exist, and some people prefer to talk about near-synonyms (Edmonds and Hirst, 2002). A near-synonym is a word that can be used instead of another one, in some contexts, without *too much* change in meaning. This leaves of lot of freedom in the degree of synonymy one is ready to accept. Other authors include "related" terms in the building of thesaurus, such as hyponyms and hypernyms, (Blondel et al., 2004) in a somewhat arbitrary way. More generally, *paraphrase* is a preferred term referring to alternative formulations of words or expressions, in the context of information retrieval or machine translation.

Then there is the question of evaluating the results. Comparing to already existing thesaurus is a debatable means when automatic construction is supposed to complement an existing one, or when a specific domain is targeted, or when simply the automatic procedure is supposed to fill a void. Manual verification of a sample of synonyms extracted is a common practice, either by the authors of a study or by independent lexicographers. This of course does not solve problems related to the definition of synonymy in the "manual" design of a thesaurus, but can help evaluate the relevance of synonyms extracted automatically, and which could have been forgotten. One can hope at best for a semi-automatic procedure were lexicographers have to weed out bad candidates in a set of proposals that is hopefully not too noisy.

A few studies have tried to use the lexical information available in a general dictionary and find patterns that would indicate synonymy relations (Blon-



*Workshop on TextGraphs, at HLT-NAACL 2006*, pages 65–72,
New York City, June 2006. ©2006 Association for Computational Linguistics

del et al., 2004; Ho and Cédrick, 2004). The general idea is that words are related by the definition they appear in, in a complex network that must be semantic in nature (this has been also applied to word sense disambiguation, albeit with limited success (Veronis and Ide, 1990; H.Kozima and Furugori, 1993)).
We present here a method exploiting the graph structure of a dictionary, where words are related by the definition they appear in, to compute a distance between words. This distance is used to isolate candidate synonyms for a given word. We present an evaluation of the relevance of the candidates on a sample of the lexicon.

## 2 Semantic distance on a dictionary graph

We describe here our method (dubbed Prox) to compute a distance between nodes in a graph. Basically, nodes are derived from entries in the dictionary or words appearing in definitions, and there are edges between an entry and the word in its definition (more in section 3). Such graphs are "small world" networks with distinguishing features and we hypothetize these features reflect a linguistic and semantic organisation that can be exploited (Gaume et al., 2005).
The idea is to see a graph as a Markov chain whose states are the graph nodes and whose transitions are its edges, valuated with probabilities. Then we send random particles walking through this graph, and their trajectories and the dynamics of their trajectories reveal their structural properties. In short, we assume the average distance a particle has made between two nodes after a given time is an indication of the semantic distance between these nodes. Obviously, nodes located in highly clustered areas will tend to be separated by smaller distance.
Formally, if $G = (V, E)$ is a reflexive graph (each node is connected to itself) with $|V| = n$, we note $[G]$ the $n \times n$ adjacency matrix of $G$ that is such that $[G]_{i,j}$ (the $i^{th}$ row and $j^{th}$ column) is non null if there is an edge between node $i$ and node $j$ and 0 otherwise. We can have different weights for the edge between nodes (cf. next section), but the method will be similar.
The first step is to turn the matrix into a Markovian matrix. We note $[\hat{G}]$ the Markovian matrix of $G$, such that

$$[\hat{G}]_{r,s} = \frac{[G]_{r,s}}{\sum_{x \in V}([G]_{r,x})}$$

The sum of each line of G is different from 0 since the graph is reflexive.
We note $[\hat{G}]^i$ the matrix $[\hat{G}]$ multiplied $i$ times by itself.
Let now PROX$(G, i, r, s)$ be $[\hat{G}]^i_{r,s}$. This is thus the probability that a random particle leaving node $r$ will be in node $s$ after $i$ time steps. This is the measure we will use to determine if a node $s$ is closer to a node $r$ than another node $t$. The choice for $i$ will depend on the graph and is explained later (cf. section 4).

## 3 Synonym extraction

We used for the experiment the XML tagged MRD *Trésor de la Langue Française informatisé* (TLFi) from ATILF (`http://atilf.atilf.fr/`), a large French dictionary with 54,280 articles, 92,997 entries and 271,166 definitions. The extraction of synonyms has been carried out only for nouns, verbs and adjectives. The basic assumption is that words with semantically close definitions are likely to be synonyms. We then designed a oriented graph that brings closer definitions that contain the same words, especially when these words occur in the beginning. We selected the noun, verb and adjective definitions from the dictionary and created a record for each of them with the information relevant to the building of the graph: the word or expression being defined (henceforth, *definiendum*); its grammatical category; the hierarchical position of the defined (sub-)sense in the article; the definition proper (henceforth *definiens*).
Definitions are made of 2 members: a *definiendum* and a *definiens* and we strongly distinguish these 2 types of objects in the graph. They are represented by 2 types of nodes: a-type nodes for the words being defined and for their sub-senses; o-type nodes for the words that occur in *definiens*.
For instance, the noun *nostalgie* 'nostalgia' has 6 defined sub-senses numbered A.1, A.2, B., C., C. – and D.:

NOSTALGIE, subst. fém.
**A. 1.** État de tristesse [...]
**2.** Trouble psychique [...]
**B.** Regret mélancolique [...] désir d'un retour dans le passé.
**C.** Regret mélancolique [...] désir insatisfait.
**–** Sentiment d'impuissance [...]
**D.** État de mélancolie [...]

The 6 sub-senses yield 6 a-nodes in the graph plus one for the article entry:

| | |
|---|---|
| `a.S.nostalgie` | article entry |
| `a.S.nostalgie.1_1` | sub-sense **A. 1.** |
| `a.S.nostalgie.1_2` | sub-sense **A. 2.** |
| `a.S.nostalgie.2` | sub-sense **B.** |
| `a.S.nostalgie.3` | sub-sense **C.** |
| `a.S.nostalgie.3_1` | sub-sense **C. –** |
| `a.S.nostalgie.4` | sub-sense **D.** |

A-node tags have 4 fields: the node type (namely `a`); its grammatical category (S for nouns, V for verbs and A for adjectives); the lemma that correponds to the *definiendum*; a representation of the hierarchical position of the sub-sense in the dictionary article. For instance, the **A. 2.** sub-sense of *nostalgie* corresponds to the hierarchical position 1_2.
O-nodes represent the types that occur in *definiens*.[1] A second example can be used to present them. The adjective *jonceux* 'rushy' has two sub-senses 'resembling rushes' and 'populated with rushes':

Jonceux, -euse,
a) Qui ressemble au jonc.
b) Peuplé de joncs.

Actually, TLFi definitions are POS-tagged and lemmatized:

Jonceux/S
a) qui/Pro ressembler/V au/D jonc/S ./X
b) peuplé/A de/Prep jonc/S ./X [2]

The 2 *definiens* yield the following o-type nodes in the graph:
`o.Pro.qui`; `o.V.ressembler`; `o.D.au`; `o.S.jonc`; `o.X..`; `o.A.peuplé`; `o.Prep.de`

[1]The tokens are represented by edges.
[2]In this sentence, *peuplé* is an adjective and not a verb.

All the types that occur in *definiens* are represented, including the function words (pronouns, determiners...) and the punctuation. Function words play an important role in the graph because they bring closer the words that belong to the same semantical referential classes (e.g. the adjectives of resemblance), that is words that are likely to be synonyms. Their role is also reinforced by the manner edges are weighted.
A large number of TLFi definitions concerns phrases and locutions. However, these definitions have been removed from the graph because:

- their tokens are not identified in the *definiens*;
- their grammatical categories are not given in the articles and are difficult to calculate;
- many lexicalized phrases are not sub-senses of the article entry.

O-node tags have 3 fields: the node type (namely `o`); the grammatical category of the word; its lemma.
The oriented graph built for the experiment then contains one a-node for each entry and each entry sub-sense (i.e. each *definiendum*) and one o-node for each type that occurs in a definition (i.e. in a *definiens*). These nodes are connected as follows:

1. The graph is reflexive;
2. Sub-senses are connected to the words of their *definiens* and vice versa (e.g. there is an edge between `a.A.jonceux.1` and `o.Pro.qui`, and another one between `o.Pro.qui` and `a.A.jonceux.1`).
3. Each a-node is connected to the a-nodes of the immediately lower hierarchical level but there is no edge between an a-node and the a-nodes of higher hierarchical levels (e.g. `a.S.nostalgie` is connected to `a.S.nostalgie.1_1`, `a.S.nostalgie.1_2`, `a.S.nostalgie.2`, `a.S.nostalgie.3` and `a.S.nostalgie.4`, but none of the sub-senses is connected to the entry).

4. Each o-node is connected to the a-node that represents its entry, but there is no edge between the a-node representing an entry and the corresponding o-node (e.g. there is an edge between `o.A.jonceux` and `a.A.jonceux`, but none between `a.A.jonceux` and `o.A.jonceux`).

All edge weights are 1 with the exception of the edges representing the 9 first words of each *definiens*. For these words, the edge weight takes into account their position in the *definiens*. The weight of the edge that represent the first token is 10; it is 9 for the second word; and so on down to 1.[3]
These characteristics are illustrated by the fragment of the graph representing the entry *jonceux* in table 1.

## 4 Experiment and results

Once the graph built, we used Prox to compute a semantic similarity between the nodes. We first turned the matrix $G$ that represent the graph into a Markovian matrix $[\hat{G}]$ as described in section 2 and then computed $[\hat{G}]^5$, that correspond to 5-steps paths in the Markovian graph.[4] For a given word, we have extracted as candidate synonyms the a-nodes (*i*) of the same category as the word (*ii*) that are the closest to the o-node representing that word in the dictionary definitions. Moreover, only the first a-node of each entry is considered. For instance, the candidate synonyms of the verb *accumuler* 'accumulate' are the a-nodes representing verbs (i.e. their tags begin in `a.V`) that are the closer to the `o.V.accumuler` node.

5-steps paths starting from an o-node representing a word $w$ reach six groups of a-nodes:

$\mathcal{A}_1$ the a-nodes of the sub-senses which have $w$ in their definition;

$\mathcal{A}_2$ the a-nodes of the sub-senses with *definiens* containing the same words as those of $\mathcal{A}_1$;

$\mathcal{A}_3$ the a-nodes of the sub-senses with *definiens* containing the same words as those of $\mathcal{A}_2$;

$\mathcal{B}_1$ the a-nodes of the sub-senses of the article of $w$. (These dummy candidates are not kept.)

$\mathcal{B}_2$ the a-nodes of the sub-senses with *definiens* containing the same words as those of $\mathcal{B}_1$;

$\mathcal{B}_3$ the a-nodes of the sub-senses with *definiens* containing the same words as those of $\mathcal{B}_2$;

The three first groups take advantage of the fact that synonyms of the *definiendum* are often used in definiens.

The question of the evaluation of the extraction of synonyms is a difficult one, as was already mentioned in the introduction. We have at our disposal several thesauri for French, with various coverages (from about 2000 pairs of synonyms, to 140,000), and a lot of discrepancies.[5] If we compare the thesaurus with each other and restrict the comparison to their common lexicon for fairness, we still have a lot of differences. The best f-score is never above 60%, and it raises the question of the proper gold standard to begin with. This is all the more distressing as the dictionary we used has a larger lexicon than all the thesaurus considered together (roughly twice as much). As our main purpose is to build a set of synonyms from the TLF to go beyond the available thesaurus, we have no other way but to have lexicographers look at the result and judge the quality of candidate synonyms. Before imposing this workload on our lexicographer colleagues, we took a sample of 50 verbs and 50 nouns, and evaluated the first ten candidates for each, using the ranking method presented above, and a simpler version with equal weights and no distinction between sense levels or node types. The basic version of the graph also excludes nodes with too many neighbours, such as "être" (be), "avoir" (have), "chose" (thing), etc. ). Two of the authors separately evaluated the candidates, with the synonyms from the existing thesauri

[3] Lexicographic definitions usually have two parts: a *genus* and a *differentia*. This edge weight is intended to favour the *genus* part of the *definiens*.

[4] The path length has been determined empirically.

[5] These seven classical dictionaries of synonyms are all available from http://www.crisco.unicaen.fr/dicosyn.html.

| | o.A.jonceux | a.A.jonceux | a.A.jonceux.1 | a.A.jonceux.2 | o.Pro.qui | o.V.ressembler | o.D.au | o.S.jonc | o.X.. | o.A.peuplé | o.Prep.de |
|---|---|---|---|---|---|---|---|---|---|---|---|
| o.A.jonceux | 1 | 1 | | | | | | | | | |
| a.A.jonceux | | 1 | 1 | 1 | | | | | | | |
| a.A.jonceux.1 | | | 1 | | 1 | 1 | 1 | 1 | 1 | | |
| a.A.jonceux.2 | | | | 1 | | | | 1 | 1 | 1 | 1 |
| o.Pro.qui | | | 10 | | 1 | | | | | | |
| o.V.ressembler | | | 9 | | | 1 | | | | | |
| o.D.au | | | 8 | | | | 1 | | | | |
| o.S.jonc | | | 7 | 8 | | | | 1 | | | |
| o.X.. | | | 6 | 7 | | | | | 1 | | |
| o.A.peuplé | | | | 10 | | | | | | 1 | |
| o.Prep.de | | | | 9 | | | | | | | 1 |

Table 1: A fragment of the graph, presented as a matrix.

already marked. It turned out one of the judge was much more liberal than the other about synonymy, but most synonyms accepted by the first were accepted by the second judge (precision of 0.85).[6]

We also considered a few baselines inspired by the method. Obviously a lot of synonyms appear in the definition of a word, and words in a definition tend to be consider close to the entry they appear in. So we tried two different baselines to estimate this bias, and how our method improves or not from this.

The first baseline considers as synonyms of a word all the words of the same category (verbs or nouns in each case) that appear in a definition of the word, and all the entry the word appear in. Then we selected ten words at random among this base.

The second baseline was similar, but restricted to the *first* word appearing in a definition of another word. Again we took ten words at random in this set if it was larger than ten, and all of them otherwise.

We show the results of precision for the first candidate ranked by prox, the first 5, and the first 10 (always excluding the word itself). In the case of the two baselines, results for the first ten are a bit misleading, since the average numbers of candidates proposed by these methods were respectively 8 and 6 for verbs and 9 and 5.6 for nouns (Table 2). Also, nouns had an average of 5.8 synonyms in the existing thesauri (when what was considered was the min between 10 and the number of synonyms), and verbs had an average of 8.9.

We can see that both baselines outperforms weighted prox on the existing thesaurus for verbs, and that the simpler prox is similar to baseline 2 (first word only). For nouns, results are close between B2 and the two proxs. It is to be noted that a lot of uncommon words appear as candidates, as they are related with very few words, and a lot of these do not appear in the existing thesauri.

By looking precisely at each candidate (see judges' scores), we can see that both baselines are slightly improved (and still close to one another), but are now beaten by both prox for the first and the first 5 words. There is a big difference between the two judges, so Judge 2 has better scores than Judge 1 for the baselines, but in each case, prox was better. It could be troubling to see how good the second baseline is for the first 10 candidates, but one must remember this baseline actually proposes 6 candidates on average (when prox was always at 10), making it actually nothing more than a variation on the 5

[6]The kappa score between the two annotators was 0.5 for both verbs and nouns, which only moderately satisfactory.

| | | Existing Thesauri (V) | Judge 1 | Judge 2 | ET (N) | J1 | J2 |
|---|---|---|---|---|---|---|---|
| baseline-1 | 1 | 0.30 | 0.42 | 0.38 | 0.06 | 0.12 | 0.12 |
| | 5 | 0.29 | 0.39 | 0.375 | 0.08 | 0.12 | 0.13 |
| | 10 | 0.31 | 0.41 | 0.39 | 0.10 | 0.14 | 0.15 |
| baseline-2 | 1 | 0.32 | 0.52 | 0.44 | 0.21 | 0.22 | 0.23 |
| | 5 | 0.36 | 0.50 | 0.446 | 0.21 | 0.24 | 0.25 |
| | 10 | 0.28 | 0.51 | 0.46 | 0.19 | 0.245 | 0.255 |
| simple prox | 1 | 0.35 | 0.67 | NA | 0.27 | 0.415 | 0.417 |
| | 5 | 0.34 | 0.52 | NA | 0.137 | 0.215 | 0.237 |
| | 10 | 0.247 | 0.375 | NA | 0.123 | 0.17 | 0.19 |
| weighted prox | 1 | 0.22 | 0.56 | 0.76 | 0.18 | 0.44 | 0.5 |
| | 5 | 0.196 | 0.44 | 0.58 | 0.148 | 0.31 | 0.39 |
| | 10 | 0.17 | 0.36 | 0.47 | 0.10 | 0.22 | 0.3 |

Table 2: Experimental results on a sample, V=verbs, N=nouns,

candidate baseline, to which it should be compared in all fairness (and we see that prox is much better there). The difference between the two versions of prox shows that a basic version is better for verbs and the more elaborate one is better for nouns, with overall better results for verbs than for nouns.

One could wonder why there was some many more candidates marked as synonyms by both judges, compared to the original compilation of thesaurus. Mainly, it seemed to us that it can be accounted for by a lot of infrequent words, or old senses of words absent for more restricted dictionaries. We are currently investigating this matter. It could also be that our sample picked out a lot of not so frequent words since they outnumber frequent words in such a large dictionary as the TLF. An indication is the average frequency of words in a corpus of ten years of the journal "Le Monde". The 50 words picked out in our sample have an average frequency of 2000 occurrences, while when we consider all our about 430 candidates for synonymy, the average frequency is 5300.

The main conclusion to draw here is that our method is able to recover a lot of synonyms that are in the definition of words, and some in definitions not directly related, which seems to be an improvement on previous attempts from dictionaries. There is some arbitrariness in the method that should be further investigated (the length of the random walk for instance), but we believe the parameters are rather intuitive wrt to graph concepts. We also have an assessment of the quality of the method, even though it is still on a sample. The precision seems fair on the first ten candidates, enough to be used in a semi-automatic way, coupled with a lexicographic analysis.

## 5 Related work

Among the methods proposed to collect synonymy information, two families can be distinguished according to the input they consider. Either a general dictionary is used (or more than one (Wu and Zhou, 2003)), or a corpus of unconstrained texts from which lexical distributions are computed (simple collocations or syntactic dependencies) (Lin, 1998; Freitag et al., 2005) . The approach of (Barzilay and McKeown, 2001) uses a related kind of resource: multiple translations of the same text, with additional constraints on availability, and problems of text alignment, for only a third of the results being synonyms (when compared to Wordnet).

A measure of similarity is almost always used to rank possible candidates. In the case of distributional approaches, similarity if determined from the appearance in similar contexts (Lin, 1998); in the case of dictionary-based methods, lexical relations are deduced from the links between words expressed in definitions of entries.

Approaches that rely on distributional data have two major drawbacks: they need a lot of data, generally syntactically parsed sentences, that is not always available for a given language (English is an exception), and they do not discriminate well among lexical relations (mainly hyponyms, antonyms, hypernyms) (Weeds et al., 2004) . Dictionary-based approaches address the first problem since dictionaries are readily available for a lot of language, even electronically, and this is the *raison d'être* of our effort. As we have seen here, it is not an obvious task to sort related terms with respect to synonymy, hypernymy, etc, just as with distribution approaches.

A lot of work has been done to extract lexical relations from the definitions taken in isolation (mostly for ontology building), see recently (Nichols et al., 2005), with a syntactic/semantic parse, with usually results around 60% of precision (that can be compared with the same baseline we used, all words in the definition with the same category), on dictionaries with very small definitions (and thus a higher proportions of synonyms and hypernyms). Estimating the recall of such methods have not been done.

Using dictionaries as network of lexical items or senses has been quite popular for word sense disambiguation (Veronis and Ide, 1990; H.Kozima and Furugori, 1993; Niwa and Nitta, 1994) before losing ground to statistical approaches, even though (Gaume et al., 2004; Mihalcea et al., 2004) tried a revival of such methods. Both (Ho and Cédrick, 2004) and (Blondel et al., 2004) build a graph of lexical items from a dictionary in a manner similar to ours. In the first case, the method used to compute similarity between two concepts (or words) is restricted to neighbors, in the graph, of the two concepts; in the second case, only directly related words are considered as potential candidates for synonymy: for two words to be considered synonyms, one has to appear in the definition of another. In both cases, only 6 or 7 words have been used as a test of synonymy, with a validation provided by the authors with "related terms" (an unclear notion) considered correct. The similarity measure itself was evaluated on a set of related terms from (Miller and Charles, 1991), as in (Budanitsky and Hirst, 2001; Banerjee and Pedersen, 2003), with seemingly good results, but semantically related terms is a very different notion ("car" and "tire" for instance are semantically related terms, and thus considered similar).
We do not know of any dictionary-based graph approach which have been given a larger evaluation of its results. Parsing definitions in isolation prevents a complete coverage (we estimated that only 30% of synonyms pairs in the TLF can be found from definitions).

As for distributional approaches, (Barzilay and McKeown, 2001) gets a very high precision (around 90%) on valid paraphrases as judged by humans, among which 35% are synonymy relations in Wordnet, 32% are hypernyms, 18% are coordinate terms. Discriminating among the paraphrases types is not addressed. Other approaches usually consider either given sets of synonyms among which one is to be chosen (for a translation for instance) (Edmonds and Hirst, 2002) or must choose a synonym word against unrelated terms in the context of a synonymy test (Freitag et al., 2005), a seemingly easier task than actually proposing synonyms. (Lin, 1998) proposes a different methodology for evaluation of candidate synonyms, by comparing similarity measures of the terms he provides with the similarity measures between them in Wordnet, using various semantic distances. This makes for very complex evaluation procedures without an intuitive interpretation, and there is no assessment of the quality of the automated thesaurus.

## 6 Conclusion

We have developed a general method to extract near-synonyms from a dictionary, improving on the two baselines. There is some arbitrariness in the parameters we used, but we believe the parameters are rather intuitive wrt to graph concepts.[7] There is room for improvement obviously, also for a combination with other methods to filter synonyms (with frequency estimates for instance, such as tf.idf or mutual information measures).

Clearly the advantage of using a dictionary is retained: there is no restriction of coverage, and we could have used a specialised dictionary to build a specialised thesaurus. We have provided an assessment of the quality of the results, although there is not much to compare it to (to the best of our knowledge), since previous accounts only had cursory evaluation.

[7]The lexical graph can be explored at http://prox.irit.fr.

## Acknowledgments

This research has been supported by the CNRS program TCAN 04N85/0025. We sincerely thank the ATILF laboratory and Pr. Jean-Marie Pierrel for the opportunity they gave us to use the *Trésor de la Langue Française informatisé*. We would also like to thank Jean-Marc Destabeaux for his crucial help in extracting the definitions from the TLFi.

## References

S. Banerjee and T. Pedersen. 2003. Extended gloss overlaps as a measure of semantic relatedness. In *Proceedings of IJCAI-03*, Acapulco, Mexico.

Regina Barzilay and Kathleen R. McKeown. 2001. Extracting paraphrases from a parallel corpus. In *Proceedings of the 39th ACL*, pages 00–00, Toulouse.

Vincent D. Blondel, Anahì Gajardo, Maureen Heymans, Pierre Senellart, and Paul Van Dooren. 2004. A measure of similarity between graph vertices: Applications to synonym extraction and web searching. *SIAM Review*, 46(4):647–666.

A. Budanitsky and G. Hirst. 2001. Semantic distance in wordnet: An experimental, application-oriented evaluation of five measures. In *Workshop on WordNet and Other Lexical Resources, NAACL 2001*, Pittsburgh.

Philip Edmonds and Graeme Hirst. 2002. Near-Synonymy and lexical choice. *Computational Linguistics*, 28(2):105–144.

Dayne Freitag, Matthias Blume, John Byrnes, Edmond Chow, Sadik Kapadia, Richard Rohwer, and Zhiqiang Wang. 2005. New experiments in distributional representations of synonymy. In *Proceedings of CoNLL*, pages 25–32, Ann Arbor, Michigan, June. Association for Computational Linguistics.

B. Gaume, N. Hathout, and P. Muller. 2004. Word sense disambiguation using a dictionary for sense similarity measure. In *Proceedings of Coling 2004*, volume II, pages 1194–1200, Genève.

B. Gaume, F. Venant, and B. Victorri. 2005. Hierarchy in lexical organization of natural language. In D. Pumain, editor, *Hierarchy in natural and social sciences*, Methodos series, pages 121–143. Kluwer.

H.Kozima and T. Furugori. 1993. Similarity between words computed by spreading activation on an english dictionary. In *Proceedings of the EACL*, pages 232–239.

Ngoc-Diep Ho and Fairon Cédrick. 2004. Lexical similarity based on quantity of information exchanged - synonym extraction. In *Proc. of Intl. Conf. RIVF'04*, Hanoi.

Irene Langkilde and Kevin Knight. 1998. Generation that exploits corpus-based statistical knowledge. In *Proceedings of COLING-ACL '98*, volume 1, pages 704–710, Montreal.

Dekang Lin. 1998. Automatic retrieval and clustering of similar words. In *Proceedings of COLING-ACL '98*, volume 2, pages 768–774, Montreal.

Rada Mihalcea, Paul Tarau, and Elizabeth Figa. 2004. PageRank on semantic networks, with application to word sense disambiguation. In *Proceedings of Coling 2004*, Geneva.

GA Miller and WG Charles. 1991. Contextual correlates of semantic similarity. *Language and Cognitive Processes*, 6(1):1–28.

Eric Nichols, Francis Bond, and Daniel Flickinger. 2005. Robust ontology acquisition from machine-readable dictionaries. In *Proceedings of IJCAI'05*.

Yoshiki Niwa and Yoshihiko Nitta. 1994. Co-occurrence vectors from corpora vs. distance vectors from dictionaries. In *Proceedings of Coling 1994*.

Sabine Ploux and Hyungsuk Ji. 2003. A model for matching semantic maps between languages (French/English, English/French). *Computational Linguistics*, 29(2):155–178.

J. Veronis and N.M. Ide. 1990. Word sense disambiguation with very large neural networks extracted from machine readable dictionaries. In *COLING-90: Proceedings of the 13th International Conference on Computational Linguistics*, volume 2, pages 389–394, Helsinki, Finland.

Julie Weeds, David Weir, and Diana McCarthy. 2004. Characterising measures of lexical distributional similarity. In *Proceedings of Coling 2004*, pages 1015–1021, Geneva, Switzerland, Aug 23–Aug 27. COLING.

Hua Wu and Ming Zhou. 2003. Optimizing synonyms extraction with mono and bilingual resources. In *Proceedings of the Second International Workshop on Paraphrasing*, Sapporo, Japan. Association for Computational Linguistics.

Ingrid Zukerman, Sarah George, and Yingying Wen. 2003. Lexical paraphrasing for document retrieval and node identification. In *Proceedings of the Second International Workshop on Paraphrasing*, Sapporo, Japan. Association for Computational Linguistics.

# Chinese Whispers - an Efficient Graph Clustering Algorithm and its Application to Natural Language Processing Problems

**Chris Biemann**
University of Leipzig, NLP Department
Augustusplatz 10/11
04109 Leipzig, Germany
biem@informatik.uni-leipzig.de

## Abstract

We introduce Chinese Whispers, a randomized graph-clustering algorithm, which is time-linear in the number of edges. After a detailed definition of the algorithm and a discussion of its strengths and weaknesses, the performance of Chinese Whispers is measured on Natural Language Processing (NLP) problems as diverse as language separation, acquisition of syntactic word classes and word sense disambiguation. At this, the fact is employed that the small-world property holds for many graphs in NLP.

## 1 Introduction

Clustering is the process of grouping together objects based on their similarity to each other. In the field of Natural Language Processing (NLP), there are a variety of applications for clustering. The most popular ones are document clustering in applications related to retrieval and word clustering for finding sets of similar words or concept hierarchies.

Traditionally, language objects are characterized by a feature vector. These feature vectors can be interpreted as points in a multidimensional space. The clustering uses a distance metric, e.g. the cosine of the angle between two such vectors. As in NLP there are often several thousand features, of which only a few correlate with each other at a time – think about the number of different words as opposed to the number of words occurring in a sentence – dimensionality reduction techniques can greatly reduce complexity without considerably losing accuracy.

An alternative representation that does not deal with dimensions in space is the *graph representation*. A graph represents objects (as nodes) and their relations (as edges). In NLP, there are a variety of structures that can be naturally represented as graphs, e.g. lexical-semantic word nets, dependency trees, co-occurrence graphs and hyperlinked documents, just to name a few.

Clustering graphs is a somewhat different task than clustering objects in a multidimensional space: There is no distance metric; the similarity between objects is encoded in the edges. Objects that do not share an edge cannot be compared, which gives rise to optimization techniques. There is no centroid or 'average cluster member' in a graph, permitting centroid-based techniques.

As data sets in NLP are usually large, there is a strong need for efficient methods, i.e. of low computational complexities. In this paper, a very efficient graph-clustering algorithm is introduced that is capable of partitioning very large graphs in comparatively short time. Especially for small-world graphs (Watts, 1999), high performance is reached in quality and speed. After explaining the algorithm in the next section, experiments with synthetic graphs are reported in section 3. These give an insight about the algorithm's performance. In section 4, experiments on three NLP tasks are reported, section 5 concludes by discussing extensions and further application areas.

## 2 Chinese Whispers Algorithm

In this section, the Chinese Whispers (CW) algorithm is outlined. After recalling important concepts from Graph Theory (cf. Bollobás 1998), we describe two views on the algorithm. The



*Workshop on TextGraphs, at HLT-NAACL 2006*, pages 73–80,
New York City, June 2006. 

second view is used to relate CW to another graph clustering algorithm, namely MCL (van Dongen, 2000).

We use the following notation throughout this paper: Let G=(V,E) be a *weighted* graph with nodes $(v_i) \in V$ and weighted edges $(v_i, v_j, w_{ij}) \in E$ with weight $w_{ij}$. If $(v_i, v_j, w_{ij}) \in E$ implies $(v_j, v_i, w_{ij}) \in E$, then the graph is *undirected.* If all weights are 1, G is called *unweighted.*

The *degree* of a node is the number of edges a node takes part in. The *neighborhood* of a node v is defined by the set of all nodes v' such that $(v,v',w) \in E$ or $(v',v,w) \in E$; it consists of all nodes that are connected to v.

The *adjacency matrix* $A_G$ of a graph G with n nodes is an n×n matrix where the entry $a_{ij}$ denotes the weight of the edge between $v_i$ and $v_j$ , 0 otherwise.

The *class matrix* $D_G$ of a Graph G with n nodes is an n×n matrix where rows represent nodes and columns represent classes $(c_i) \in C$. The value $d_{ij}$ at row i and column j represents the amount of $v_i$ as belonging to a class $c_j$. For convention, class matrices are row-normalized; the i-th row denotes a distribution of $v_i$ over C. If all rows have exactly one non-zero entry with value 1, $D_G$ denotes a *hard partitioning* of V, *soft partitioning* otherwise.

### 2.1 Chinese Whispers algorithm

CW is a very basic – yet effective – algorithm to partition the nodes of weighted, undirected graphs. It is motivated by the eponymous children's game, where children whisper words to each other. While the game's goal is to arrive at some funny derivative of the original message by passing it through several noisy channels, the CW algorithm aims at finding groups of nodes that broadcast the same message to their neighbors. It can be viewed as a simulation of an agent-based social network; for an overview of this field, see (Amblard 2002).

The algorithm is outlined in figure 1:

```
initialize:
 forall v_i in V: class(v_i)=i;
while changes:
 forall v in V, randomized order:
   class(v)=highest ranked class
               in neighborhood of v;
```

Figure 1: The Chinese Whispers algorithm

Intuitively, the algorithm works as follows in a bottom-up fashion: First, all nodes get different classes. Then the nodes are processed for a small number of iterations and inherit the strongest class in the local neighborhood. This is the class whose sum of edge weights to the current node is maximal. In case of multiple strongest classes, one is chosen randomly. Regions of the same class stabilize during the iteration and grow until they reach the border of a stable region of another class. Note that classes are updated immediately: a node can obtain classes from the neighborhood that were introduced there in the same iteration.

Figure 2 illustrates how a small unweighted graph is clustered into two regions in three iterations. Different classes are symbolized by different shades of grey.

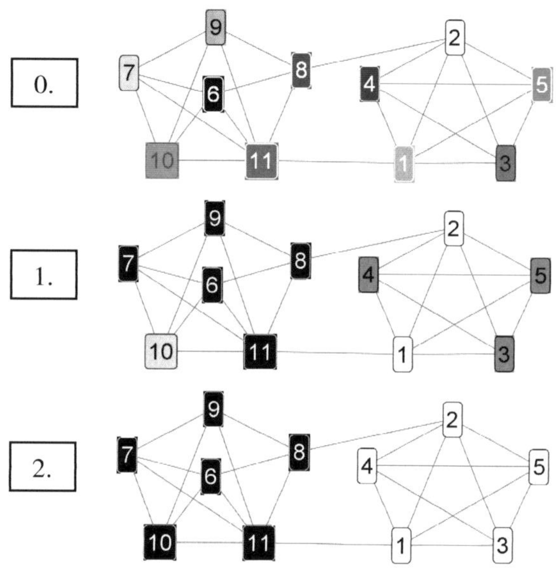


Figure 2: Clustering an 11-nodes graph with CW in two iterations

It is possible to introduce a random mutation rate that assigns new classes with a probability decreasing in the number of iterations as described in (Biemann & Teresniak 2005). This showed having positive effects for small graphs because of slower convergence in early iterations.

The CW algorithm cannot cross component boundaries, because there are no edges between nodes belonging to different components. Further, nodes that are not connected by any edge are discarded from the clustering process, which possibly leaves a portion of nodes unclustered.

Formally, CW does not converge, as figure 3 exemplifies: here, the middle node's neighborhood consists of a tie which can be decided in assigning the class of the left or the class of the right nodes in any iteration all over again. Ties, however, do not play a major role in weighted graphs.

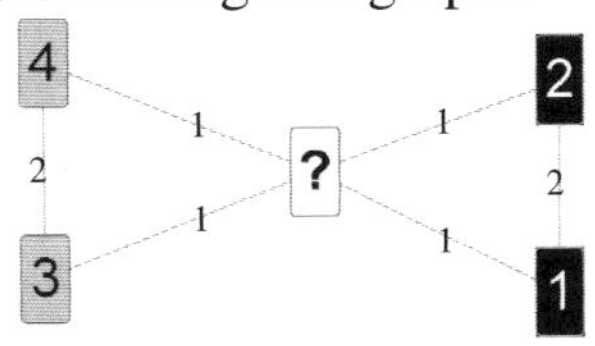


Figure 3: The middle node gets the grey or the black class. Small numbers denote edge weights.

Apart from ties, the classes usually do not change any more after a handful of iterations. The number of iterations depends on the diameter of the graph: the larger the distance between two nodes is, the more iterations it takes to percolate information from one to another.

The result of CW is a hard partitioning of the given graph into a number of partitions that emerges in the process – CW is parameter-free. It is possible to obtain a soft partitioning by assigning a class distribution to each node, based on the weighted distribution of (hard) classes in its neighborhood in a final step.

The outcomes of CW resemble those of *Min-Cut* (Wu & Leahy 1993): Dense regions in the graph are grouped into one cluster while sparsely connected regions are separated. In contrast to *Min-Cut*, CW does not find an optimal hierarchical clustering but yields a non-hierarchical (flat) partition. Furthermore, it does not require any threshold as input parameter and is more efficient.

Another algorithm that uses only local contexts for time-linear clustering is DBSCAN as, described in (Ester et al. 1996), needing two input parameters (although the authors propose an interactive approach to determine them). DBSCAN is especially suited for graphs with a geometrical interpretation, i.e. the objects have coordinates in a multidimensional space. A quite similar algorithm to CW is MAJORCLUST (Stein & Niggemann 1996), which is based on a comparable idea but converges slower.

## 2.2 Chinese Whispers as matrix operation

As CW is a special case of Markov-Chain-Clustering (MCL) (van Dongen, 2000), we spend a few words on explaining it. MCL is the parallel simulation of all possible random walks up to a finite length on a graph G. The idea is that random walkers are more likely to end up in the same cluster where they started than walking across clusters. MCL simulates flow on a graph by repeatedly updating transition probabilities between all nodes, eventually converging to a transition matrix after k steps that can be interpreted as a clustering of G. This is achieved by alternating an expansion step and an inflation step. The expansion step is a matrix multiplication of $M_G$ with the current transition matrix. The inflation step is a column-wise non-linear operator that increases the contrast between small and large transition probabilities and normalizes the column-wise sums to 1. The k matrix multiplications of the expansion step of MCL lead to its time-complexity of $O(k \cdot n^2)$.

It has been observed in (van Dongen, 2000), that only the first couple of iterations operate on dense matrices – when using a strong inflation operator, matrices in the later steps tend to be sparse. The author further discusses pruning schemes that keep only some of the largest entries per column, leading to drastic optimization possibilities. But the most aggressive sort of pruning is not considered: only keeping one single largest entry. Exactly this is conducted in the basic CW process. Let `maxrow(.)` be an operator that operates row-wise on a matrix and sets all entries of a row to zero except the largest entry, which is set to 1. Then the algorithm is denoted as simple as this:

$$
\begin{aligned}
&D^0 = I_n \\
&\texttt{for } t=1 \texttt{ to iterations} \\
&\qquad D^{t-1} = \texttt{maxrow}(D^{t-1}) \\
&\qquad D^t \;= D^{t-1}A_G
\end{aligned}
$$

Figure 4: Matrix Chinese Whispers process. t is time step, $I_n$ is the identity matrix of size n×n, $A_G$ is the adjacency matrix of graph G.

By applying `maxrow(.)`, $D^{t-1}$ has exactly n non-zero entries. This causes the time-complexity to be dependent on the number of edges, namely $O(k \cdot |E|)$. In the worst case of a fully connected graph, this equals the time-complexity of MCL.

A problem with the matrix CW process is that it does not necessarily converge to an iteration-invariant class matrix D, but rather to a pair of oscillating class matrices. Figure 5 shows an example.

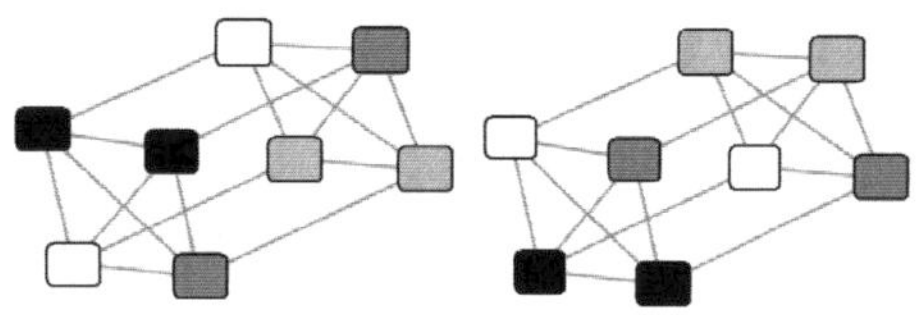

Figure 5: oscillating states in matrix CW for an unweighted graph

This is caused by the stepwise update of the class matrix. As opposed to this, the CW algorithm as outlined in figure 1 *continuously* updates D after the processing of each node. To avoid these oscillations, one of the following measures can be taken:

- Random mutation: with some probability, the maxrow-operator places the 1 for an otherwise unused class
- Keep class: with some probability, the row is copied from $D^{t-1}$ to $D^t$
- Continuous update (equivalent to CW as described in section 2.1.)

While converging to the same limits, the continuous update strategy converges the fastest because prominent classes are spread much faster in early iterations.

## 3 Experiments with synthetic graphs

The analysis of the CW process is difficult due to its nonlinear nature. Its run-time complexity indicates that it cannot directly optimize most global graph cluster measures because of their NP-completeness (Šíma and Schaeffer, 2005). Therefore we perform experiments on synthetic graphs to empirically arrive at an impression of our algorithm's abilities. All experiments were conducted with an implementation following figure 1. For experiments with synthetic graphs, we restrict ourselves to unweighted graphs, if not stated explicitly.

### 3.1 Bi-partite cliques

A cluster algorithm should keep dense regions together while cutting apart regions that are sparsely connected. The highest density is reached in fully connected sub-graphs of n nodes, a.k.a. *n-cliques*. We define an *n-bipartite-clique* as a graph of two n-cliques, which are connected such that each node has exactly one edge going to the clique it, does not belong to.

Figures 5 and 6 are n-partite cliques for n=4,10.

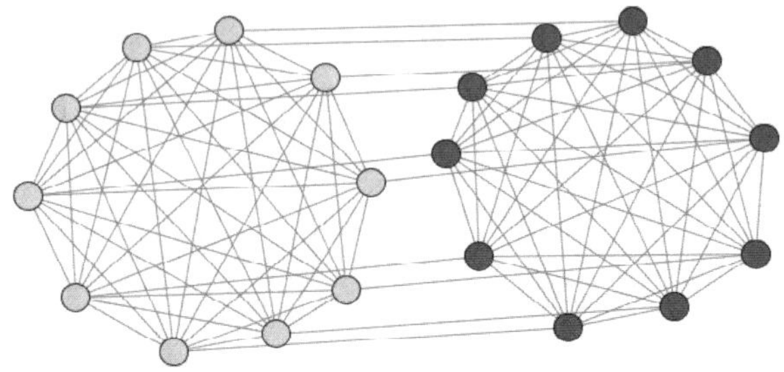

Figure 6: The 10-bipartite clique.

We clearly expect a clustering algorithm to cut the two cliques apart. As we operate on unweighted graphs, however, CW is left with two choices: producing two clusters or grouping all nodes into one cluster. This is largely dependent on the random choices in very early iterations - if the same class is assigned to several nodes in both cliques, it will finally cover the whole graph. Figure 7 illustrates on what rate this happens on n-bipartite-cliques for varying n.

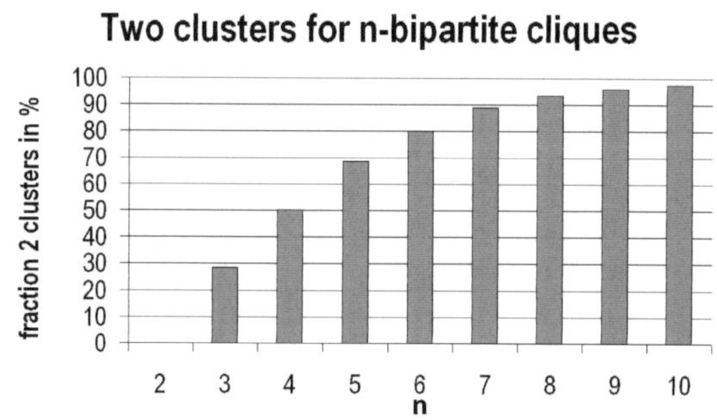


Figure 7: Percentage of obtaining two clusters when applying CW on n-bipartite cliques

It is clearly a drawback that the outcome of CW is non-deterministic. Only half of the experiments with 4-bipartite cliques resulted in separation. However, the problem is most dramatic on small graphs and ceases to exist for larger graphs as demonstrated in figure 7.

### 3.2 Small world graphs

A structure that has been reported to occur in an enormous number of natural systems is the *small world (SW) graph*. Space prohibits an in-depth discussion, which can be found in (Watts 1999). Here, we restrict ourselves to SW-graphs in language data. In (Ferrer-i-Cancho and Sole, 2001), co-occurrence graphs as used in the experiment section are reported to possess the small world property, i.e. a high clustering co-efficient and short average path length between arbitrary nodes. Steyvers and Tenenbaum (2005) show that association networks as well as semantic resources are *scale-free* SW-graphs: their degree distribution follows a power law. A generative model is provided that generates undirected, scale-free SW-graphs in the following way: We start with a small number of fully connected nodes. When adding a new node, an existing node v is chosen with a probability according to its degree. The new node is connected to M nodes in the neighborhood of v. The generative model is parameterized by the number of nodes n and the network's mean connectivity, which approaches 2M for large n.

Let us assume that we deal with natural systems that can be characterized by small world graphs. If two or more of those systems interfere, their graphs are joined by merging some nodes, retaining their edges. A graph-clustering algorithm should split up the resulting graph in its previous parts, at least if not too many nodes were merged.

We conducted experiments to measure CW's performance on SW-graph mixtures: We generated graphs of various sizes, merged them by twos to a various extent and measured the amount of cases where clustering with CW leads to the reconstruction of the original parts. When generating SW-graphs with the Steyvers-Tenenbaum model, we fixed M to 10 and varied n and the merge rate r, which is the fraction of nodes of the smaller graph that is merged with nodes of the larger graph.

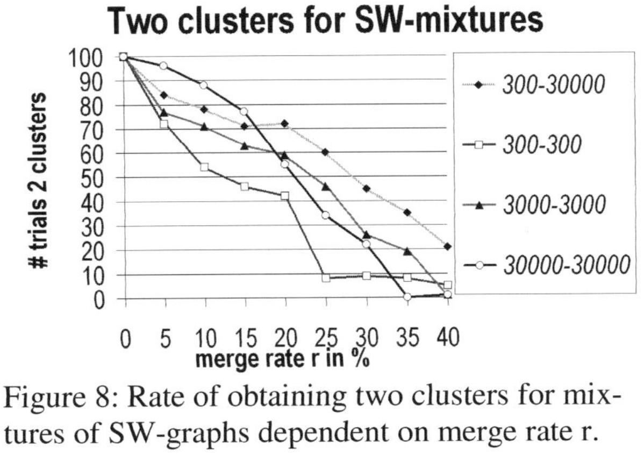


Figure 8: Rate of obtaining two clusters for mixtures of SW-graphs dependent on merge rate r.

Figure 8 summarizes the results for equisized mixtures of 300, 3,000 and 30,000 nodes and mixtures of 300 with 30,000 nodes.

It is not surprising that separating the two parts is more difficult for higher r. Results are not very sensitive to size and size ratio, indicating that CW is able to identify clusters even if they differ considerably in size – it even performs best at the skewed mixtures. At merge rates between 20% and 30%, still more then half of the mixtures are separated correctly and can be found when averaging CW's outcome over several runs.

## 3.3 Speed issues

As formally, the algorithm does not converge, it is important to define a stop criterion or to set the number of iterations. To show that only a few iterations are needed until almost-convergence, we measured the normalized Mutual Information (MI)[1] between the clustering in the $50^{th}$ iteration and the clusterings of earlier iterations. This was conducted for two unweighted SW-graphs with 1,000 (1K) and 10,000 (10K) nodes, M=5 and a weighted 7-lingual co-occurrence graph (cf. section 4.1) with 22,805 nodes and 232,875 edges. Table 1 indicates that for unweighted graphs, changes are only small after 20-30 iterations. In iterations 40-50, the normalized MI-values do not improve any more. The weighted graph converges much faster due to fewer ties and reaches a stable plateau after only 6 iterations.

| *Iter* | *1* | *2* | *3* | *5* | *10* | *20* | *30* | *40* | *49* |
|---|---|---|---|---|---|---|---|---|---|
| *1K* | 1 | 8 | 13 | 20 | 37 | 58 | 90 | 90 | 91 |
| *10K* | 6 | 27 | 46 | 64 | 79 | 90 | 93 | 95 | 96 |
| *7ling* | 29 | 66 | 90 | 97 | 99.5 | 99.5 | 99.5 | 99.5 | 99.5 |

Table 1: normalized Mutual Information values for three graphs and different iterations in %.

# 4 NLP Experiments

In this section, some experiments with graphs originating from natural language data are presented. First, we define the notion of co-occurrence graphs, which are used in sections 4.1 and 4.3: Two words co-occur if they can both be found in a certain unit of text, here a sentence. Employing a significance measure, we determine whether their co-occurrences are significant or random. In this case, we use the log-likelihood measure as described in (Dunning 1993). We use the words as nodes in the graph. The weight of an

[1] defined for two random variables X and Y as (H(X)+H(Y)-H(X,Y))/max(H(X),H(Y)) with H(X) entropy. A value of 0 denotes indepenence, 1 is perfect congruence.

edge between two words is set to the significance value of their co-occurrence, if it exceeds a certain threshold. In the experiments, we used significances from 15 on. The entirety of words that are involved in at least one edge together with these edges is called *co-occurrence graph* (cf. Biemann et al. 2004).

In general, CW produces a large number of clusters on real-world graphs, of which the majority is very small. For most applications, it might be advisable to define a minimum cluster size or something alike.

### 4.1 Language Separation

This section shortly reviews the results of (Biemann and Teresniak, 2005), where CW was first described. The task was to separate a multilingual corpus by languages, assuming its tokenization in sentences.

The co-occurrence graph of a multilingual corpus resembles the synthetic SW-graphs: Every language forms a separate co-occurrence graph, some words that are used in more than one language are members of several graphs, connecting them. By CW-partitioning, the graph is split into its monolingual parts. These parts are used as word lists for word-based language identification. (Biemann and Teresniak, 2005) report almost perfect performance on getting 7-lingual corpora with equisized parts sorted apart as well as highly skewed mixtures of two languages.

In the process, language-ambiguous words are assigned to only one language, which did not hurt performance due to the high redundancy of the task. However, it would have been possible to use the soft partitioning to acquire a distribution over languages for each word.

### 4.2 Acquisition of Word Classes

For the acquisition of word classes, we use a different graph: the second-order graph on neighboring co-occurrences. To set up the graph, a co-occurrence calculation is performed which yields significant word pairs based on their occurrence as immediate neighbors. This can be perceived as a bipartite graph, figure 9a gives a toy example. Note that if similar words occur in both parts, they form two distinct nodes.

This graph is transformed into a second-order graph by comparing the number of common right and left neighbors for two words. The similarity (edge weight) between two words is the sum of common neighbors. Figure 9b depicts the second-order graph derived from figure 9a and its partitioning by CW. The word-class-ambiguous word "drink" (to drink the drink) is responsible for all intra-cluster edges. The hypothesis here is that words sharing many neighbors should usually be observed with the same part-of-speech and get high weights in the second order graph. In figure 9, three clusters are obtained that correspond to different parts-of-speech (POS).

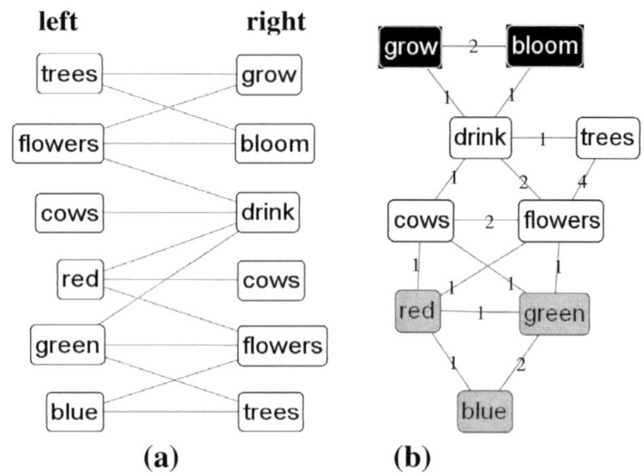


Figure 9: Bi-partite neighboring co-occurrence graph (a) and second-order graph on neighboring co-occurrences (b) clustered with CW.

To test this on a large scale, we computed the second-order similarity graph for the British National Corpus (BNC), excluding the most frequent 2000 words and drawing edges between words if they shared at least four left and right neighbors. The clusters are checked against a lexicon that contains the most frequent tag for each word in the BNC. The largest clusters are presented in table 2 .

| *size* | *tags:count* | *sample words* |
|---|---|---|
| 18432 | NN:17120<br>AJ: 631 | secret, officials, transport, unemployment, farm, county, wood, procedure, grounds, ... |
| 4916 | AJ: 4208<br>V: 343 | busy, grey, tiny, thin, sufficient, attractive, vital, ... |
| 4192 | V: 3784<br>AJ: 286 | filled, revealed, experienced, learned, pushed, occurred, ... |
| 3515 | NP: 3198<br>NN: 255 | White, Green, Jones, Hill, Brown, Lee, Lewis, Young, ... |
| 2211 | NP: 1980<br>NN: 174 | Ian, Alan, Martin, Tony, Prince, Chris, Brian, Harry, Andrew, |

| | | |
|---|---|---|
| | | Christ, Steve, ... |
| 1855 | NP: 1670<br>NN: 148 | Central, Leeds, Manchester, Australia, Yorkshire, Belfast, Glasgow, Middlesbrough, ... |

Table 2: the largest clusters from partitioning the second order graph with CW.

In total, CW produced 282 clusters, of which 26 exceed a size of 100. The weighted average of cluster purity (i.e. the number of predominant tags divided by cluster size) was measured at 88.8%, which exceeds significantly the precision of 53% on word type as reported by Schütze (1995) on a related task. How to use this kind of word clusters to improve the accuracy of POS-taggers is outlined in (Ushioda, 1996).

### 4.3 Word Sense Induction

The task of word sense induction (WSI) is to find the different senses of a word. The number of senses is not known in advance, therefore has to be determined by the method.

Similar to the approach as presented in (Dorow and Widdows, 2003) we construct a word graph. While there, edges between words are drawn iff words co-occur in enumerations, we use the co-occurrence graph. Dorow and Widdows construct a graph for a target word w by taking the sub-graph induced by the neighborhood of w (without w) and clustering it with MCL. We replace MCL by CW. The clusters are interpreted as representations of word senses.

To judge results, the methodology of (Bordag, 2006) is adopted: To evaluate word sense induction, two sub-graphs induced by the neighborhood of different words are merged. The algorithm's ability to separate the merged graph into its previous parts can be measured in an unsupervised way. Bordag defines four measures:

- retrieval precision (rP): similarity of the found sense with the gold standard sense
- retrieval recall (rR): amount of words that have been correctly assigned to the gold standard sense
- precision (P): fraction of correctly found disambiguations
- recall (R): fraction of correctly found senses

We used the same program to compute co-occurrences on the same corpus (the BNC). Therefore it is possible to directly compare our results to Bordag's, who uses a triplet-based hierarchical graph clustering approach. The method was chosen because of its appropriateness for unlabelled data: without linguistic pre-processing like tagging or parsing, only the disambiguation mechanism is measured and not the quality of the preprocessing steps. We provide scores for his test 1 (word classes separately) and test 3 (words of different frequency bands). Data was obtained from BNC's raw text; evaluation was performed for 45 test words.

| % | *(Bordag, 2006)* | | | | *Chinese Whispers* | | | |
|---|---|---|---|---|---|---|---|---|
| *POS* | *P* | *R* | *rP* | *rR* | *P* | *R* | *rP* | *rR* |
| *N* | 87.0 | **86.7** | 90.9 | 64.2 | **90.0** | 79.5 | **94.8** | **71.3** |
| *V* | **78.3** | 64.3 | 80.2 | 55.2 | 77.6 | **67.1** | **87.3** | **57.9** |
| *A* | 88.6 | **71.0** | 88.0 | 65.4 | **92.2** | 61.9 | **89.3** | **71.9** |

Table 3: Disambiguation results in % dependent on word class (nouns, verbs, adjectives)

| % | *(Bordag, 2006)* | | | | *Chinese Whispers* | | | |
|---|---|---|---|---|---|---|---|---|
| *freq* | *P* | *R* | *rP* | *rR* | *P* | *R* | *rP* | *rR* |
| *high* | *93.7* | **78.1** | 90.3 | **80.7** | *93.7* | 72.9 | **95.0** | 73.8 |
| *med* | **84.6** | **85.2** | 89.9 | 54.6 | 80.7 | 83.8 | **91.0** | **55.7** |
| *low* | **74.8** | 49.5 | 71.0 | 41.7 | 74.1 | **51.4** | **72.9** | **56.2** |

Table 4: Disambiguation results in % dependent on frequency

Results (tables 3 and 4) suggest that both algorithms arrive at about equal overall performance (P and R). Chinese Whispers clustering is able to capture the same information as a specialized graph-clustering algorithm for WSI, given the same input. The slightly superior performance on rR and rP indicates that CW leaves fewer words unclustered, which can be advantageous when using the clusters as clues in word sense disambiguation.

## 5 Conclusion

Chinese Whispers, an efficient graph-clustering algorithm was presented and described in theory and practice. Experiments with synthetic graphs showed that for small graphs, results can be inconclusive due to its non-deterministic nature. But while there exist plethora of clustering approaches that can deal well with small graphs, the power of CW lies in its capability of handling very large graphs in reasonable time. The application field of CW rather lies in size regions, where other approaches' solutions are intractable.

On the NLP data discussed, CW performs equally or better than other clustering algorithms. As CW – like other graph clustering algorithms – chooses the number of classes on its own and can handle clusters of different sizes, it is especially suited for NLP problems, where class distributions are often highly skewed and the number of classes (e.g. in WSI) is not known beforehand.

To relate the partitions, it is possible to set up a hierarchical version of CW in the following way: The nodes of equal class are joined to hyper-nodes. Edge weights between hyper-nodes are set according to the number of inter-class edges between the corresponding nodes. This results in flat hierarchies.

In further works it is planned to apply CW to other graphs, such as the co-citation graph of Citeseer, the co-citation graph of web pages and the link structure of Wikipedia.


## Acknowledgements

Thanks go to Stefan Bordag for kindly providing his WSI evaluation framework. Further, the author would like to thank Sebastian Gottwald and Rocco Gwizdziel for a platform-independent GUI implementation of CW, which is available for download from the author's homepage.


## References


F. Amblard. 2002. *Which ties to choose? A survey of social networks models for agent-based social simulations.* In Proc. of the 2002 SCS International Conference On Artificial Intelligence, Simulation and Planning in High Autonomy Systems, pp.253-258, Lisbon, Portugal.

C. Biemann, S. Bordag, G. Heyer, U. Quasthoff, C. Wolff. 2004. *Language-independent Methods for Compiling Monolingual Lexical Data*, Proceedings of CicLING 2004, Seoul, Korea and Springer LNCS 2945, pp. 215-228, Springer, Berlin Heidelberg

B. Bollobás. 1998. *Modern graph theory*, Graduate Texts in Mathematics, vol. 184, Springer, New York

S. Bordag. 2006. *Word Sense Induction: Triplet-Based Clustering and Automatic Evaluation.* Proceedings of EACL-06. Trento

C. Biemann and S. Teresniak. 2005. *Disentangling from Babylonian Confusion – Unsupervised Language Identification.* Proceedings of CICLing-2005, Mexico City, Mexico and Springer LNCS 3406, pp. 762-773

S. van Dongen. 2000. *A cluster algorithm for graphs.* Technical Report INS-R0010, National Research Institute for Mathematics and Computer Science in the Netherlands, Amsterdam.

T. Dunning. 1993. *Accurate Methods for the Statistics of Surprise and Coincidence*, Computational Linguistics 19(1), pp. 61-74

M. Ester, H.-P. Kriegel, J. Sander and X. Xu. 1996. *A Density-Based Algorithm for Discovering Clusters in Large Spatial Databases with Noise.* In Proceedings of the 2nd Int. Conf. on Knowledge Discovery and Datamining (KDD'96) Portland, USA, pp. 291-316.

B. Dorow and D. Widdows. 2003. *Discovering Corpus-Specific Word Senses.* In EACL-2003 Conference Companion (research notes and demos), pp. 79-82, Budapest, Hungary

R. Ferrer-i-Cancho and R.V. Sole. 2001. *The small world of human language.* Proceedings of The Royal Society of London. Series B, Biological Sciences, 268(1482):2261-2265

H. Schütze. 1995. *Distributional part-of-speech tagging.* In EACL 7, pages 141–148

J. Šíma and S.E. Schaeffer. 2005. *On the np-completeness of some graph cluster measures.* Technical Report cs.CC/0506100, arXiv.org e-Print archive, http://arxiv.org/.

B. Stein and O. Niggemann. 1999. *On the Nature of Structure and Its Identification.* Proceedings of WG'99, Springer LNCS 1665, pp. 122-134, Springer Verlag Heidelberg

M. Steyvers, J. B. Tenenbaum. 2005. *The large-scale structure of semantic networks: statistical analyses and a model of semantic growth.* Cognitive Science, 29(1).

Ushioda, A. (1996). *Hierarchical clustering of words and applications to NLP tasks.* In Proceedings of the Fourth Workshop on Very Large Corpora, pp. 28-41. Somerset, NJ, USA

D. J. Watts. 1999. *Small Worlds: The Dynamics of Networks Between Order and Randomness*, Princeton Univ. Press, Princeton, USA

Z. Wu and R. Leahy (1993): *An optimal graph theoretic approach to data clustering: Theory and its application to image segmentation.* IEEE Transactions on Pattern Analysis and Machine Intelligence

# Matching Syntactic-Semantic Graphs for Semantic Relation Assignment

**Vivi Nastase**[1] and **Stan Szpakowicz**[1,2]
[1] School of Information Technology and Engineering,
University of Ottawa, Ottawa, Canada
[2] Institute of Computer Science,
Polish Academy of Sciences, Warsaw, Poland
{vnastase,szpak}@site.uottawa.ca

## Abstract

We present a graph-matching algorithm for semantic relation assignment. The algorithm is part of an interactive text analysis system. The system automatically extracts pairs of syntactic units from a text and assigns a semantic relation to each pair. This is an incremental learning algorithm, in which previously processed pairs and user feedback guide the process. After each assignment, the system adds to its database a syntactic-semantic graph centered on the main element of each pair of units. A graph consists of the main unit and all syntactic units with which it is syntactically connected. An edge contains information both about syntax and about semantic relations for use in further processing. Syntactic-semantic graph matching is used to produce a list of candidate assignments for 63.75% of the pairs analysed, and in 57% of situations the correct relations is one of the system's suggestions; in 19.6% of situations it suggests only the correct relation.

## 1 Introduction

When analysing texts, it is essential to see how elements of meaning are interconnected. This is an old idea. The first chronicled endeavour to connect text elements and organise connections between them goes back to the $5^{th}$ century B.C. and the work of Panini[1]. He was a grammarian who analysed Sanskrit (Misra, 1966). The idea resurfaced forcefully at several points in the more recent history of linguistic research (Tesnière, 1959; Gruber, 1965; Fillmore, 1968). Now it has the attention of many researchers in natural language processing, as shown by recent research in semantic parsing and semantic role labelling (Baker et al., 1998; Kipper et al., 2000; Carreras and Marquez, 2004; Carreras and Marquez, 2005; Atserias et al., 2001; Shi and Mihalcea, 2005).

Graph-like structures are a natural way of organising one's impressions of a text seen from the perspective of connections between its simpler constituents of varying granularity, from sections through paragraphs, sentences, clauses, phrases, words to morphemes.

In this work we pursue a well-known and often tacitly assumed line of thinking: connections at the syntactic level reflect connections at the semantic level (in other words, syntax carries meaning). Anecdotal support for this stance comes from the fact that the grammatical notion of case is the basis for semantic relations (Misra, 1966; Gruber, 1965; Fillmore, 1968). Tesnière (1959), who proposes a grouping of verb arguments into *actants* and *circumstances*, gives a set of rules to connect specific types of *actants* – for example, *agent* or *instrument* – to such grammatical elements as subject, direct object, indirect object. This idea was expanded to include nouns and their modifiers through verb nominalizations (Chomsky, 1970; Quirk et al., 1985).

We work with sentences, clauses, phrases and words, using syntactic structures generated by a parser. Our system incrementally processes a text, and extracts pairs of text units: two clauses, a verb and each of its arguments, a noun and each of its modifiers. For each pair of units, the system builds a syntactic graph surrounding the main element (main clause, head verb, head noun). It then tries to find among the previously processed instances another main element with a matching syntactic graph. If such a graph is found, then the system maps previously assigned semantic relations onto the current syntactic graph. We have a list of 47 relations that manifest themselves in compound clauses, inside a simple clause or in noun phrases. The list, a synthesis of a number of relation lists cited in the literature, has been designed to be general, domain-independent (Barker et al., 1997a).

Section 2 overviews research in semantic relation analysis. Section 3 describes the text we used in ex-

[1]The sources date his work variously between the $5^{th}$ and $7^{th}$ century.



*Workshop on TextGraphs, at HLT-NAACL 2006*, pages 81–88,
New York City, June 2006. 

periments, and the semantic relation list. Section 4 looks in detail at the graph-matching heuristic. Section 5 describes the experimental setting and shows how often the heuristic was used when processing the input text. We show in detail our findings about syntactic levels (how often graph matching helped assign a relation between two clauses, a verb and its arguments, or a noun and its modifier) and about the accuracy of the suggestion. Discussion and conclusions appear in Section 6.

## 2 Related Work

Some methods of semantic relation analysis rely on predefined templates filled with information from processed texts (Baker et al., 1998). In other methods, lexical resources are specifically tailored to meet the requirements of the domain (Rosario and Hearst, 2001) or the system (Gomez, 1998). Such systems extract information from some types of syntactic units (clauses in (Fillmore and Atkins, 1998; Gildea and Jurafsky, 2002; Hull and Gomez, 1996); noun phrases in (Hull and Gomez, 1996; Rosario et al., 2002)). Lists of semantic relations are designed to capture salient domain information.

In the Rapid Knowledge Formation Project (RKF) a support system was developed for domain experts. It helps them build complex knowledge bases by combining components: events, entities and modifiers (Clark and Porter, 1997). The system's interface facilitates the expert's task of creating and manipulating structures which represent domain concepts, and assigning them relations from a relation dictionary.

In current work on semantic relation analysis, the focus is on semantic roles – relations between verbs and their arguments. Most approaches rely on *VerbNet* (Kipper et al., 2000) and *FrameNet* (Baker et al., 1998) to provide associations between verbs and semantic roles, that are then mapped onto the current instance, as shown by the systems competing in semantic role labelling competitions (Carreras and Marquez, 2004; Carreras and Marquez, 2005) and also (Gildea and Jurafsky, 2002; Pradhan et al., 2005; Shi and Mihalcea, 2005).

These systems share two ideas which make them different from the approach presented here: they all analyse verb-argument relations, and they all use machine learning or probabilistic approaches (Pradhan et al., 2005) to assign a label to a new instance. Labelling every instance relies on the same previously encoded knowledge (see (Carreras and Marquez, 2004; Carreras and Marquez, 2005) for an overview of the systems in the semantic role labelling competitions from 2004 and 2005). Pradhan et al. (2005) combine the outputs of multiple parsers to extract reliable syntactic information, which is translated into features for a machine learning experiment in assigning semantic roles.

Our system analyses incrementally pairs of units coming from three syntactic levels – clause (CL), intra-clause (or verb-argument, IC), noun-phrase (NP). There are no training and testing data sets. Instead of using previously built resources, the system relies on previously processed examples to find the most appropriate relation for a current pair. Because the system does not rely on previously processed or annotated data, it is flexible. It allows the user to customize the process for a specific domain by choosing the syntactic units of interest and her own list of relations that best fit the domain.

It is also interesting to assess, using the current system configuration, the effect of syntactic information and incremental learning on semantic analysis. This is described in section 5.

Because of these differences in the type of data used, and in the learning approach, the results we obtain cannot be compared to previous approaches. In order to show that the system does learn, we show that the number of examples for which it provides the correct answer increases with the number of examples previously analysed.

## 3 Input data and semantic relations

### 3.1 Input data

We work with a semi-technical text on meteorological phenomena (Larrick, 1961), meant for primary school students. The text gradually introduces concepts related to precipitation, and explains them. Its nature makes it appropriate for the semantic analysis task in an incremental approach. The system will mimic the way in which a human reader accumulates knowledge and uses what was written before to process ideas introduced later in the text.

The text contains 513 sentences, with an average length of 9.13 words. There are 4686 word tokens and 969 types. The difference between the number of types (2850) and tokens (573) in the extracted pairs (which contain only open-class words) shows that the same concepts recur, as expected in a didactic text.

The syntactic structures of the input data are produced by a parser with good coverage and detailed syntactic information, DIPETT (Delisle and Szpakowicz, 1995). The parser, written in Prolog, implements a classic constituency English grammar from Quirk et al. (1985). Pairs of syntactic units connected by grammatical relations are extracted from the parse trees. A dependency parser would produce a similar output, but DIPETT also provides verb subcategorization information (such as, for example, subject-verb-object or subject-verb-object-indirect_object), which we use to select the (best) matching syntactic structures.

To find pairs, we use simple structural information. If a unit is directly embedded in another unit, we assume a subordinate relation between them; if the two units are coordinate, we assume a coordinate relation. These assumptions are safe if the parse is correct. A modifier is subordinate to its head noun, an argument to its head verb, and a clause perhaps to the main clause in the sentence.

If we conclude that two units should interact, we seek an appropriate semantic relation to describe this interaction. The system uses three heuristics to find one or more semantic relation candidates for the current pair.

1. **Word match** – the system will propose the semantic relation(s) that have previously been assigned to a pair containing the same lemmas.
2. **Syntactic graph match** – we elaborate this heuristic in Section 4.
3. **Marker** – the system uses a manually built dictionary of markers (prepositions, coordinators, subordinators) associated with the semantic relations they indicate. The dictionary contains 325 markers, and a total of 662 marker-relation associations.

If neither of the three heuristics yield results, the system will present an empty list, and expect the user to input the appropriate relation. When at least one relation is proposed, the user can *accept* a unique relation, *choose* among several options, or *supply* a new one. The system records which action took place, as well as the heuristic that generated the options presented to the user. The pair is also analysed to determine the syntactic level from which it came, to allow for a more detailed analysis of the behaviour of the system.

### 3.2 Semantic relations

The list of semantic relations with which we work is based on extensive literature study (Barker et al., 1997a). Three lists of relations for three syntactic levels – inter-clause, intra-clause (case) and noun-modifier relations – were next combined based on syntactic and semantic phenomena. The resulting list is the one used in the experiments we present in this paper. The relations are grouped by general similarity into 6 relation classes (H denotes the head of a base NP, M denotes the modifier).

1. CAUSAL groups relations enabling or opposing an occurrence. Examples:

   **cause** - H causes M: *flu virus*;

   **effect** - H is the effect (was caused by) M: *exam anxiety*;

   **purpose** - H is for M: *concert hall*;

2. CONJUNCTIVE includes relations that describe the conjunction or disjunction of occurrences (events/act/actions/states/activities), entities or attributes:

   **conjunction** - both H and M occur or exist (and nothing more can be said about that from the point of view of causality or temporality): *running and swimming (are good for you)*;

   **disjunction** - either one or both H and M occur or exist: *painting or drawing*;

3. PARTICIPANT groups relations between an occurrence and its participants or circumstances. Examples:

   **agent** - M performs H: *student protest*;

   **object** - M is acted upon by H: *metal separator*;

   **beneficiary** - M benefits from H: *student discount*;

4. SPATIAL groups relations that place an occurrence at an absolute or relative point in space. Examples:

   **direction** - H is directed towards M: *outgoing mail*;

   **location** - H is the location of M: *home town*;

   **location at** - H is located at M: *desert storm*;

5. TEMPORAL groups relations that place an occurrence at an absolute or relative point in time. Examples:

   **frequency** - H occurs every time M occurs: *weekly game*;

   **time at** - H occurs when M occurs: *morning coffee*;

   **time through** - H existed while M existed: *2-hour trip*;

6. QUALITY groups the remaining relations between a verb or noun and its arguments. Examples:

   **manner** - H occurs as indicated by M: *stylish writing*;

**material** - H is made of M: *brick house*;
**measure** - M is a measure of H: *heavy rock*;

There is no consensus in the literature on a list of semantic relations that would work in all situations. This is, no doubt, because a general list of relations such as the one we use would not be appropriate for the semantic analysis of texts in a specific domain, such as for example medical texts. All the relations in the list we use were necessary, and sufficient, for the analysis of the input text.

## 4 Syntactic-semantic graph-matching

Our system begins operation with a minimum of manually encoded knowledge, and accumulates information as it processes the text. This design idea was adopted from TANKA (Barker et al., 1997b). The only manually encoded knowledge is a dictionary of markers (subordinators, coordinators, prepositions). This resource does not affect the syntactic-semantic graph-matching heuristic.

Because the system gradually accumulates knowledge as it goes through the input text, it uses a form of memory-based learning to make predictions about the semantic relation that fits the current pair. The type of knowledge that it accumulates consists of previously analysed pairs, together with the semantic relation assigned, and a syntactic-semantic graph centered on each word in a sentence which appears as the main element in a processed pair.

To process a pair $P$ not encountered previously, the system builds a graph centered on the main element (often the head) of $P$. This idea was inspired by Delisle et al. (1993), who used a list of arguments surrounding the main verb together with the verb's subcategorization information and previously processed examples to analyse semantic roles (case relations). In recent approaches, syntactic information is translated into features which, together with information from *FrameNet, WordNet* or *VerbNet*, will be used with ML tools to make predictions for each example in the test set (Carreras and Marquez, 2004; Carreras and Marquez, 2005).

Our system builds a (simple) graph surrounding a head word (which may be a verb – representing the predicate of a sentence, or representing a clause – or noun), and matches it with previously analysed examples.

A graph $G(w)$ centered on word $w$ consists of the following: a node for $w$; a set of nodes for each of the words $w_i$ in the sentence with which $w$ is connected by a grammatical relation (including situations when $w$ is a modifier/argument); edges that connect $w$ with each $w_i$, tagged with grammatical relation $GR$ (such as *subject, object, complement*) and connective information $Con$ (prepositions, coordinators, subordinators, or *nil*). The nodes also contain part-of-speech information for the corresponding word, and other information from the parser (such as subcategorization structure for the verb, if it is available).

Graph matching starts with the central node, and continues with edge matching. If $G(w)$ is the graph centered on word $w$ whose pairs are currently being processed, the system selects from the collection of previously stored graphs, a set of graphs $\{G(w_i)\}$, which satisfy the following conditions:

- The central nodes match. The matching is guided by a set of contraints. We choose the graphs centered on the nodes that satisfy the most constraints, presented here in the order of their importance:
  - $w$ and $w_i$ must have the same part of speech.
  - $w$ and $w_i$ have the same syntactic properties. If $w$ and $w_i$ are verbs, they must have the same subcategorization structure.
  - $w$ and $w_i$ are the same lemma. We emphasize that a graph centered on a different lemma, but with the same subcategorization structure is preferred to a graph with the same lemma, but a different subcategorization structure.
- The edge representing the word pair to which we want to assign a semantic relation has a match in $G(w_i)$. From all graphs that comply with this constraint, the ones that have the lowest distance – corresponding to the highest matching score – are chosen. The graphs are matched edge by edge. Two edges match if the grammatical relation and the connectives match. Figure 1 shows the formula that computes the distance between two graphs. We note that edge matching uses only edge information – grammatical and connective information. Using the node information as is (lemmas and their part of speech) is too restrictive. We are looking into using word similarity as a solution of node matching.

If no matching graph has been found, the system searches for a simpler match, in which the current word pair is matched against previously processed pairs, using the same formula as for edge distance, and preferring the pairs that have the same modifier.

This algorithm will retrieve the set of graphs $\{G(w_i)\}$, which give the same score when matched

Definition of a graph centered on $w$:

$$G(w) = \{w_i, edge(w, w_i) \text{ or } edge(w_i, w) | w_i \text{appears in sent. S, and is connected to } w\}$$

$$edge(w, w_i) = \{GR_i, Con_i\}\ ; \quad GR_i \in \{subject, object, complement, ...\} \quad Con_i \in \{at, in, on, with, for, ...\}$$

Distance metric between two graphs:

$$dist(G(w_1), G(w_2)) = \sum_{k=1}^{N} d(edge_{1k}, edge_{2k}); \qquad edge_{ik} \in G(w_i), N \text{ is the number of edges in } G(w_i)$$

$$d(edge_{1k}, edge_{2k}) = d(\{GR_{1k}, Con_{1k}\}, \{GR_{2k}, Con_{2k}\}) = d_1(GR_{1k}, GR_{2k}) + d_1(Con_{1k}, Con_{2k})$$

$$d_1(x, y) = \begin{cases} 0 & : \ x = y \\ 1 & : \ x \neq y \end{cases}$$

Figure 1: Distance between two graphs

with the current graph. The set of possible semantic relations presented to the user consists of the semantic relation on the edge of each $G(w_i)$ that matches the edge (of the current graph) corresponding to the word pair which we are analysing.

To the sentence:

*When you breathe out on a cold day, you make a cloud.*

corresponds the following syntactic graph:

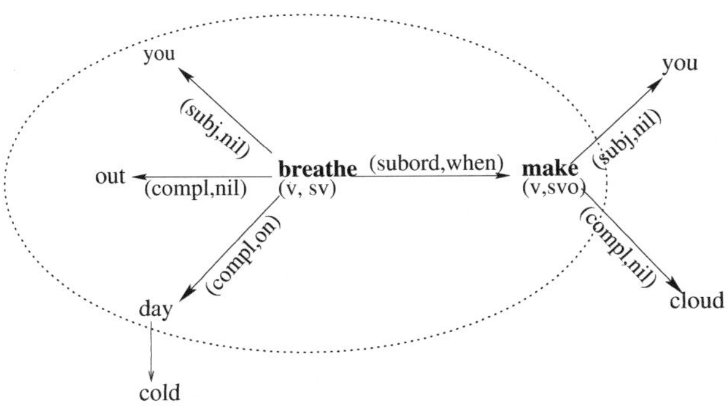


When we focus on the graph centered on a specific word, such as *breathe*, we look only at the node corresponding to the word *breathe*, and the nodes adjacent to it.

To process a pair $P = (w_H, w_M)$, the system first builds $G(w_H)$, and then searches through previously stored graphs for those which have the same center $w_H$, or have the same part of speech as $w_H$ assigned to its central node. For each graph found, we compute a distance that gives a measure of the match between the two graphs. The best match will have the smallest distance.

For example, for the sentence:

*Weathermen watch the clouds day and night.*

the system builds the following network centered on the predicate *watch*[2]:

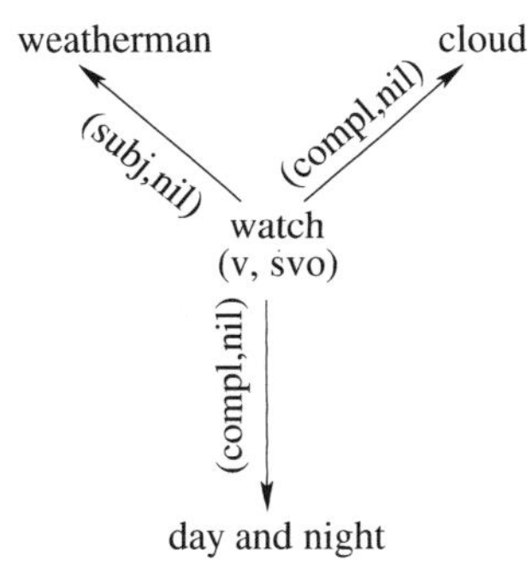


The system locates among previously stored networks those centered around verbs[3]. For the sentence above, the system uses the following graph,

[2]The *nil* value on the edges means that no preposition or other connective explicitly links the two words or the corresponding syntactic structures.

[3]If more detailed information is available, the system will choose only networks associated with verbs that have the same subcategorisation pattern (svo, svoi and so on).

built from the immediately preceding sentence in the text:
*Air pilots know that clouds can bring rain, hail, sleet and snow.*

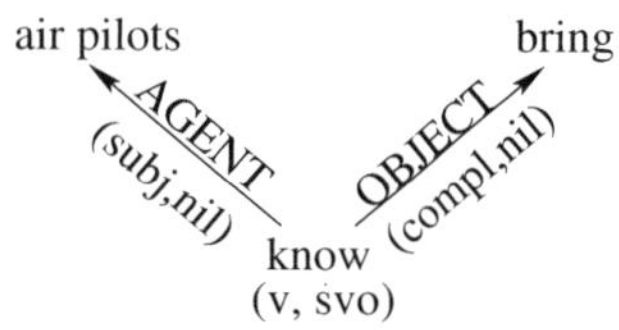


According to the metric, the networks match and the pairs **(watch, weatherman)** and **(know, air pilots)** match, so the semantic relation for the pair **(know, air pilots)** is proposed as a possible relation for pair **(watch, weatherman)** .

## 5 Experiments

The system processes the 513 sentences interactively. It begins by running the DIPETT parser. Next, it extracts syntactic units (clauses, phrases, words) and pairs them up according to the information in the parse tree. Each unit is represented by its head word. Next, the system checks if the same pair of word lemmas has already been processed, to propose the same relation(s) to the user as options. If not, the system builds a graph centered on the head word, and proceeds with the matching on previously encountered instances, as described in section 4. When a set of candidates has been found, the system goes through a dialogue with the user.

The system generated 2020 pairs from the 513 sentences. The experiment was run in 5 interactive sessions of approximately 3 hours each. The total net processing time was 6 hours, 42 minutes and 52 seconds[4]. While it would have been instructive to run the system several times with different users, it was not feasible. The experiment was run once, with two cooperating users. They were instructed on the set of semantic relations, and told how the system works. They discussed the semantic relation assignment and, once agreed, compared the system's suggestion with their decision.

DIPETT did not produce a complete parse for all sentences. When a complete parse (correct or incorrect) was not possible, DIPETT produced fragmentary parses. The semantic analyser extracted units even from tree fragments, although sometimes the fragments were too small to accommodate any pairs. Of the 513 input sentences, 441 had a parse tree that allowed the system to extract pairs.

[4]The time difference accounts for system processing times, and user interaction for other steps of the analysis.

| | | | |
|---|---|---|---|
| # of analyzed examples | 1475 | | |
| level statistics | CL | IC | NP |
| | 64 | 978 | 433 |
| user actions | accept | choose | supply |
| | 459 | 393 | 623 |
| avg. # of suggestions | 2.81 | | |
| graph-matching usage | 933 | | |
| level/action statistics | CL | IC | NP |
| accept 183 (19.61%) | 9 | 141 | 33 |
| choose 349 (37.41%) | 23 | 314 | 12 |
| supply 401 (42.98%) | 27 | 316 | 58 |

Table 1: Summary of semantic analysis

Of 2020 pairs generated, the users discarded 545 in the dialogue step. An example of an erroneous pair comes from the sentence:
*Tiny clouds drift across like feathers on parade.*
The semantic analyser produced the pair *(drift,parade)*, because of a parsing error: *parade* was parsed as a complement of *drift*, instead of a post-modifier for *feathers*. The correct pairing *(feather,parade)* is missing, because it cannot be inferred from the parse tree.

Table 1 gives a summary of the processing statistics. We observe that graph-matching was used to process a clear majority of the total pairs extracted – 63.25% (933/1475) , leaving the remaining 36.75% for the other two heuristics and for cases where no suggestion could be made. In 57.02% of the situations when graph-matching was used, the system's suggestion contained the correct answer (user's action was either *accept* or *choose*), and in 19.61% of the situations a single correct semantic relation was proposed (user action was *accept*).

When the system presents multiple suggestions to the user, including the correct one, the average number of suggestions is 3.75. The small number of suggestions shows that the system does not simply add to the list relations that it has previously encountered, but it learns from past experience and graph-matching helps it make good selections. Figure 2 plots the difference between the number of examples for which the system gives the correct answer (possibly among other suggestions) and the number of examples when the user must supply the correct relation, from the first example processed until the end of the experiment. We observe a steady increase in the number of correctly processed examples.

Our system does not differentiate between syntactic levels, but based on the structures of the syntactic units in each pair we can decide which syntactic level it pertains to. For a more in-depth analysis, we have separated the results for each syntactic level,

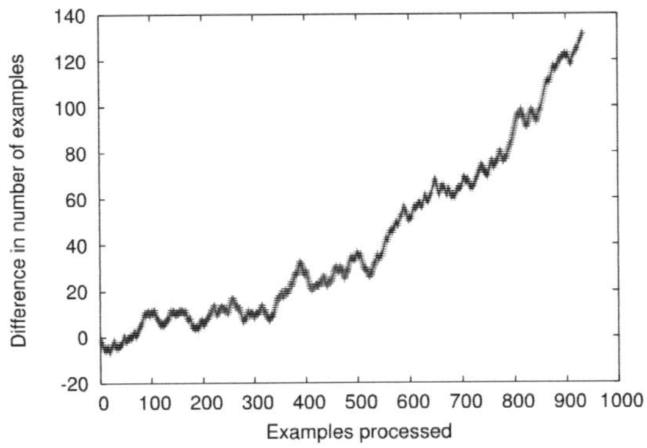


Figure 2: Difference between the number of situations in which the user *accepts* or *chooses* from the system's suggestions, and when it must *supply* the correct relation

and present them for comparison in Figure 3.

We observe that the intra-clause level – verbs and their arguments – makes the best use of graph-matching, with the curve showing the cumulative number of situations in which the system makes correct predictions becoming steeper as more text is processed. At the same time, the curve that plots the cumulative number of cases in which the user has to supply a correct answer begins to level off. As expected, at the noun-phrase level where the syntactic structures are very simple, often consisting of only the noun and its modifier (without even a connective), the graph-matching algorithm does not help as much. At the inter-clause level the heuristic helps, as shown by the marginally higher curve for cumulative *accept/choose* user actions, compared to *supply* actions.

## 6 Conclusions

We have shown through the results gathered from an interactive and incremental text processing system that syntactic-semantic graph-matching can be used with good results for semantic analysis of texts. The graph-matching heuristic clearly dominates other heuristics used, and it learns to make better predictions as more examples accumulate.

Graph-matching is most useful for assigning semantic relations between verbs and their arguments, but it also gives good results for inter-clause relations. At the noun-phrase level, we could only tackle noun-modifier pairs that exhibit a modicum of syntactic structure – a connective. For base NPs there is practically nothing that syntactic information can bring to the semantic analysis process.

The graph-matching process could be improved by bringing into play freely available lexical re-

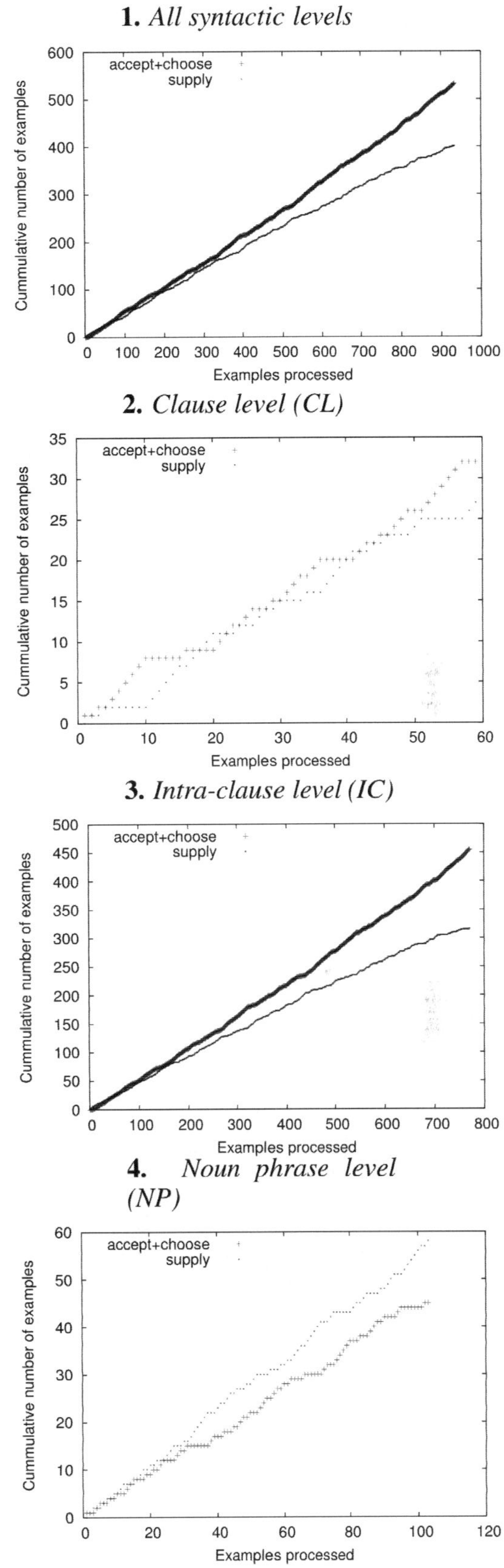


Figure 3: Graph-matching for different syntactic levels

sources. For now, the actual words in the graph nodes are not used at all. We could use *WordNet* to compute word similarities, to select closer matching graphs. *VerbNet* or *FrameNet* information could help choose graphs centered on verbs with similar syntactic behaviour, as captured by Levin's verb groups (Levin, 1993) which are the basis of *VerbNet*.

## References


Jordi Atserias, L. Padró, and German Rigau. 2001. Integrating multiple knowledge sources for robust semantic parsing. In *Proceedings of RANLP - 2001*, Tsigov Czark, Bulgaria.

Collin F. Baker, Charles J. Fillmore, and John B. Lowe. 1998. The Berkeley FrameNet project. In *COLING-ACL*, pages 86–90, Montreal, Canada.

Ken Barker, Terry Copeck, Sylvain Delisle, and Stan Szpakowicz. 1997a. Systematic construction of a versatile case system. *Journal of Natural Language Engineering*, 3(4):279–315.

Ken Barker, Sylvain Delisle, and Stan Szpakowicz. 1997b. Test-driving TANKA: Evaluating a semi-automatic system of text analysis for knowledge acquisition. In *Proceedings of CAI 1997*, pages 60–71, Vancouver, BC, Canada.

Xavier Carreras and Lluis Marquez, editors. 2004. *Introduction to the CoNLL-2004 Shared Task: Semantic Role Labelling*. Boston, MA, USA.

Xavier Carreras and Lluis Marquez, editors. 2005. *Introduction to the CoNLL-2005 Shared Task: Semantic Role Labelling*. Ann Arbour, MI, USA.

Noam Chomsky. 1970. Remarks on nominalizations. In Roderick Jacobs and Peter Rosenbaum, editors, *Readings in English Transformational Grammar*, pages 184–221. Ginn and Co., Waltham, MA, USA.

Peter Clark and Bruce Porter. 1997. Building concept reprezentations from reusable components. In *AAAI*, pages 367–376, Providence, Rhode Island.

Sylvain Delisle and Stan Szpakowicz. 1995. Realistic parsing: Practical solutions of difficult problems. In *PACLING*, Brisbane, Queensland, Australia.

Sylvain Delisle, Terry Copeck, Stan Szpakowicz, and Ken Barker. 1993. Pattern matching for case analysis: A computational definition of closeness. In *ICCI*, pages 310–315, Sudbury, ON, Canada.

Charles Fillmore and Beryl T. Atkins. 1998. FrameNet and lexicographic relevance. In *Proceedings of the 1st International Conference on Language Resources and Evaluation*, Granada, Spain.

Charles Fillmore. 1968. The case for case. In Emmond Bach and Robert T. Harms, editors, *Universals in Linguistic Theory*, pages 1–88. Holt, Rinehart and Winston.

Daniel Gildea and Daniel Jurafsky. 2002. Automatic labeling of semantic roles. *Computational Linguistics*, 28(3):245–288.

Fernando Gomez. 1998. A representation of complex events and processes for the acquisition of knowledge from text. *Kowledge-Based Systems*, 10(4):237–251.

Jeffrey Gruber. 1965. *Studies in Lexical Relations*. Ph.D. thesis, MIT, Cambridge, MA. Reprinted in Jeffrey Gruber. 1976. *Lexical Structures in Syntax and Semantics*. Part I. North-Holland Publishing Company, Amsterdam.

Richard D. Hull and Fernando Gomez. 1996. Semantic interpretation of nominalizations. In *13th National Conference on Artificial Intelligence*, pages 1062–1068, Portland, Oregon, USA.

Karin Kipper, Hoa Trang Dang, and Martha Palmer. 2000. Class-based construction of a verb lexicon. In *AAAI/IAAI*, pages 691–696.

Nancy Larrick. 1961. *Junior Science Book of Rain, Hail, Sleet and Snow*. Garrard Publishing Company, Champaign, Illinois.

Beth Levin. 1993. *English Verb Classes and Alternations*. University of Chicago Press.

Vidya Niwas Misra. 1966. *The Descriptive Technique of Panini*. Mouton, The Hague.

Sameer Pradhan, Wayne Ward, Kadri Hacioglu, James H. Martin, and Daniel Jurafsky. 2005. Semantic role labelling using different syntactic views. In *Proceedings of ACL 2005*, pages 581–588, Ann Arbour, MI, USA.

Randolph Quirk, Sidney Greenbaum, Geoffrey Leech, and Jan Svartvik. 1985. *A Comprehensive Grammar of the English Language*. Longman, London and New York.

Barbara Rosario and Marti Hearst. 2001. Classifying the semantic relations in noun-compounds via a domain specific hierarchy. In *EMNLP*, pages 82–90, Pittsburg, PA, USA.

Barbara Rosario, Marti Hearst, and Charles Fillmore. 2002. The descent of hierarchy and selection in relational semantics. In *ACL*, Philadelphia, PA, USA.

Lei Shi and Rada Mihalcea. 2005. Putting pieces together: Combining framenet, verbnet and wordnet for robust semantic parsing. In *Proceedings of CICLing 2005*, pages 100–111, Mexico City, Mexico.

Lucien Tesnière. 1959. *Éléments de syntaxe structurale*. C. Klincksieck, Paris.

# Evaluating and optimizing the parameters of an unsupervised graph-based WSD algorithm

**Eneko Agirre, David Martínez, Oier López de Lacalle and Aitor Soroa**
IXA NLP Group
University of Basque Country
Donostia, Basque Contry
a.soroa@ehu.es

## Abstract

Véronis (2004) has recently proposed an innovative unsupervised algorithm for word sense disambiguation based on small-world graphs called *HyperLex*. This paper explores two sides of the algorithm. First, we extend Véronis' work by optimizing the free parameters (on a set of words which is different to the target set). Second, given that the empirical comparison among unsupervised systems (and with respect to supervised systems) is seldom made, we used hand-tagged corpora to map the induced senses to a standard lexicon (WordNet) and a publicly available gold standard (Senseval 3 English Lexical Sample). Our results for nouns show that thanks to the optimization of parameters and the mapping method, HyperLex obtains results close to supervised systems using the same kind of bag-of-words features. Given the information loss inherent in any mapping step and the fact that the parameters were tuned for another set of words, these are very interesting results.

## 1 Introduction

Word sense disambiguation (WSD) is a key enabling technology. Supervised WSD techniques are the best performing in public evaluations, but need large amounts of hand-tagging data. Existing hand-annotated corpora like SemCor (Miller et al., 1993), which is annotated with WordNet senses (Fellbaum, 1998) allow for a small improvement over the simple most frequent sense heuristic, as attested in the all-words track of the last Senseval competition (Snyder and Palmer, 2004). In theory, larger amounts of training data (SemCor has approx. 500M words) would improve the performance of supervised WSD, but no current project exists to provide such an expensive resource.

Supervised WSD is based on the "fixed-list of senses" paradigm, where the senses for a target word are a closed list coming from a dictionary or lexicon. Lexicographers and semanticists have long warned about the problems of such an approach, where senses are listed separately as discrete entities, and have argued in favor of more complex representations, where, for instance, senses are dense regions in a continuum (Cruse, 2000).

Unsupervised WSD has followed this line of thinking, and tries to induce word senses directly from the corpus. Typical unsupervised WSD systems involve clustering techniques, which group together similar examples. Given a set of induced clusters (which represent word *uses* or senses[1]), each new occurrence of the target word will be compared to the clusters and the most similar cluster will be selected as its sense.

Most of the unsupervised WSD work has been based on the vector space model (Schütze, 1998; Pantel and Lin, 2002; Purandare and Pedersen, 2004), where each example is represented by a vector of features (e.g. the words occurring in the context). Recently, Véronis (Véronis, 2004) has

[1]Unsupervised WSD approaches prefer the term 'word uses' to 'word senses'. In this paper we use them interchangeably to refer to both the induced clusters, and to the word senses from some reference lexicon.



*Workshop on TextGraphs, at HLT-NAACL 2006*, pages 89–96,
New York City, June 2006. 

proposed HyperLex, an application of graph models to WSD based on the small-world properties of cooccurrence graphs. Hand inspection of the clusters (called hubs in this setting) by the author was very positive, with hubs capturing the main senses of the words. Besides, hand inspection of the disambiguated occurrences yielded precisions over 95% (compared to a most frequent baseline of 73%) which is an outstanding figure for WSD systems.

We noticed that HyperLex had some free parameters and had not been evaluated against a public gold standard. Besides, we were struck by the few works where supervised and unsupervised systems were evaluated on the same test data. In this paper we use an automatic method to map the induced senses to WordNet using hand-tagged corpora, enabling the automatic evaluation against available gold standards (Senseval 3 English Lexical Sample S3LS (Mihalcea et al., 2004)) and the automatic optimization of the free parameters of the method. The use of hand-tagged corpora for tagging makes this algorithm a mixture of unsupervised and supervised: the method to induce senses in completely unsupervised, but the mapping is supervised (albeit very straightforward).

This paper is structured as follows. We first present the graph-based algorithm as proposed by Véronis, reviewing briefly the features of small-world graphs. Section 3 presents our framework for mapping and evaluating the induced hubs. Section 4 introduces parameter optimization. Section 5 shows the experiment setting and results. Section 6 analyzes the results and presents related work. Finally, we draw the conclusions and advance future work.

## 2 HyperLex

Before presenting the HyperLex algorithm itself, we briefly introduce small-world graphs.

### 2.1 Small world graphs

The small-world nature of a graph can be explained in terms of its *clustering coefficient* and *characteristic path length*. The clustering coefficient of a graph shows the extent to which nodes tend to form connected groups that have many edges connecting each other in the group, and few edges leading out of the group. On the other side, the characteristic path length represents "closeness" in a graph. See (Watts and Strogatz, 1998) for further details on these characteristics.

Randomly built graphs exhibit low clustering coefficients and are believed to represent something very close to the minimal possible average path length, at least in expectation. Perfectly ordered graphs, on the other side, show high clustering coefficients but also high average path length. According to Watts and Strogatz (1998), small-world graphs lie between these two extremes: they exhibit high clustering coefficients, but short average path lengths.

Barabasi and Albert (1999) use the term "scale-free" to graphs whose degree probability follow a power-law[2]. Specifically, scale free graphs follow the property that the probability $P(k)$ that a vertex in the graph interacts with $k$ other vertices decays as a power-law, following $P(k) \sim k^{-\alpha}$. It turns out that in this kind of graphs there exist nodes centrally located and highly connected, called *hubs*.

### 2.2 The HyperLex algorithm for WSD

The HyperLex algorithm builds a cooccurrence graph for all pairs of words cooccurring in the context of the target word. Véronis shows that this kind of graph fulfills the properties of small world graphs, and thus possess highly connected components in the graph. The centers or prototypes of these components, called hubs, eventually identify the main word uses (senses) of the target word.

We will briefly introduce the algorithm here, check (Véronis, 2004) for further details. For each word to be disambiguated, a text corpus is collected, consisting of the paragraphs where the word occurs. From this corpus, a cooccurrence graph for the target word is built. Nodes in the graph correspond to the words[3] in the text (except the target word itself). Two words appearing in the same paragraph are said to cooccur, and are connected with edges. Each edge is assigned with a weight which measures the relative frequency of the two words cooccurring. Specifically, let $w_{ij}$ be the weight of the edge[4] connecting

[2]Although scale-free graphs are not necessarily small worlds, a lot of real world networks are both scale-free and small worlds.

[3]Following Véronis, we only work on nouns for the time being.

[4]Note that the cooccurrence graph is undirected, i.e. $w_{ij} = w_{ji}$

nodes $i$ and $j$, then

$$w_{ij} = 1 - \max[P(i \mid j), P(j \mid i)]$$

$$P(i \mid j) = \frac{\text{freq}_{ij}}{\text{freq}_j} \quad \text{and} \quad P(j \mid i) = \frac{\text{freq}_{ij}}{\text{freq}_i}$$

The weight of an edge measures how tightly connected the two words are. Words which always occur together receive a weight of 0. Words rarely cooccurring receive weights close to 1.

Once the cooccurrence graph is built, a simple iterative algorithm is executed to obtain its hubs. At each step, the algorithm finds the vertex with highest relative frequency[5] in the graph, and, if it meets some criteria, it is selected as a hub. These criteria are determined by a set of heuristic parameters, that will be explained later in Section 4. After a vertex is selected to be a hub, its neighbors are no longer eligible as hub candidates. At any time, if the next vertex candidate has a relative frequency below a certain threshold, the algorithm stops.

Once the hubs are selected, each of them is linked to the target word with edges weighting 0, and the *Minimum Spanning Tree* (MST) of the whole graph is calculated and stored.

The MST is then used to perform word sense disambiguation, in the following way. For every instance of the target word, the words surrounding it are examined and confronted with the MST. By construction of the MST, words in it are placed under exactly one hub. Each word in the context receives a set of scores $s$, with one score per hub, where all scores are 0 except the one corresponding to the hub where it is placed. If the scores are organized in a score vector, all values are 0, except, say, the $i$-th component, which receives a score $d(h_i, v)$, which is the distance between the hub $h_i$ and the node representing the word $v$. Thus, $d(h_i, v)$ assigns a score of 1 to hubs and the score decreases as the nodes move away from the hub in the tree.

For a given occurrence of the target word, the score vectors of all the words in the context are added, and the hub that receives the maximum score is chosen.

[5]In cooccurrence graphs, the relative frequency of a vertex and its degree are linearly related, and it is therefore possible to avoid the costly computation of the degree.

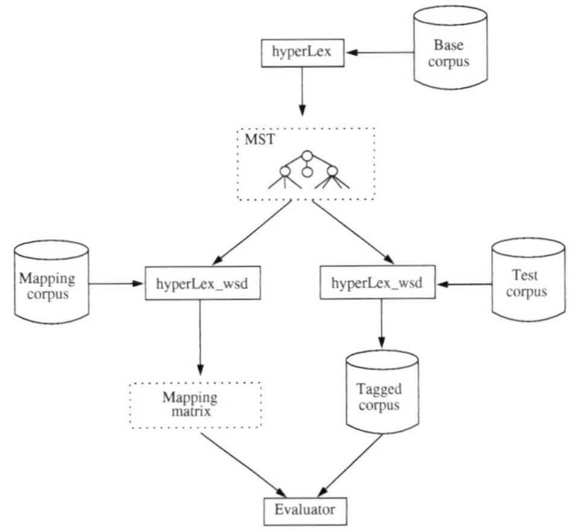


Figure 1: Design for the automatic mapping and evaluation of HyperLex algorithm against a gold standard (test corpora).

## 3 Evaluating unsupervised WSD systems

All unsupervised WSD algorithms need some addition in order to be evaluated. One alternative, as in (Véronis, 2004), is to manually decide the correctness of the hubs assigned to each occurrence of the words. This approach has two main disadvantages. First, it is expensive to manually verify each occurrence of the word, and different runs of the algorithm need to be evaluated in turn. Second, it is not an easy task to manually decide if an occurrence of a word effectively corresponds with the use of the word the assigned hub refers to, especially considering that the person is given a short list of words linked to the hub. We also think that instead of judging whether the hub returned by the algorithm is correct, the person should have independently tagged the occurrence with hubs, which should have been then compared to the hub returned by the system.

A second alternative is to evaluate the system according to some performance in an application, e.g. information retrieval (Schütze, 1998). This is a very attractive idea, but requires expensive system development and it is sometimes difficult to separate the reasons for the good (or bad) performance.

A third alternative would be to devise a method to map the hubs (clusters) returned by the system to the senses in a lexicon. Pantel and Lin (2002) automatically map the senses to WordNet, and then measure the quality of the mapping. More recently, the mapping has been used to test the system on publicly available benchmarks (Purandare and Ped-

| | Default value | p180 Range | p180 Best | p1800 Range | p1800 Best | p6700 Range | p6700 Best |
|---|---|---|---|---|---|---|---|
| p1 | 5 | 2-3 | 2 | 1-3 | 2 | 1-3 | 1 |
| p2 | 10 | 3-4 | 3 | 2-4 | 3 | 2-4 | 3 |
| p3 | 0.9 | 0.7-0.9 | 0.7 | 0.5-0.7 | 0.5 | 0.3-0.7 | 0.4 |
| p4 | 4 | 4 | 4 | 4 | 4 | 4 | 4 |
| p5 | 6 | 6-7 | 6 | 3-7 | 3 | 1-7 | 1 |
| p6 | 0.8 | 0.5-0.8 | 0.6 | 0.4-0.8 | 0.7 | 0.6-0.95 | 0.95 |
| p7 | 0.001 | 0.0005-0.001 | 0.0009 | 0.0005-0.001 | 0.0009 | 0.0009-0.003 | 0.001 |

Table 1: Parameters of the HyperLex algorithm

ersen, 2004; Niu et al., 2005). See Section 6 for more details on these systems.

Yet another possibility is to evaluate the induced senses against a gold standard as a clustering task. Induced senses are clusters, gold standard senses are classes, and measures from the clustering literature like entropy or purity can be used. As we wanted to focus on the comparison against a standard data-set, we decided to leave aside this otherwise interesting option.

In this section we present a framework for automatically evaluating unsupervised WSD systems against publicly available hand-tagged corpora. The framework uses three data sets, called Base corpus, Mapping corpus and Test corpus:

- The *Base Corpus*: a collection of examples of the target word. The corpus is not annotated.
- The *Mapping Corpus*: a collection of examples of the target word, where each corpus has been manually annotated with its sense.
- The *Test Corpus*: a separate collection, also annotated with senses.

The evaluation framework is depicted in Figure 1. The first step is to execute the HyperLex algorithm over the *Base corpus* in order to obtain the hubs of a target word, and the generated MST is stored. As stated before, the *Base Corpus* is not tagged, so the building of the MST is completely unsupervised.

In a second step (left part in Figure 1), we assign a hub score vector to each of the occurrences of target word in the *Mapping corpus*, using the MST calculated in the previous step (following the WSD algorithm in Section 2.2). Using the hand-annotated sense information, we can compute a mapping matrix $M$ that relates hubs and senses in the following way. Suppose there are $m$ hubs and $n$ senses for the target word. Then, $M = \{m_{ij}\}$ $1 \leq i \leq m, 1 \leq j \leq n$, and each $m_{ij} = P(s_j|h_i)$, that is, $m_{ij}$ is the probability of a word having sense $j$ given that it has been assigned hub $i$. This probability can be computed counting the times an occurrence with sense $s_j$ has been assigned hub $h_i$.

This mapping matrix will be used to transform any hub score vector $\bar{h} = (h_1, \ldots, h_m)$ returned by the WSD algorithm into a sense score vector $\bar{s} = (s_1, \ldots, s_n)$. It suffices to multiply the score vector by $M$, i.e., $\bar{s} = \bar{h}M$.

In the last step (right part in Figure 1), we apply the WSD algorithm over the *Test corpus*, using again the MST generated in the first step, and returning a hub score vector for each occurrence of the target word in the test corpus. We then run the *Evaluator*, which uses the $M$ mapping matrix in order to convert the hub score vector into a sense score vector. The *Evaluator* then compares the sense with highest weight in the sense score vector to the sense that was manually assigned, and outputs the precision figures.

Preliminary experiments showed that, similar to other unsupervised systems, HyperLex performs better if it sees the test examples when building the graph. We therefore decided to include a copy of the training and test corpora in the base corpus (discarding all hand-tagged sense information, of course). Given the high efficiency of the algorithm this poses no practical problem (see efficiency figures in Section 6).

## 4 Tuning the parameters

As stated before, the behavior of the HyperLex algorithm is influenced by a set of heuristic parameters, that affect the way the cooccurrence graph is built, the number of induced hubs, and the way they are extracted from the graph. There are 7 parameters in total:

p1 Minimum frequency of edges (occurrences)
p2 Minimum frequency of vertices (words)
p3 Edges with weights above this value are removed
p4 Context containing fewer words are not processed

| word | train | test | MFS | default | p180 | p1800 | p6700 |
|---|---|---|---|---|---|---|---|
| argument | 221 | 111 | **51.4** | **51.4** | **51.4** | **51.4** | **51.4** |
| arm | 266 | 133 | 82.0 | 82.0 | 80.5 | 82.0 | **82.7** |
| atmosphere | 161 | 81 | 66.7 | 67.9 | **70.4** | **70.4** | 67.9 |
| audience | 200 | 100 | 67.0 | 69.0 | 71.0 | 74.0 | **77.0** |
| bank | 262 | 132 | 67.4 | 69.7 | 75.0 | **76.5** | 75.0 |
| degree | 256 | 128 | 60.9 | 60.9 | 60.9 | 62.5 | **63.3** |
| difference | 226 | 114 | 40.4 | 40.4 | 41.2 | 46.5 | **49.1** |
| difficulty | 46 | 23 | 17.4 | 30.4 | 30.4 | **39.1** | 26.1 |
| disc | 200 | 100 | 38.0 | 66.0 | 75.0 | 70.0 | **76.0** |
| image | 146 | 74 | 36.5 | 63.5 | 62.2 | **67.6** | 64.9 |
| interest | 185 | 93 | 41.9 | 49.5 | 41.9 | 47.3 | **51.6** |
| judgment | 62 | 32 | 28.1 | 28.1 | 28.1 | **53.1** | 50.0 |
| organization | 112 | 56 | **73.2** | **73.2** | **73.2** | 71.4 | **73.2** |
| paper | 232 | 117 | 25.6 | 42.7 | 39.3 | 47.9 | **53.8** |
| party | 230 | 116 | 62.1 | **67.2** | 64.7 | 65.5 | **67.2** |
| performance | 172 | 87 | 32.2 | 44.8 | 46.0 | 54.0 | **59.8** |
| plan | 166 | 84 | 82.1 | 81.0 | 79.8 | 81.0 | **83.3** |
| shelter | 196 | 98 | 44.9 | 45.9 | 49.0 | 48.0 | **54.1** |
| sort | 190 | 96 | **65.6** | 64.6 | 64.6 | **65.6** | 64.6 |
| source | 64 | 32 | **65.6** | 59.4 | 56.2 | 62.5 | 62.5 |
| | | Average: | 54.5 | 59.9 | 60.3 | 63.0 | **64.6** |
| | | (Over S2LS) | 51.9 | 56.2 | 57.5 | 58.7 | **60.0** |

Table 2: Precision figures for nouns over the test corpus (S3LS). The second and third columns show the number of occurrences in the train and test splits. The *MFS* column corresponds to the most frequent sense. The rest of columns correspond to different parameter settings: *default* for the default setting, *p180* for the best combination over 180, etc.. The last rows show the micro-average over the S3LS run, and we also add the results on the S2LS dataset (different sets of nouns) to confirm that the same trends hold in both datasets.

p5 Minimum number of adjacent vertices a hub must have
p6 Max. mean weight of the adjacent vertices of a hub
p7 Minimum frequency of hubs

Table 1 lists the parameters of the HyperLex algorithm, and the default values proposed for them in the original work (second column).

Given that we have devised a method to efficiently evaluate the performance of HyperLex, we are able to tune the parameters against the gold standard. We first set a range for each of the parameters, and evaluated the algorithm for each combination of the parameters on a collection of examples of different words (Senseval 2 English lexical-sample, S2LS). This ensures that the chosen parameter set is valid for any noun, and is not overfitted to a small set of nouns.[6] The set of parameters that obtained the best results in the S2LS run is then selected to be run against the S3LS dataset.

We first devised ranges for parameters amounting to 180 possible combinations (p180 column in Table 2), and then extended the ranges to amount to 1800 and 6700 combinations (columns p1800 and p6700).

[6]In fact, previous experiments showed that optimizing the parameters for each word did not yield better results.

## 5 Experiment setting and results

To evaluate the HyperLex algorithm in a standard benchmark, we applied it to the 20 nouns in S3LS. We use the standard training-test split. Following the design in Section 3, we used both the training and test sets as the *Base Corpus* (ignoring the sense tags, of course). The *Mapping Corpus* comprised the training split only, and the *Test corpus* the test split only. The parameter tuning was done in a similar fashion, but on the S2LS dataset.

In Table 2 we can see the number of examples of each word in the different corpus and the results of the algorithm. We indicate only precision, as the coverage is 100% in all cases. The left column, named *MFS*, shows the precision when always assigning the most frequent sense (relative to the train split). This is the baseline of our algorithm as our algorithm does see the tags in the mapping step (see Section 6 for further comments on this issue).

The *default* column shows the results for the HyperLex algorithm with the default parameters as set by Véronis, except for the minimum frequency of the vertices (*p2* in Table 1), which according to some preliminary experiments we set to 3. As we can see, the algorithm with the default settings outperforms

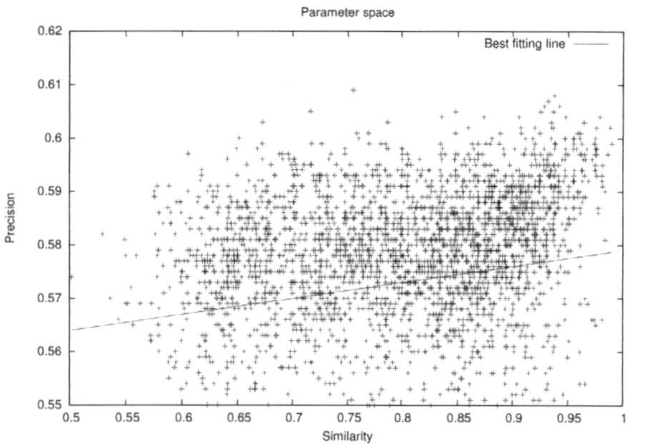


Figure 2: Dispersion plot of the parameter space for 6700 combinations. The horizontal axis shows the similarity of a parameter set w.r.t. the best parameter set using the cosine. The vertical axis shows the precision in S2LS. The best fitting line is also depicted.

the MFS baseline by 5.4 points average, and in almost all words (except *plan, sort* and *source*).

The results for the best of 180 combinations of the parameters improve the default setting (0.4 overall), Extending the parameter space to 1800 and 6700 improves the precision up to 63.0 and 64.6, 10.1 over the MFS (MFS only outperforms HyperLex in the best setting for two words). The same trend can be seen on the S2LS dataset, where the gain was more modest (note that the parameters were optimized for S2LS).

## 6 Discussion and related work

We first comment the results, doing some analysis, and then compare our results to those of Véronis. Finally we overview some relevant work and review the results of unsupervised systems on the S3LS benchmark.

### 6.1 Comments on the results

The results show clearly that our exploration of the parameter space was successful, with the widest parameter space showing the best results.

In order to analyze whether the search in the parameter space was making any sense, we drew a dispersion plot (see Figure 2). In the top right-hand corner we have the point corresponding to the best performing parameter set. If the parameters were not conditioning the good results, then we would have expected a random cloud of points. On the contrary, we can see that there is a clear tendency for those parameter sets most similar to the best one to obtain better results, and in fact the best fitting line shows a clearly ascending slope.

| | default | p180 | p1800 | p6700 |
|---|---|---|---|---|
| hubs defined | 9.2 ±3.8 | 15.3 ±5.7 | 38.6 ±11.8 | 77.7±18.7 |
| used | 8.4 ±3.5 | 14.4 ±5.3 | 30.4 ±9.3 | 45.2±13.3 |
| senses defined | 5.4 ±1.5 | 5.4 ±1.5 | 5.4 ±1.5 | 5.4 ±1.5 |
| used | 2.6 ±1.2 | 2.5 ±1 | 3.1 ±1.1 | 3.2±1.2 |
| senses in test | 5.1 ±1.3 | - | - | - |

Table 3: Average number of hubs and senses (along with the standard deviation) for three parameter settings. Defined means the number of hubs induced, and used means the ones actually returned by HyperLex when disambiguating the test set. The same applies for senses, that is, defined means total number of senses (equal for all columns), and used means the senses that were actually used by HyperLex in the test set. The last row shows the actual number of senses used by the hand-annotators in the test set.

Regarding efficiency, our implementation of HyperLex is extremely fast. Doing the 1800 combinations takes 2 hours in a 2 AMD Opteron processors at 2GHz and 3Gb RAM. A single run (building the MST, mapping and tagging the test sentences) takes only 16 sec. For this reason, even if an on-line version would be in principle desirable, we think that this batch version is readily usable.

### 6.2 Comparison to (Véronis, 2004)

Compared to Véronis we are inducing larger numbers of hubs (with different parameters), using less examples to build the graphs and obtaining more modest results (far from the 90's). Regarding the latter, our results are in the range of other S3LS WSD systems (see below), and the discrepancy can be explained by the way Véronis performed his evaluation (see Section 3).

Table 3 shows the average number of hubs for the four parameter settings. The average number of hubs for the default setting is larger than that of Véronis (which ranges between 4 and 9 per word), but quite close to the average number of senses. The exploration of the parameter space prefers parameter settings with even larger number of hubs, and the figures shows that most of them are actually used for disambiguation. The table also shows that, after the mapping, less than half of the senses are actually used, which seems to indicate that the mapping tends to favor the most frequent senses.

Regarding the actual values of the parameters used (c.f. Table 1), we had to reduce the value of some parameters (e.g. the minimum frequency of vertices) due to the smaller number of of examples (Véronis used from 1900 to 8700 examples per word). In theory, we could explore larger parameter spaces, but Table 1 shoes that the best setting for the 6700 combinations has no parameter in a range boundary (except *p5*, which cannot be further reduced).

All in all, the best results are attained with smaller and more numerous hubs, a kind of micro-senses. A possible explanation for this discrepancy with Véronis could be that he was inspecting by hand the hubs that he got, and perhaps was biased by the fact that he wanted the hubs to look more like standard senses. At first we were uncomfortable with this behavior, so we checked whether HyperLex was degenerating into a trivial solution. We simulated a clustering algorithm returning one hub per example, and its precision was 40.1, well below the MFS baseline. We also realized that our results are in accordance with some theories of word meaning, e.g. the "indefinitely large set of prototypes-within-prototypes" envisioned in (Cruse, 2000). We now think that the idea of having many micro-senses is very attractive for further exploration, especially if we are able to organize them into coarser hubs.

### 6.3 Comparison to related work

Table 4 shows the performance of different systems on the nouns of the S3LS benchmark. When not reported separately, we obtained the results for nouns running the official scorer program on the filtered results, as available in the S3LS web page. The second column shows the type of system (supervised, unsupervised).

We include three supervised systems, the winner of S3LS (Mihalcea et al., 2004), an in-house system (kNN-all, CITATION OMITTED) which uses optimized kNN, and the same in-house system restricted to bag-of-words features only (kNN-bow), i.e. discarding other local features like bigrams or trigrams (which is what most unsupervised systems do). The table shows that we are one point from the bag-of-words classifier kNN-bow, which is an impressive result if we take into account the information loss of the mapping step and that we tuned our parameters on a different set of words. The full kNN system is state-of-the-art, only 4 points below the S3LS winner.

| System | Type | Prec. | Cov. |
|---|---|---|---|
| S3LS-best | Sup. | 74.9 | 0.99 |
| kNN-all | Sup. | 70.3 | 1.0 |
| kNN-bow | Sup. | 65.7 | 1.0 |
| **HyperLex** | Unsup(S3LS) | 64.6 | 1.0 |
| Cymfony | Unsup(10%-S3LS) | 57.9 | 1.0 |
| Prob0 | Unsup. (MFS-S3) | 55.0 | 0.98 |
| **MFS** | - | 51.5 | 1.0 |
| Ciaosenso | Unsup (MFS-Sc) | 53.95 | 0.90 |
| clr04 | Unsup (MFS-Sc) | 48.86 | 1.0 |
| duluth-senserelate | Unsup | 47.48 | 1.0 |
| (Purandare and Pedersen, 2004) | Unsup (S2LS) | - | - |

Table 4: Comparison of HyperLex and MFS baseline to S3LS systems for nouns. The last system was evaluated on S2LS.

Table 4 also shows several unsupervised systems, all of which except Cymfony and (Purandare and Pedersen, 2004) participated in S3LS (check (Mihalcea et al., 2004) for further details on the systems). We classify them according to the amount of "supervision" they have: some have have access to most-frequent information (MFS-S3 if counted over S3LS, MFS-Sc if counted over SemCor), some use 10% of the S3LS training part for mapping (10%-S3LS), and some use the full amount of S3LS training for mapping (S3LS). Only one system (Duluth) did not use in any way hand-tagged corpora.

Given the different typology of unsupervised systems, it's unfair to draw definitive conclusions from a raw comparison of results. The system coming closer to ours is that described in (Niu et al., 2005). They use hand tagged corpora which does not need to include the target word to tune the parameters of a rather complex clustering method which does use local information (an exception to the rule of unsupervised systems). They do use the S3LS training corpus for mapping. For every sense the target word, three of its contexts in the train corpus are gathered (around 10% of the training data) and tagged. Each cluster is then related with its most frequent sense. Only one cluster may be related to a specific sense, so if two or more clusters map to the same sense, only the largest of them is retained. The mapping method is similar to ours, but we use all the available training data and allow for different hubs to be assigned to the same sense.

Another system similar to ours is (Purandare and Pedersen, 2004), which unfortunately was evaluated on Senseval 2 data. The authors use first and second order bag-of-word context features to represent each instance of the corpus. They apply several clustering algorithms based on the vector space model, limiting the number of clusters to 7. They also use all available training data for mapping, but given their small number of clusters they opt for a one-to-one mapping which maximizes the assignment and discards the less frequent clusters. They also discard some difficult cases, like senses and words with low frequencies (10% of total occurrences and 90, respectively). The different test set and mapping system make the comparison difficult, but the fact that the best of their combinations beats MFS by 1 point on average (47.6% vs. 46.4%) for the selected nouns and senses make us think that our results are more robust (nearly 10% over MFS).

## 7 Conclusions and further work

This paper has explored two sides of HyperLex: the optimization of the free parameters, and the empirical comparison on a standard benchmark against other WSD systems. We use hand-tagged corpora to map the induced senses to WordNet senses.

Regarding the optimization of parameters, we used a another testbed (S2LS) comprising different words to select the best parameter. We consistently improve the results of the parameters by Véronis, which is not perhaps so surprising, but the method allows to fine-tune the parameters automatically to a given corpus given a small test set.

Comparing unsupervised systems against supervised systems is seldom done. Our results indicate that HyperLex with the supervised mapping is on par with a state-of-the-art system which uses bag-of-words features only. Given the information loss inherent to any mapping, this is an impressive result. The comparison to other unsupervised systems is difficult, as each one uses a different mapping strategy and a different amount of supervision.

For the future, we would like to look more closely the micro-senses induced by HyperLex, and see if we can group them into coarser clusters. We also plan to apply the parameters to the Senseval 3 all-words task, which seems well fit for HyperLex: the best supervised system only outperforms MFS by a few points in this setting, and the training corpora used (Semcor) is not related to the test corpora (mainly Wall Street Journal texts).

Graph models have been very successful in some settings (e.g. the PageRank algorithm of Google), and have been rediscovered recently for natural language tasks like knowledge-based WSD, textual entailment, summarization and dependency parsing. We would like to test other such algorithms in the same conditions, and explore their potential to integrate different kinds of information, especially the local or syntactic features so successfully used by supervised systems, but also more heterogeneous information from knowledge bases.

## References


A. L. Barabasi and R. Albert. 1999. Emergence of scaling in random networks. *Science*, 286(5439):509–512, October.

D. A. Cruse, 2000. *Polysemy: Theoretical and Computational Approaches*, chapter Aspects of the Microstructure of Word Meanings. OUP.

C. Fellbaum. 1998. *WordNet: An Electronic Lexical Database*. MIT Press.

R. Mihalcea, T. Chklovski, and A. Kilgarriff. 2004. The senseval-3 english lexical sample task. In R. Mihalcea and P. Edmonds, editors, *Senseval-3 proceedings*, pages 25–28. ACL, July.

G.A. Miller, C. Leacock, R. Tengi, and R.Bunker. 1993. A semantic concordance. In *Proc. of the ARPA HLT workshop*.

C. Niu, W. Li, R. K. Srihari, and H. Li. 2005. Word independent context pair classification model for word sense disambiguation. In *Proc. of CoNLL-2005*.

P. Pantel and D. Lin. 2002. Discovering word senses from text. In *Proc. of KDD02*.

A. Purandare and T. Pedersen. 2004. Word sense discrimination by clustering contexts in vector and similarity spaces. In *Proc. of CoNLL-2004*.

H. Schütze. 1998. Automatic word sense discrimination. *Computational Linguistics*, 24(1):97–123.

B. Snyder and M. Palmer. 2004. The english all-words task. In *Proc. of SENSEVAL*.

J. Véronis. 2004. HyperLex: lexical cartography for information retrieval. *Computer Speech & Language*, 18(3):223–252.

D. J. Watts and S. H. Strogatz. 1998. Collective dynamics of 'small-world' networks. *Nature*, 393(6684):440–442, June.

# Context Comparison as a Minimum Cost Flow Problem

**Vivian Tsang and Suzanne Stevenson**
Department of Computer Science
University of Toronto
Canada
{vyctsang,suzanne}@cs.utoronto.ca

## Abstract

Comparing word contexts is a key component of many NLP tasks, but rarely is it used in conjunction with additional ontological knowledge. One problem is that the amount of overhead required can be high. In this paper, we provide a graphical method which easily combines an ontology with contextual information. We take advantage of the intrinsic graphical structure of an ontology for representing a context. In addition, we turn the ontology into a metric space, such that subgraphs within it, which represent contexts, can be compared. We develop two variants of our graphical method for comparing contexts. Our analysis indicates that our method performs the comparison efficiently and offers a competitive alternative to non-graphical methods.

## 1 Introduction

Many natural language problems can be cast as a problem of comparing "contexts" (units of text). For example, the local context of a word can be used to resolve its ambiguity (e.g., Schütze, 1998), assuming that words used in similar contexts are closely related semantically (Miller and Charles, 1991). Extending the meaning of context, the content of a document may reveal which document class(es) it belongs to (e.g., Xu et al., 2003). In any application, once a sensible view of context is formulated, the next step is to choose a representation that makes comparisons possible. For example, in word sense disambiguation, a context of an ambiguous instance can be represented as a vector of the frequencies of words surrounding it. Until recently, the dominant approach has been a non-graphical one—context comparison is reduced to a task of measuring distributional distance between context vectors. The difference in the frequency characteristics of contexts is used as an indicator of the semantic distance between them.

We present a graphical alternative that combines both distributional and ontological knowledge. We begin with the use of a different context representation that allows easy incorporation of ontological information. Treating an ontology as a network, we can represent a context as a set of nodes in the network (i.e., concepts in the ontology), each with a weight (i.e., frequency). To contrast our work with that of Navigli and Velardi (2005) and Mihalcea (2006), the goal is not merely to provide a graphical representation for a context in which the relevant concepts are connected. Rather, contexts are treated as weighted subgraphs within a larger graph in which they are connected via a set of paths. By incorporating the semantic distance between individual concepts, the graph (representing the ontology) becomes a metric space in which we can measure the distance between subgraphs (representing the contexts to be compared).

More specifically, measuring the distance between two contexts can be viewed as solving a minimum cost flow (MCF) problem by calculating the amount of "effort" required for transporting the flow from one context to the other. Our method has the advantage of including semantic information (by making use of the graphical structure of an ontology) without losing distributional information (by



*Workshop on TextGraphs, at HLT-NAACL 2006*, pages 97–104,
New York City, June 2006. 

using the concept frequencies derived from corpus data).

This network flow formulation, though supporting the inclusion of an ontology in context comparison, is not flexible enough. The problem is rooted in the choice of concept-to-concept distance (i.e., the distance between two concepts, to contrast it from the overall semantic distance between two contexts). Certain concept-to-concept distances may result in a difficult-to-process network which severely compromises efficiency. To remedy this, we propose a novel network transformation method for constructing a pared-down network which mimics the structure of the more precise network, but without the expensive processing or any significant information loss as a result of the transformation.

In the remainder of this paper, we first present the underlying network flow framework, and develop a more efficient variant of it. We then evaluate the robustness of our methods on a context comparison task. Finally, we conclude with an analysis and some future directions.

## 2 The Network Flow Method

### 2.1 Minimum Cost Flow

As a standard example of an MCF problem, consider the graphical representation of a route map for delivering fresh produce from grocers (supply nodes) to homes (demand nodes). The remaining nodes (e.g., intersections, gas stations) have neither a supply nor a demand. Assuming there are sufficient supplies, the optimal solution is to find the cheapest set of routes from grocers to homes such that all demands are satisfied.

Mathematically, let $G = (N, E)$ be a connected network, where $N$ is the set of nodes, and $E$ is the set of edges.[1] Each edge has a cost $c : E \rightarrow \mathbb{R}$, which is the distance of the edge. Each node $i \in N$ is associated with a value $b(i)$ such that $b : N \rightarrow \mathbb{R}$ indicates its available supply ($b(i) > 0$), its demand ($b(i) < 0$), or neither ($b(i) = 0$). The goal is to find a solution for each node $i$ such that all the flow passing through $i$ satisfies its supply or demand requirement ($b(i)$). The flow passing through node $i$ is captured by $x : E \rightarrow \mathbb{R}$ such that we can observe the combined incoming flow, $\sum_{(h,i) \in IN_i} x(h, i)$, from the entering edges $IN_i$, as well as the combined outgoing flow, $\sum_{(i,j) \in OUT_i} x(i, j)$, via the exiting edges $OUT_i$. (See Figure 1.) If a feasible solution can be found, the net flow (the difference between the entering and exiting flow) at each node must fulfill the corresponding supply or demand requirement.

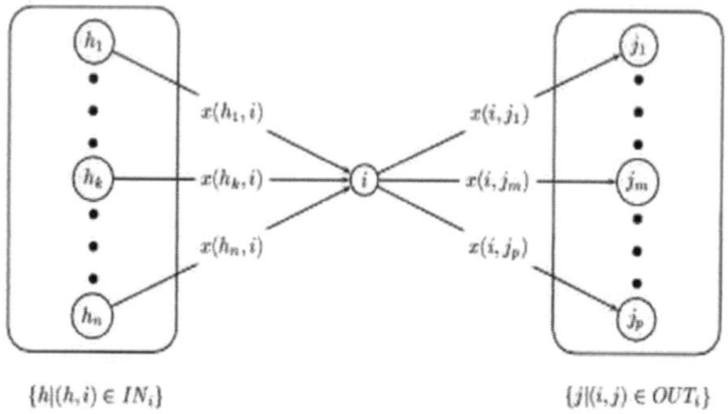


Figure 1: An illustration of flow entering and exiting node $i$.

Formally, the MCF problem can be stated as:

Minimize

$$z(\vec{x}) = \sum_{(i,j) \in E} c(i, j) \cdot x(i, j) \quad (1)$$

subject to

$$\sum_{(i,j) \in OUT_i} x(i, j) - \sum_{(h,i) \in IN_i} x(h, i) = b(i), \forall i \in N \quad (2)$$

$$x(i, j) \geq 0, \forall (i, j) \in E \quad (3)$$

The constraint specified by (2) ensures that the difference between the flow entering and exiting each node $i$ matches its supply or demand $b(i)$ exactly. The next constraint (3) ensures that the flow is transported from the supply to the demand but not in the opposite direction. Finally, selecting route $(i, j)$ requires a transportation "effort" of $c(i, j)$ (cost of the route) multiplied by the amount of supply transported $x(i, j)$ (the term inside the summation in eqn. (1)). Taking the summation of the effort, $c(i, j) \cdot x(i, j)$, of cheapest routes yields the desired distance between the supply and the demand.

### 2.2 Semantic Distance as MCF

To cast our context comparison task into this framework, we first represent each context as a vector of concept frequencies (or a *context profile* for the remainder of this paper). The profile of one context is chosen as the supply and the other as the demand. The concept frequencies of the profiles are normalized, so that the total supply always equals the total

[1]Most ontologies are hierarchical, thus, in the case of a forest, adding an arbitrary root node yields a connected graph.

demand. The cost of the routes between nodes is determined by a semantic distance measure defined over any two nodes in the ontology. Now, as in the grocery delivery domain, the goal is to find the MCF from supply to demand.

We can treat any ontology as the transport network. A relation (such as hyponymy) between two concepts $i$ and $j$ is represented by an edge $(i, j)$, and the cost $c$ on each edge can be defined as the semantic distance between the two concepts. This semantic distance can be as simple as the number of edges separating the concepts, or more sophisticated, such as Lin's (1998) information-theoretic measure. (See Budanitsky and Hirst (2006) for a survey of such measures).

Numerous methods are possible for converting the word frequency vector of a context to a concept frequency vector (i.e., a context profile). One simple method is to transfer each element in the word vector (i.e., the frequency of each word) to the corresponding concepts in the ontology, resulting in a vector of concept frequencies. In this paper, we have chosen a uniform distribution of word frequency counts among concepts, instead of a weighted distribution towards the relevant concepts for a particular text. Since we wish to evaluate the strength of our method alone without any additional NLP effort, we bypass the issue of approximating the true distribution of the concepts via word sense disambiguation or class-based approximation methods, such as those by Li and Abe (1998) and Clark and Weir (2002).

To calculate the distance between two profiles, we need to cast one profile as the supply ($S$) and the other as the demand ($D$). Note that our distance is symmetric, so the choice of the supply and the demand is arbitrary. Next, we must determine the value of $b(i)$ at each concept node $i$; this is just the difference between the (normalized) supply frequency $f_S(i)$ and demand frequency $f_D(i)$:

$$b(i) = f_S(i) - f_D(i) \tag{4}$$

This formula yields the net supply/demand, $b(i)$, at node $i$. Recall that our goal is to transport all the supply to meet the demand—the final step is to determine the cheapest routes between $S$ and $D$ such that the constraints in (2) and (3) are satisfied. The total distance of the routes, or the MCF, $z(\vec{x})$ in eqn. (1), is the distance between the two context profiles.

Finally, it is important to note that the MCF formulation does not simply find the shortest paths from the concept nodes in the supply to those in the demand. Because a profile is a frequency-weighted concept vector, some concept nodes are weighted more heavily than others, and the routes between such nodes across the two profiles are also weighted more heavily. Indeed, in eqn. (1), the cost of each route, $c(i, j)$, is weighted by $x(i, j)$ (how much supply, or frequency weight, is transported between nodes $i$ and $j$).

## 3 Graphical Issues

As alluded to in the introduction, certain concept-to-concept distances pose a problem to solving the MCF problem easily. The details are described next.

### 3.1 Additivity

In theory, our method has the flexibility to incorporate different concept-to-concept distances. The issue lies in the algorithms for solving MCF problems. Existing algorithms are greedy—they take a stepwise "localist" approach on the set of edges connecting the supply and the demand; i.e., at each node, the cheapest outgoing edge is selected. The assumption is that the concept-to-concept distance function is additive. Mathematically, for any path from node $i$ to node $k$, $\{(j_0, j_1), \ldots, (j_{n-1}, j_n)\}$, where $i = j_0$ and $k = j_n$, the distance between nodes $i$ and $k$ is the sum of the distance of the edges along the path:

$$dist(i, k) = \sum_{m=0}^{n-1} dist(j_m, j_{m+1}) \tag{5}$$

The additivity of a concept-to-concept distance entails that selecting the cheapest edge at each step (i.e., locally) yields the overall cheapest set of routes (i.e., globally). Note that some of the most successful concept-to-concept distances proposed in the CL literature are non-additive (e.g., Lin, 1998; Resnik, 1995). This poses a problem in solving our network flow problem—the global distance between any concepts, $i$ and $k$, cannot be correctly determined by the greedy method.

### 3.2 Constructing an Equivalent Bipartite Network

The issue of non-additive distances can be addressed in the following way. We map the relevant portion

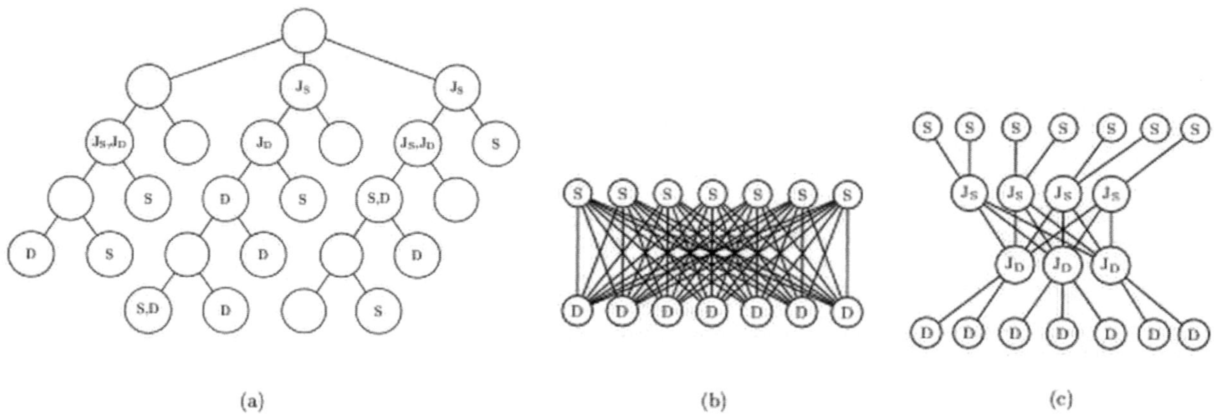


Figure 2: An illustration of the transformations (left to right) from the original network (a) to the bipartite network (b), and finally, to the network produced by our transformation (c), given two profiles S and D. Nodes labelled with either "S" or "D" belong to the corresponding profile. Nodes labelled with "$J_S$" or "$J_D$" are junction nodes (see section 4.2).

of the network into a new network such that the concept-to-concept distance is preserved, but without the problem introduced by non-additivity. One possible solution is to construct a complete bipartite graph between the supply nodes and the demand nodes (the nodes in the two context profiles). We set the cost of each edge $(s, d)$ in the bipartite graph to be the concept-to-concept distance between $s$ and $d$ in the original network. Since there is exactly one edge between any pair of nodes, the non-additivity is removed entirely. (See Figures 2(a) and 2(b).) Now, we can apply a network flow solver on the new graph.

However, one problem arises from performing the above mapping—there is a processing bottleneck as a result of the quadratic increase in the number of edges in the new network. Unfortunately, though tractable, polynomial complexity is not always practical. For example, with an average of 900 nodes per profile, making 120 profile comparisons in addition to network re-structuring can take as long as 10 days.[2] If we choose to use a non-additive distance, the method described above does not scale up well for a large number of comparisons. Next, we present a method to alleviate the complexity issue.

## 4 Network Transformation

One method of alleviating the bottleneck is to reduce the processing load from generating a large number of edges. Instead of generating a complete bipartite network, we generate a network which approximates both the structure of the original network as well as that of the complete bipartite network. The goal is to construct a pared-down network such that (a) a reduction in the number of edges improves efficiency, and (b) the resulting distance distortion does not hamper performance significantly.

### 4.1 Path Shape in a Hierarchy

To understand our transformation method, let us further examine the graphical properties of an ontology as a network. In a hierarchical network (e.g., WordNet, Gene Ontology, UMLS), calculating the distance between two concept nodes usually involves travelling "up" and "down" the hierarchy. The simplest route is a single hop from a child to its parent or vice versa. Generally, travelling from one node $i$ to another node $j$ consists of an A-shaped path ascending from node $i$ to a common ancestor of $i$ and $j$, and then descending to node $j$.

Interestingly, our description of the A-shaped path matches the design of a number of concept-to-concept distances. For example, distances that incorporate Resnik's (1995) information content (IC), $-\log(p(concept))$, such as those of Jiang and Conrath (1997) and Lin (1998), consider both the (lowest) common ancestor as well as the two nodes of interest in their calculation.

The complete bipartite graph considered in section 3.2 directly connects each node s in profile $S$ to node $d$ in profile $D$, eliminating the typical A-shaped path in an ontology. This structure solves the

[2]This is tested on a context comparison task not reported in this paper. The code is scripted in perl. The experiment was performed on a machine with two P4 Xeon CPUs running at 3.6GHz, with a 1MB cache and 6GB of memory.

non-additivity issue, by generating an edge with the exact concept-to-concept distance for each potential node comparison, but, as noted above, is too inefficient. Our solution here is to construct a network that uses the idea of a pared-down A-shaped path to mostly avoid non-additivity, but without the inefficiency of the complete bipartite graph. Thus, as explained in more detail in the following subsections, we trade off the exactness of the distance calculation against the efficiency of the network construction.

### 4.2 Network Construction

In our network construction, we exploit the general notion of an A-shaped path between any two nodes, but replace the "tip" of the A with two nodes. Then for each node $s$ and $d$ in profiles $S$ and $D$, we generate an edge from s to an ancestor $a_s$ of $s$ (the left "branch" of the A), an edge from d to an ancestor $a_d$ of $d$ (the right "branch" of the A), and an edge between $a_s$ and $a_d$ (the two nodes forming the "elongated tip" of the A). Each edge has the exact concept-to-concept distance from the original network, so that the distance between any two nodes $s$ and $d$ is the sum of three exact distances.

The set of ancestor nodes, $a_s$ and $a_d$, comprise the "junction" points at which the supply from $S$ can be transported across to the nodes in $D$ to satisfy their demand. The set of junction nodes, $J_P$, for a profile $P$, must be selected such that for each node $i$ in $P$, $J_P$ contains at least one ancestor of $i$. (See section 4.4 for details on the junction selection process.) The resulting network is constructed by directly connecting each profile to its corresponding junction, then connecting the two junctions in the middle (Figure 2(c)).

The difference between the complete bipartite network and the transformed network here is that, instead of connecting each node in $S$ to every node in $D$, we connect each node in $J_S$ to every node in $J_D$. Compare the transformed network in Figure 2(c) with the complete bipartite network in Figure 2(b). The complete bipartite component in the transformed network (the middle portion between the junction nodes labelled $J_S$ and $J_D$) is considerably smaller in size. Thus, the number of edges in the transformed network is significantly fewer as well.

Next, we can proceed to define the cost function on the transformed network. Observe that each edge $(s, d)$, with cost $dist(s, d)$, in the complete bipartite network, where $s \in S$, $d \in D$, is now instead represented by three edges: $(s, a_s)$, $(a_s, a_d)$, and $(a_d, d)$, where $a_s \in J_S$ and $a_d \in J_D$. Thus, the transformed distance between $s$ and $d$, $dist_{trans}(s, d)$, becomes:

$$dist_{trans}(s, d) = dist(s, a_s) + dist(a_s, a_d) + dist(a_d, d) \quad (6)$$

where $dist(i, j)$ is the precise concept-to-concept distance between $i$ and $j$ in the original network. Once we have set up the transformed network, we can solve the MCF in this network, yielding the distance between the two (supply and demand) profiles.

### 4.3 Distance Distortion

Because the distance between nodes $s$ and $d$ is now calculated as the sum of three distances (eqn. (6)), some distortion may result for non-additive concept-to-concept distances. To illustrate the distortion effect, consider Jiang and Conrath's (1997) distance:

$$dist_{jc}(i, j) = IC(i) + IC(j) - 2IC(LCS(i, j)) \quad (7)$$

where $IC(i)$ is the information content of a node $i$, and $LCS(i, j)$ is the lowest common subsumer of nodes $i$ and $j$. This distance measures the difference in information content between the concepts and their lowest common subsumers.

After the transformation, the distance is distorted in the following way. If $i$ and $j$ have no common junction ancestor, then $dist_{jc_{trans}}(i, j)$ becomes:

$$\begin{aligned} dist_{jc_{trans}}(i, j) &= [IC(i) + IC(a_i) - 2IC(a_i)] + \\ &\quad [IC(j) + IC(a_j) - 2IC(a_j)] + \\ &\quad [IC(a_i) + IC(a_j) - 2IC(LCS(a_i, a_j))] \\ &= IC(i) + IC(j) - 2IC(LCS(a_i, a_j)) \quad (8) \end{aligned}$$

where $a_i$ and $a_j$ are the junction ancestors of $i$ and $j$, respectively. Otherwise, if $i$ and $j$ share a common ancestor $a$ at the junction, then $dist_{jc_{trans}}(i, j)$ becomes $IC(i) + IC(j) - 2IC(a)$, where the term $2IC(LCS(a_i, a_j))$ in eqn. (8) is replaced by $2IC(a)$. In either case, the transformation replaces the lowest common subsumer $LCS(i, j)$ in eqn. (7) with some other common subsumer $CS(i, j)$ ($LCS(a_i, a_j)$ or $a$, mentioned above). Unless $CS(i, j) = LCS(i, j)$, the distance is distorted by using a less precise quantity, $IC(CS(i, j))$.

Note that the information content of a concept is given by its maximum likelihood estimate based on its frequency in a large corpus. An increment in the frequency of a concept leads to an increment in the frequency of all its ancestors. Due to the frequency percolation, concepts with a small depth tend to accumulate higher counts than those deeper in the hierarchy (note the difference in depth: $depth_{CS(i,j)} \leq depth_{LCS(i,j)}$). Thus, we expect the information content of a concept to be higher than its ancestors, i.e., a concept is more semantically specific than its ancestors, which is captured by the use of the negative log function in the definition of IC. The transformed distance is distorted accordingly $(IC(CS(i,j)) \leq IC(LCS(i,j)))$.

### 4.4 Junction Selection

Selection of junction nodes is a key component of the network transformation. Trivially, a junction consisting of profile nodes yields a network equivalent to the complete bipartite network. The key is to select a junction that is considerably smaller in size than its corresponding profile, hence, cutting down the number of edges generated, which results in significant savings in complexity.

Note that there is a tradeoff between the overall computational efficiency and the similarity between the transformed network and the complete bipartite network. The closer the junctions are to the corresponding profiles, the closer the transformed network resembles the complete bipartite network. Though the distance calculation is more accurate, such a network is also more expensive to process. On the other hand, there are fewer nodes in a junction as it approaches the root level, but there is more distortion in the transformed concept-to-concept distance. Clearly, it is important to balance the two factors.

Selecting junction nodes involves finding a smaller set of ancestor nodes representing the profile nodes in a hierarchy. In other words, the junction can be viewed as an alternative representation which is a generalization of the profile nodes. In addition to the profile nodes, the junction nodes are also included in the transformed network. They may provide extra information about the corresponding context.

Finding a generalization of a profile is explored in the works of Clark and Weir (2002) and Li and Abe (1998). Unfortunately, the complexity of these algorithms is quadratic (the former) or cubic (the latter) in the number of nodes in a network, which is unacceptably expensive for our transformation method. Note that to ensure every profile node has an ancestor node in the junction, the selection process has a linear lower bound. To keep the cost low, it is best to keep a linear complexity for the junction selection process. However, if this is not possible, it should be significantly less expensive than a quadratic complexity. We will empirically explore the process further in section 5.3.

## 5 Context Comparison

As alluded to earlier, our network flow method provides an alternative to a purely distributional and non-graphical approach to context comparison. In this paper, we will test both variants of our method (with or without the transformation in section 4) in a name disambiguation task in which the context words within a small window surrounding the ambiguous words are compared. Our preliminary analysis shows that our general network flow framework is robust and efficient.

### 5.1 Name Disambiguation

The goal for name disambiguation is to classify each ambiguous instance on the basis of its surrounding context. One approach is to use an unsupervised method such as clustering. This involves making a large number of pairwise comparisons between individual contexts. Given that there is an overhead to incorporating ontological information, our network flow method does not compute distances as efficiently as calculating a purely arithmetic distance such as cosine or Euclidean distance. Our alternative approach is to use minimal training data. Using a handful of contexts, we can build a "gold standard" profile for each sense of an ambiguous name by using the context words of a small number of instances. We then compare the context profile of each instance to the gold standards. Each instance is given the label of the gold standard profile to which its context profile is the closest.

### 5.2 Experimental Setup

In our name disambiguation experiment, we use the data collected by Pedersen et al. (2005) for their name discrimination task. This data is taken from

| Name Pairs | Baseline | 200 (Full) | 200 (Trans) | 100 (Full) | 100 (Trans) |
|---|---|---|---|---|---|
| Ronaldo/David Beckham | 0.69 | 0.80 | 0.88 | 0.79 | 0.84 |
| Tajik/Rolf Ekeus | 0.74 | 0.97 | 0.99 | 0.98 | 0.99 |
| Microsoft/IBM | 0.59 | 0.73 | 0.75 | 0.73 | 0.71 |
| Shimon Peres/Slobodan Milosevic | 0.56 | 0.96 | 0.99 | 0.97 | 0.99 |
| Jordan/Egyptian | 0.54 | 0.77 | 0.76 | 0.74 | 0.76 |
| Japan/France | 0.51 | 0.75 | 0.82 | 0.75 | 0.83 |
| Weighted Average | 0.53 | 0.77 | 0.82 | 0.76 | 0.82 |

Table 1: Name disambiguation results (accuracy/F-measure) at a glance. The baseline is the relative frequency of the majority name. "200" and "100" give the averaged results (over five different runs) using 200 and 100 randomly selected training instances per ambiguous name. The weighted average is calculated based on the number of test instances per task. "Full" and "Trans" refer to the results using the full network (pre-transformation) or the pared-down network (with transformation), respectively.

the Agence France Press English Service portion of the GigaWord English corpus distributed by the Linguistic Data Consortium. It consists of the contexts of six pairs of names, including: the names of two soccer players (Ronaldo and David Beckham); an ethnic group and a diplomat (Tajik and Rolf Ekeus); two companies (Microsoft and IBM); two politicians (Shimon Peres and Slobodan Milosevic); a nation and a nationality (Jordan and Egyptian); and two countries (France and Japan). These name pairs are selected by Pedersen et al. (2005) to reflect a range of confusability between names.

Each pair of names serves as one of six name disambiguation tasks. Each name instance consists of a context window of 50 words (25 words to the left and to the right of the target name), with the target name obfuscated. For example, for the task of distinguishing "David Beckham" and "Ronaldo", the target name in each instance becomes "David_BeckhamRonaldo". The goal is to recover the correct target name in each instance.

### 5.3 Junction Selection

We reported earlier that a complete bipartite graph with 900 nodes is too expensive to process. Our first attempt is to select a junction on the basis of the number of nodes it contains. Here, the junctions we select are simple to find by taking a top-down approach. We start at the top nine root nodes of WordNet (nodes of zero depth) and proceed downwards. We limit the search within the top two levels because the second level consists of 158 nodes, while the following level consists of 1307 nodes, which, clearly, exceeds 900 nodes. Here, we select the junction which consists of eight of the top root nodes (siblings of *entity*) and the children of *entity*, given that *entity* is semantically more general than its siblings.[3]

In our current experiment, we use Jiang and Conrath's distance for its ease of analysis. As shown in section 4.3, only one term in the distance, $IC(LCS(i,j))$, is replaced because of the use of the junction nodes. Any change in the performance (in comparison to our method *without* the transformation) can be attributed to the distance distortion as a result of this term being replaced. The analysis of experimental results (next section) is made easy because we can assess the goodness of the transformation given the selected junction—a significant degradation in performance is an indication that the junction nodes should be brought closer to the profile nodes, yielding a more precise distance.

## 6 Results and Analysis

To compare the two variants of our method, we perform our name disambiguation experiment using 100 and 200 training instances per ambiguous name to create the gold standard profiles. See Table 1 for the results. Comparing the results using the full network and the transformed network, observe that there is very little performance degradation; in fact, in most cases, there is an increase in accuracy (the difference is significant, paired t-test with $p \ll 0.05$).

**Distance Transformation** In Jiang and Conrath's formulation, the network transformation replaces the term $2IC(LCS(i,j))$ with $2IC(CS(i,j))$, where $CS(i,j)$ is some common ancestor of $i$ and

[3]Note that the complexity of this selection process is linear, since all profile nodes must be examined to ensure they have an ancestor in the junction; any profile node of which no junction node is an ancestor is added to the junction. This process can only be avoided by using junction nodes of zero depth exclusively.

$j$, whose depth is small. Junction nodes with a small depth distort the distance more than those with a larger depth. Surprisingly, our experiment indicates that using such nodes produces equally good or better performance. This suggests that selecting a junction with a larger depth, at least for the data in this task, is not necessary.

**Speed Improvement** In comparison to our reported running time on the pre-transformation network (120 comparisons running for 10 days), on the same machine, making 12,000 comparisons can now be accomplished within two hours. In terms of complexity, if we have $n$ profile nodes and $j$ junction nodes, the number of edges to be processed is $O(n + j^2)$. Given that our junctions have significantly fewer nodes than the original profiles, the running time is significantly less than quadratic in the number of profile nodes.

## 7 Conclusions

We have given an overview of our network flow formalism which seamlessly combines distributional and ontological information. Given a suitable ontology, a context vector of word frequencies can be transformed into a context profile—a frequency distribution over the concepts in the ontology. In contrast to traditional non-graphical approaches to measuring only the distributional distance between context vectors, we provide a graphical formalism which incorporates both the semantic distance of the component nodes as well as the distributional differences between the context profiles. By taking advantage of the graphical structure of an ontology, our method allows a systematic and meaningful way of abstracting over words in a context, and by extension, a meaningful way of comparing contexts.

One concern with our method in its pre-transformation form is its inability to incorporate sophisticated concept-to-concept semantic distances efficiently. To remedy this, we propose a novel technique that mimics the structure of the more computationally intensive network. Our preliminary evaluation shows that the transformation does not hamper the method's ability to make fine-grained semantic distinctions, and the computational complexity is drastically reduced as well. Generally, our network flow method presents a highly competitive alternative to a purely distributional and non-graphical approach.

In our on-going work, we are further exploring how the choice of junction influences the performance of different types of concept-to-concept semantic distances. For example, would a bottom-up junction selection approach (from the profile nodes instead of from the root level) result in better performance? In addition, we intend to examine the graphical properties of the individual profiles as well as the routes between the concepts across profiles selected by our network flow methods. Such analyses will help us gain insight into the strengths (and weaknesses) of taking advantage of a graphical representation of contexts as well as treating an ontology as a metric space for context comparisons.

## References


Budanitsky, A. and Hirst, G. (2006). Evaluating WordNet-based measures of semantic distance. *Computational Linguistics*. To appear.

Clark, S. and Weir, D. (2002). Class-based probability estimation using a semantic hierarchy. *Computational Linguistics*, 28(2):187–206.

Jiang, J. and Conrath, D. (1997). Semantic similarity based on corpus statistics and lexical taxonomy. In *Proceedings on the International Conference on Research in Computational Linguistics*, pages 19–33.

Li, H. and Abe, N. (1998). Word clustering and disambiguation based on co-occurrence data. In *Proceedings of COLING-ACL 1998*, pages 749–755.

Lin, D. (1998). An information-theoretic definition of similarity. In *Proceedings of International Conference on Machine Learning*.

Mihalcea, R. (2006). Random walks on text structures. In *Proceedings of CICLing 2006*, pages 249–262.

Miller, G. A. and Charles, W. G. (1991). Contextual correlates of semantic similarity. *Language and Cognitive Processes*, 6(1):1–28.

Navigli, R. and Velardi, P. (2005). Structural semantic interconnections: A knowledge-based approach to word sense disambiguation. *IEEE Transactions on Pattern Analysis and Machine Intelligence*, 27(7).

Pedersen, T., Purandare, A., and Kulkarni, A. (2005). Name discrimination by clustering similar context. In *Proceedings of the Sixth International Conference on Intelligent Text Processing and Computational Linguistics*.

Resnik, P. (1995). Using information content to evaluate semantic similarity in a taxonomy. In *Proceedings of the 14th International Joint Conference on Artificial Intelligence*.

Schütze, H. (1998). Automatic word sense discrimination. *Computational Linguistics*, 24(1):97–123.

Xu, W., Liu, X., and Gong, Y. (2003). Document clustering based on non-negative matrix factorization. In *Proceedings of the 26th ACM SIGIR Conference*.

# Author Index

**Association for Computational Linguistics**
209 N. Eighth Street
Stroudsburg, Pennsylvania 18360